PLAYING IN EMPTINESS

PLAYING IN EMPTINESS

An Introduction to Zen Buddhist Discourse

CARL OLSON

WIPF & STOCK · Eugene, Oregon

PLAYING IN EMPTINESS
An Introduction to Zen Buddhist Discourse

Copyright © 2024 Carl Olson. All rights reserved. Except for brief quotations in critical publications or reviews, no part of this book may be reproduced in any manner without prior written permission from the publisher. Write: Permissions, Wipf and Stock Publishers, 199 W. 8th Ave., Suite 3, Eugene, OR 97401.

Wipf & Stock
An Imprint of Wipf and Stock Publishers
199 W. 8th Ave., Suite 3
Eugene, OR 97401

www.wipfandstock.com

PAPERBACK ISBN: 979-8-3852-1599-7
HARDCOVER ISBN: 979-8-3852-1600-0
EBOOK ISBN: 979-8-3852-1601-7

10/10/24

This book is dedicated to the following old tennis bums of the college on the hill: Marty Serra, Glenn Rogers, Tony Moskwa, and to the memories of Steve Bowser, Chuck Cable, and Pinky Bates.

Contents

	Preface	ix
1	Introduction	1
2	Buddhism in China and Japan: An Overview	34
3	Getting the Goose Out of the Bottle	73
4	Violence, Beatings, Shouts, and Finger Raising	107
5	A Painting of a Rice Cake Can Satisfy Hunger	130
6	Madness, the Erotic, Humor, and Play	151
7	Zen and Japanese Fine Arts	178
8	Zen, Death, and the Martial Arts	209
	Bibliography	227
	Index	235

PREFACE

This book is the product of a college level course that I have taught for many years at the undergraduate level. Thus, it is intended to serve as supplemental reading for a course on Buddhism within the context of undergraduate survey courses on Buddhism. To meet this purpose for the book, I have chosen the theme of play as it appears in Zen Buddhist discourse and narratives.

An introductory chapter devoted to the historical development of Buddhism and the major features of Zen are intended to ground this work in its historical and cultural context, I propose to take a thematic approach to the subject by focusing on the notion of play and its connection to other phenomena. This approach presents Zen as a dynamic path to liberation. An advantage of this approach is the enhancement of a student's understanding of the trap of rationality and the representative mode of thinking. Besides, a reader will be able to grasp its emphasis on what is natural, ordinary, and concrete. Moreover, a reader will be able to understand why and how Zen Buddhism is iconoclastic, playful, and comic.

The second chapter is a historical survey of the development of Zen in China and Japan to the late medieval period. The cultural context in which Zen developed is considered in both China and Japan. The chapter incorporates some of the most recent scholarship on the history of Chan/Zen, resulting in a less idealized, stereotypical, and romantic portrait of the religion as evident in the work of D. T. Suzuki and others influenced by him. Throughout the book, I use a narrative approach in part because it allows practitioners an opportunity to tell their own stories and do less violence to the religion because it avoids to a large degree the imposition of western categories on an eastern religion that might distort it. This narrative approach is combined with the theme of play.

The third chapter looks at the Zen understanding of language as it pertains to achieving enlightenment via the use of *kōans*; the disruptive nature of language, meditation, and monastic life in general; and ritual and politics. The third chapter is grounded in two major works that reflect the major divisions of Chan: Baizhang's monastic regulations and the Sōtō master Dōgen's similar text. Building on chapter 3, the fourth chapter examines unusual and violent teaching methods used by Zen masters and a discussion of the interconnection between Zen, violence, and play.

The fifth chapter looks at the thought of Dōgen, the greatest Sōtō master, by reviewing his philosophy of perception, the importance of seated meditation, the relationship of existence and time, non-thinking, and the authentic and inauthentic self. A reader will see that Dōgen is an excellent example of a Zen thinker playing in emptiness. The sixth chapter introduces an examination of madness, the erotic, humor as examples of play, focusing on the eccentric monk Ikkyū. The final two chapters are devoted to the ways that Zen Buddhism influenced Japanese culture by examining the various artistic ways. This goal will be accomplished by reviewing *haiku* poetry, the Nō theater, the tea ceremony, landscape painting, rock gardens, swordsmanship, and the art of archery. The final chapter on the martial arts is introduced by a discussion of death in the Zen tradition.

Some western readers of this book may get the impression that I am applying a western category—play—on an eastern religion and thus superimposing a foreign feature on the tradition. I disagree with such a claim because of the nature of play, which is a universal cultural phenomenon. In other words, I am unaware of any culture that does not have examples of play. From childhood to old age, people around the globe engage in spontaneous episodes of play, flights of fantasy that transport one to a sphere of play, card games with friends or family members, vicariously participating in a sport by watching amateur or professional athletes perform, or by attending bingo at a local church. The many forms of play extend to rites, festivals, language, and thinking of a religion.

Parts of this book were begun in my apartment at Clare Hall at the University of Cambridge where I was enjoying a sabbatical leave before riding off to the Pure Land of Retirement. My gratitude and thanks go to the many helpful and friendly folks at Clare Hall. They always make one's stay enjoyable. The fellows from around the globe afford stimulating conversation. My good friend Julius Lipner and his lovely wife Anita are always fun to see while enjoying the fruits of a visiting fellowship. Email correspondence from my wife, Peggy, and daughters Holly and Kelly and their love kept me going during periods of loneliness. Besides, Peggy has functioned as a super nurse as evident by her selfless efforts assisting me to get my left foot back to health after walking on too many cobblestones in central Europe. I also want to thank my undergraduate students at Allegheny College for their enthusiastic support over the years by constantly filling my courses on Zen. I can only hope that the subject has been as much fun for me as it has been for them. My friend and colleague Glenn Holland has been a steadfast dialogical partner over the years, and he has never failed to be a source of amusement and good cheer. My other colleagues—EB, Eric, Steven, Adrienne, Rabbi Ron, Tal, Younus, Patrick, and Jane Ellen—have enriched my life in many ways. The department will miss the contributions of Tal and Younus as they move to other venues. I am sorry about not being able to watch the struggles of the hoops team with my old buddy La Lloyd because of my stay at Cambridge. Finally, this book is dedicated to some good friends and to memories of tennis matches that were never broadcast on national television for obvious reasons.

1

INTRODUCTION

IT IS COMMON WISDOM that those leading a Buddhist monastic lifestyle live a disciplined, detached, sober, and regimented way of life with the purpose of attaining spiritual goals. Being detached from the ordinary pleasures of life found in sense pleasures and bodily comforts, a monk or nun exists apart from society in isolated circumstances or in monastic communities set apart from society. Thus, it is a bit surprising when one finds counter evidence to what might be expected from these monastics. The Chan/Zen Buddhist tradition is an excellent example of the exception to some aspects of monastic life.

The Blue Cliff Record, an important source of information about the lives, interactions, and teachings of leaders and disciples of the tradition, depicts monks engaged in various types of play. According to one episode, layman Pang took leave of Yaoshan after staying with the master for a time and was joined by ten students to say good-bye. During this departing episode, Pang noticed that it was snowing and called this fact to everyone's attention. A student named Quan asked where the snowflakes fell. In response, Pang slapped the student. Thus, the falling snow was used as a teaching moment.[1] Sometimes, Chan monks play with words such as the time when a monk said to Guanxi ("Pouring Mountain Stream") that he had long heard of him, but now sees that he is a flax soaking pool. Although the monk expressed disappointment after meeting Guanxi and denigrated him, the master asked the monk why he did not see the pouring mountain stream. In response, the monk asks Guanxi

---

1. Cleary, *Blue Cliff Record*, 211–13.

to identify what he meant, and the master replied, "Swift as a whistling arrow."[2] Another similar story follows the previous tale with Huanglong ("Yellow Dragon") being questioned in a similar vein by a monk, who says that what he sees is a red-striped snake. The monk inquires what would happen if the yellow dragon met a dragon-eating bird; Huanglong replies that it would be difficult for the dragon to remain alive. After the monk essentially agrees that it would be eaten by the bird, Huanglong says, "Thanks for feeding me."[3] With these examples from the Chan tradition, we see masters using words to playfully interact with students.

There are episodes from the text that suggest a playfulness that is more spontaneous. Jinniu is reported to have danced when taking the rice pail to feed the monks in their hall; laughing, he would tell the monks, "Bodhisattvas come eat!"[4] The commentator explains this episode by saying that Chan practitioners operate outside of normal patterns.[5] In another example, a monk arrived at the hermitage of Tongfeng, and asked him what he would do if he encountered a tiger at this remote location. The hermit responded to the question by roaring like a tiger, and the monk acted frightened with the hermit responding with laughter.[6] A third spontaneous example of play relates Yaoshan reacting to a question from a monk about shooting "the elk of elks." Yaoshan responds "Look—an arrow!" In response, the monk collapses.[7] In *The Recorded Sayings of Linji*, Puhua was eating some raw vegetables in the front of the monk's hall. The master Linji saw him and said, "Just like a donkey." Puhua imitated the braying of a donkey. Linji called him a thief, and Puhua replied "Thief! Thief!" and walked out.[8] A reader will notice that these encounters share spontaneity in common.

These types of dialogical exchanges, dancing, imitation, and laughter are typical of the element of play in Chan/Zen Buddhism. From ancient times, as the examples from *The Blue Cliff Record* illustrate, Zen Buddhism has embraced the notion of play into its ethos. By examining the notion of play within the tradition, it is possible to shine a new light on a complex religious tradition. This purpose will begin to be fulfilled

2. Cleary, *Blue Cliff Record*, 254.
3. Cleary, *Blue Cliff Record*, 255.
4. Cleary, *Blue Cliff Record*, 329.
5. Cleary, *Blue Cliff Record*, 331.
6. Cleary, *Blue Cliff Record*, 374.
7. Cleary, *Blue Cliff Record*, 357.
8. Sasaki, *Record of Linji*, 48.

beginning with chapter 3. In the remainder of this chapter, I want to place Zen into its historical context by starting with the life and teachings of the historical Buddha and moving to developments in China and Japan in chapter 2.

Chapter 3 looks at Chan masters' unusual and often violent teaching methods and how the notion of play elucidates these harsh techniques. Chapter 4 examines the teaching method of *kōan* use and how it is playful, while chapter 5 looks at the thought and practice of the Rinzai school. Chapter 6 is devoted to understanding the thought of Dōgen of the Sōtō school, the other major branch of Zen in Japan. The themes of play, madness, and erotic are reviewed in chapter 7, whereas chapter 8 looks at the relationship between play and humor. In the final two chapters, the book turns to the relationship between Zen and Japanese culture. By examining the element of play in the Zen tradition, I am not asserting that it is the only or the best way to grasp Zen. But it is certainly a neglected aspect of Zen that needs to be examined with the purpose of understanding the tradition more fully.

OVERVIEW OF INDIAN BUDDHISM

After renouncing his wife, child, kingdom, social status, wealth, and predictions of future political and military prestige, a man named Siddhartha, who received, according to legend, a series of consecutive signs concerning sickness, old age, and death that caused his profound mental and emotional turmoil, took a spiritual quest to find answers to the fundamental problems of human existence like the following: Why is there so much mental and physical suffering in the world? Is there anything that a person can do about it? Does death represent the end of human existence? Is there a way to escape the sting of death? What is the meaning of human life? To find answers to these kinds of questions and others, Siddhartha set forth on a six-year regimen of asceticism that nearly killed him. After moving away from extreme forms of asceticism, Siddhartha developed his own spiritual method that he called the middle path that was grounded in meditation, leading to four trance states and eventual liberation from pain and suffering. Upon achieving the state of *nirvāṇa* (ultimate freedom) by means of arduous meditation, Siddhartha became a Buddha (a fully enlightened being).

It is precisely this emphasis on meditation that later Zen Buddhists wanted to emphasize and recapture, because Buddhism had strayed from its roots in the practice of meditation. From this perspective, Zen Buddhism can be viewed as a revival of a pristine Buddhism. From the Zen perspective, Buddhism had strayed from its meditative foundation and evolved into a cult of devotion and obtuse speculative metaphysics. Therefore, Buddhism needed to be reinvigorated by returning to its roots of a way of life characterized by meditation and discipline of the body, mind, and speech, although in actual practice in China and Japan Zen incorporated elements from folk religion, Pure Land practice, Confucianism, and Daoism. The point being made from the Zen perspective is manifested in the very name of Zen itself, which is the Japanese translation for Chan in Chinese, a translation of the Sanskrit term *dhyāna* (meditation). The historical development of this movement will be fully explored in the next chapter, whereas this chapter will review some general characteristics of Zen along with a brief review of the formative Buddhist period and the later development of Mahāyāna Buddhism, a broad designation for many different types of schools within Buddhism including Zen.

BASIC TEACHINGS OF THE BUDDHA

After attaining enlightenment, the Buddha proceeded to the Deer Park in the city of Benares to share with others what he learned on his religious quest. Since he was already liberated by means of his enlightenment experience, his decision to teach was an act of compassion for those still captive to the cycle of life and death. The initial truth that he discovered and shared with his audience was that all life was suffering, a truth based on his observations of sickness, old age, death, and causality. The initial three observations are connected to the legend of the four signs that he witnessed while riding on his horse in the countryside on successive days when he witnessed an ill man, an old, frail, and bent over man, and a corpse by the side of the road. The truth about the operation of causality was discovered by the Buddha in a state of insightful trance. These observations are interconnected because they are connected to the law of karma (cause and effect) and the cycle of rebirth (*saṁsāra*).

The Buddha's basic insight into the nature of causation means that the cycle of human existence is determined by the law of karma (cause and effect) because the kinds of action that we perform produce either positive or negative karmic consequences that produce results within this present life or a future lifetime in an apparently never-ending cycle. The law of karma is like a natural law that is built into the universe that operates automatically for actions performed with either one's body, speech, or mind in any of three temporal modes: past, present, and future. If a person is negligent, neglectful, or mistaken when performing an action that harms another person or creature, the consequences are not as severe as when a person intentionally commits a harmful act. This means that the Buddha conceived of an intimate connection between a deed or action and human intention. Thus, karmic results of actions performed without intention are not as severe as those committed with intention. A slip of the tongue is not, for instance, as karmically consequential as willfully lying or intentionally hiding the truth. The doctrine of karma suggests necessarily that there are no accidental occurrences within the universe. It also implies that everything in the universe is causally conditioned or produced. Therefore, there is nothing in the world from an apple pie to a zebra that is not causally produced or conditioned by something else.

Depending on a person's karmic condition during their present and past lives, their future rebirth destiny will be determined by their actions. Even if a person led a virtuous life, this does not mean that their rebirth will result in a favorable condition because negative karmic consequences from an earlier birth could override the virtuous deeds performed in a person's present life. The important points from the perspective of the Buddha were that this process was unending, led to suffering, and was part of a broader cycle of causation. To be captive to the cycle of rebirth was conceived as suffering.

The entire process of karma and rebirth was an integral part of a larger process called conditioned genesis, a twelve-linked chain of causation discovered by the Buddha. This meant that karma operated within the context of this larger chain of causation and closely interacted with it. The twelve links of causation created a circular chain without beginning and end that functioned as a prison for human beings. The overall theory was important because it explained how suffering arose and how it could be ended. The theory also explained that human existence was determined by innumerable interrelated processes, and it demonstrated how each moment within the process of causation is determined by other conditions. Moreover, the theory of causation demonstrated that everything within the world was impermanent and that all things were interdependent. With its automatic mode of operation and its formation for the context of suffering, causation was a difficult cycle from which humans could escape. It was analogous to being condemned by a person's actions to eternally riding an ever-revolving carousel. When the ride ends, a person changes their vehicle, but they can never leave the carousel that continues to turn because it is fed by the energy of hatred, delusion, ignorance, and greed.

With relentless causation as the foundation of suffering, the Buddha taught about how life was unsatisfactory because of such events as the frustration of our desires, sickness, degeneration of our mental and physical faculties, old age, anxiety, fear, and death. Suffering was also connected to change and the temporary nature of things. The passing away of a pleasant event or feeling, for instance, leads to sorrow. By clinging to notions like self, I, or ego, a person suffered from conditioned states, which functioned as the support for the initial two levels of suffering. The Buddha taught that it was essential to recognize that the self is nothing more than combination of ever-changing physical and mental forces without any permanence or enduring substance.

The second truth shared by the Buddha was the identity of the cause of suffering that he traced to ignorant craving, thirst, or desire (*tanhā*). Humans craved for sense pleasures, existence, and non-existence or no rebirth. Any form of craving was considered counter-productive to a person's spiritual liberation because they were examples of attachment and led to rebirth. Even though ignorant craving is the second noble truth, it was not considered the first cause of suffering because it was dependent for its origin within the larger context of the entire cycle of causation. However, ignorant craving was centered in the false idea of the self, which entailed eradicating attachment to the self to make any spiritual progress. To think that a person could satisfy their ego or self represented a fundamental misconception because there was no permanent ego or self to satisfy. From the Buddha's perspective, there was no spiritual substance, soul, or eternal self that endured beyond this present mode of existence, which was called the non-self (*anatta*) doctrine. What a person mistakenly assumed to be a self was really a group of five aggregates that consisted of matter, sensations, perceptions, impulses to action, and consciousness that were in a constant state of flux and impermanence, whereas death represented the complete dissolution of these five aggregates leaving no distinctive physical or mental identity that endured. Therefore, becoming detached from the five aggregates was essential for escaping the world of suffering and pain.

The cycle of suffering ended with the achievement of *nirvāṇa* as expressed in the third noble truth. In short, *nirvāṇa* represented the opposite of this world because it was described as uncompounded, unconditioned, causeless, the absence of desire, cessation, the extinction of craving, and the end of rebirth. Being beyond logic and reason, *nirvāṇa* was unthinkable and incomprehensible. From a more positive perspective, *nirvāṇa* was absolute freedom in the sense of liberation from evil, craving, hatred, ignorance, duality, relativity, space, and time. The attainment of *nirvāṇa* was analogous to a deathless calm, which was free of decay, aging, and death, that enabled a person to gain an insight into the absolute truth that there was nothing absolute in the world because everything was relative, conditioned, and impermanent within the world. This flash of intuitive insight was an experience that occurred during the life of a person while embodied. With the death of a person's body, the enlightened person passed away because their life energy was exhausted, but a person was not reborn due to being beyond the cycle of causation.

To attain *nirvāṇa*, a person needed to follow a path that was explained by the fourth noble truth, which the Buddha called the eightfold path. This was described as a middle way between the extremes of asceticism and hedonism. The path consisted of an integration of elements of wisdom, moral/ethical virtue, and meditation. The elements of wisdom were identified as right understanding and thought, which represented understanding of the four noble truths and thought devoid of lust, ill-will, and cruelty. The ethical/moral aspects of the path were represented by right speech, which meant refraining from falsehood and other types of harmful speech, right action, which involved avoiding violence, stealing, lying, sex, and intoxications of any kind, and finally right livelihood, which suggested refraining from a mode of occupation that harmed others. The final three steps on the path involved meditation. The sixth step of right effort involved cleansing the mind of evil thought and the prevention of others from arising, whereas the seventh step of right mindfulness implied becoming astutely aware of one's body and mind. Finally, right concentration involved practicing meditation that culminated in the four trance states in the intuitive vision associated with the attainment of *nirvāṇa*.

MAHĀYĀNA BUDDHISM

Within a hundred years after the death of the Buddha, the movement that he established began to split initially over issues of monastic discipline and later over issues of discipline and doctrine. At one point, some eighteen different schools existed. It is not possible to assert with absolute certainty that any of these schools represented precursors of Mahāyāna Buddhism. It appears to be more likely that the Mahāyāna school arose between 150 BCE and 100 CE as a loose community of individuals and groups adhering to revered texts that were believed to embody the truth. With roots in India, Mahāyāna spread north to Tibet and east to China, Korea, and Japan. Within the overall umbrella term of Mahāyāna, there were many different schools that often represented very different views about the nature of Buddhism. The school of Zen was one such movement that was shaped by a new type of wisdom literature that emphasized the notion of emptiness, the philosophical insights of Mādhyamika, and the thought and practice of the Yogācāra and its emphasis on consciousness-only as the sole reality.

The wisdom (*prajñā*) literature represented texts (*sūtras*) by different unknown authors of various lengths with some texts entitled by their length, such as the *Prajñāpāramitā of Eight Thousand Lines*. Among the shorter works, there were such texts as the *Heart Sūtra* and the *Diamond Sūtra* that were composed between 300–500 CE. The format of these texts represented a continuous dialogue between the Buddha and other figures like disciples, gods, spirits, or humans. These texts were believed to represent the word of the Buddha, an association that gave these texts their authority. If we look at the briefer *Heart Sūtra*, it will be possible to survey some of the major notions discussed.

According to the text, the ultimate facts of reality are called *dharmas*, of which there are two types: conditioned (generally the world of causation) and unconditioned. There are only two unconditioned types of *dharmas*: *nirvāṇa* and space. The text proceeds to teach that there are two ways of viewing *dharmas* (elements of reality) that are essential for a person's salvation. The first way is an act of differentiation that involves breaking apart the apparent unified ego or self and its experiences, and being able to recognize that wisdom views the aggregates that constitute the self as something constructed by the mind, whereas ignorance imagines a unified self. The second step involves an act of depersonalization that eliminates all references to ego, me, or mine. Finally, there is an act of evaluation in which one realizes that the Buddha's teaching regarding the self is superior to an unenlightened and ordinary understanding of the self.

But when a person really views the *dharmas* (elements of reality) she sees them in their own-being (*svabhāva*), a term that can refer to the essence of a thing. A good example would be to say that fire is a thing of which heat is its essence (own-being). The term is also used to refer to an essential feature of a thing in the sense that own-being embodies its own mark. An example would be to assert that consciousness is being aware. A third usage of the term is to claim that it is the opposite of other-being, which means that the former is dependent only on itself, whereas other-being is contingent and tied to conditions. It is possible to illustrate this point by noting that heat is an essential feature of fire, although it also depends on fuel, oxygen, and other elements. To truly have own-being (*svabhāva*) a thing must possess full control over itself that is independent of conditions. But what is the point of this torturous type of philosophical exercise?

The author of the text wants to make clear that *dharmas* (elements of reality) are empty of any own-being, meaning that they are not ultimate facts. They are merely imagined because each *dharma* is dependent on something other than itself for its existence. In and by itself, it is nothing. Therefore, elements of reality (*dharmas*) do not exist as separate entities, have no relationship to other entities, are isolated, and are not made or produced because they have never left original emptiness. The most that a person can assert about *dharmas* is that they have a nominal existence as mere words. In fact, from the perspective of an enlightened being, *dharmas* (elements of reality) are empty. Therefore, the notion of emptiness conveys the idea that what appears to be something is really nothing. They are analogous to a dream state.

The *Heart Sūtra* develops a three-stage dialectic that begins with the five aggregates that mistakenly give a person the false sense of a self and each is identified with emptiness. The text makes it clear that emptiness is a transcendent reality when it states the following: "Form is emptiness, emptiness is not different from form, neither is form different from emptiness, indeed, emptiness is form."[9] Even though emptiness is beyond all that is, it is also immanent, which suggests that it is also identical with its exact opposite, for instance, the five aggregates that constitute the self.

---

9. Conze, *Heart Sutra*, 81.

Therefore, emptiness is nowhere, and there is also nowhere it is not. This implies that it is identical with the world. In short, the world and everything within it are empty.

In the second stage of the dialectic of emptiness, the text affirms: "All things having the nature of emptiness have no beginning and no ending."[10] This remark suggests a couple of points. It implies that emptiness is the essential and exclusive trait of all entities and that it is all-comprehensive. Moreover, *dharmas* (elements of reality) are empty of anything that could distinguish a separate existence for each one of them. In other words, they do not have any separate existence. The third stage of dialectics denies the initial assertion of the first stage because all *dharmas* are nothing but emptiness. The overall purpose of this three-stage dialectic is to remove false views to enable a person to view everything lucidly.

A similar type of dialectic is operative in the *Diamond Sūtra* where eight types of misconceptions are identified and eliminated. These misconceptions are related to erroneous notions regarding the self, soul, being, person and four false perceptions about discoveries that cannot be grasped in its objective or subjective forms. In fact, the *dharma* (truth) cannot be discussed, expressed, or reached because it is not a separate thing accessible to discriminative thought. A person is left without negation or affirmation, neither reality nor unreality. A person is left with only emptiness or suchness, another way to express emptiness.

MĀDHYAMIKA AND YOGĀCĀRA

The basic insights of the wisdom texts were made more systematic by the Mādhyamika school inspired by a brilliant philosophical monk named Nāgārjuna (ca. 150–250 CE). Inspired by more idealistic Mahāyāna texts like the *Gandavyūha Sūtra* (Flower Ornament Text) and the *Lankāvatāra Sūtra*, the Yogācāra school, which was founded by the monk Asanga in the fourth century and his brother Vasubandhu, attempted to correct some of the perceived shortcomings of the Mādhyamika school that did not address issues like the process used by the monk to create objective fictions, error, how memory occurs, the identity of experiences that are free from discrimination, and the origin of suffering.

In a fashion, like the Buddha, Nāgārjuna envisions a middle way between affirmation (is) and negation (is not), occupying a transcendental

---

10. Conze, *Heart Sutra*, 85.

position that is beyond concepts and speech. This middle way clings to neither existence nor non-existence, implying a position of total detachment in which no philosophical view is ultimate. The ruthlessness of Nāgārjuna's dialectical method is intended to put an end to all theorizing, knowing and philosophizing. From his perspective, this is the practice of the perfection of wisdom (*prajñāpāramitā*), which is equivalent in Mahāyāna Buddhism to the attainment of *nirvāṇa*.

A crucial feature of understanding the thought of Nāgārjuna is coming to grips with his distinction between conventional truth and ultimate truth. The first kind of truth deals with knowledge that is valid for practical purposes. It is useful to know, for instance, that rice and bread can satisfy a person's hunger and that a stone is uneatable and will not cure one's hunger. But this everyday type of knowing does have its limits because when a person pushes it there is a tendency for it to become self-contradictory or illusory. Why is this true? It is due to ignorance (*avidyā*) that tends to obscure the real nature of things or construct a false appearance. This does not imply, however, that ignorance possesses any reality because it is in fact characterized as unreal (*māyā*) much like a mirage in the desert or a pregnant virgin. In contrast, ultimate truth is a non-dual type of knowledge that represents an intuition devoid of content. Beyond ordinary knowledge or rationality, it represents a dissolution of the conceptual aspect of the mind. The freedom suggested by this type of truth does not necessarily imply a complete rejection of conventional truth because a person still finds it pragmatically useful to know how to cook, what to eat, how to use a hammer, how to communicate, and many other valuable forms of practical knowing that gets us through the day successfully and may even improve our lives.

With the dawning of the realization that all distinctions are empty, a person's mode of awareness is transformed. Such an awakened person sees things as they really are in fact, which means to see things as empty (*śūnyatā*), which suggests an intuitive vision of everything as swollen or lacking in self-existence (*svabhāva*), a feature that is non-contingent and without relation to anything else. Wetness is, for instance, never encountered apart from water or moisture. Therefore, wetness is created and is not self-existent. The lack of self-existence (*svabhāva*) represents the true nature of all things. This does not suggest that emptiness is a superior viewpoint, something or represents ultimate reality because Nāgārjuna defines emptiness as empty. This means that emptiness is non-substantial and non-perceptible. This suggests that emptiness checks the inclination to transform phenomena into something substantial by means of conceptualizing them and making them something that they are not. The wisdom that a person gains from the intuitive insight into emptiness releases a person from attachment to things, to dissolve any absolute notions about something, and to realize that one attains nothing. However, intuitive insight does destroy illusion created by attributing self-existence to things, and it affords a person freedom, detachment, cessation of problems, and purification from things like hatred, greed, and anxiety.

In contrast to the Mādhyamika school, the Yogācāra school more clearly defined the problematic nature of the human condition by specifying craving (*tanhā*) as the root cause of misery, although craving needs a subject (craver) and an object (something craved) for it to be effective. The other basic problem is ignorance (*avidyā*), which exists because humans regard the objectifications of their minds as a world solely independent of their minds. To overcome this problem, humans need to realize that their minds are the source of all objectifications. If you can imagine an animal with the body of a zebra, the legs of an elephant, the tail of a peacock, and the head of a lion, it would be possible to create an object of such a strange creature. The objectification of such a weird creature could be traced directly to our minds, suggesting that this false creature is nothing more than a phantom created by the mind. Just as humans can create strange creatures by using their mental powers like imagination, they can also make strange creatures or objects disappear without a trace. The Yogācāra philosophers claim that this type of mental operation occurs all the time with the objects of the external world and the world itself. Thus, the only thing that truly exists is mind-only or consciousness-only.

It is not possible to become aware of this either from the standpoint of a mentally constructed level of reality nor from a relative level of reality, because the former fabricates objects, and the latter is dependent on a duality of a perceiver and a thing perceived. It is essential for one to reach perfect knowledge and to see things as they really are in fact in a fulfilled state of reality that is beyond all discrimination and duality. The fulfilled state means to see everything as mind or consciousness only, which implies that the fundamental dichotomy between subject and object is extinguished as a person's consciousness sees only consciousness. With the identity of the seer (mind or consciousness) with itself by the extinction of an external object, there arises an identity of the consciousness and object. Yogācāra thinkers call the negation of the seer no-mind and the negation of the object nothing-grasped. This represents the end of thinking that objectifies or conceptualizes. A person's thinking is now characterized or equated with wisdom. Thus, if a person can still conceive of a subject and an object, such a person is not liberated and does not possess wisdom. But the truly wise person who sees consciousness-only does not allow craving to arise because such a person is liberated from objects as well as a self that craves objects. Consciousness-only is pure in the sense that there are no objects and not even being conscious of consciousness. Moreover, pure consciousness is equated with sheer emptiness.

If there is consciousness-only or just mind, how can a person account for the variety of ideas and impressions that exist in their mind? Why can different people agree that an object represents a chair and another object a glass? The Yogācāra thinkers account for such questions by pointing to the store-house consciousness (*ālaya-vijñāna*), which is a kind of repository for ideas and impressions associated with the activity of the mind that is traced to an endless past. Since the beginning of time, every human that has ever lived has made deposits in this store-house consciousness in the form of universal and private seeds. The former type of seeds accounts for things that we recognize and share with others, while the latter accounts for differences. In addition, there are pure and impure seeds, which along with the other types of seeds are deposited on the store-house consciousness in a process called perfuming, which affects other types of consciousness. In its perfected state, which is gained by the practice of yoga and meditation, the store-house consciousness represents pure consciousness that is equated with the state of *nirvāṇa*.

In summary, it is possible to witness the influence of these schools on Zen Buddhism. The Mādhyamika school and its philosophy of emptiness along with its dialectical method exerted a strong influence upon Zen. The emphasis on meditation and pure consciousness by the Yogācāra was also influential on the development of Zen thought and method. As we will learn in the next chapter, Chinese culture exerted a powerful influence on shaping the nature of Zen with its preexisting schools of Confucianism and especially Taoism.

THE IDEAL OF THE *BODHISATTVA*

In contrast to the ideal of the *Arhat* (fully enlightened being) in the Pāli text tradition of the Theravāda school, the Mahāyāna school countered with the paradigm of the *bodhisattva* (literally, enlightened being). The term *bodhisattva* is a bit misleading because this individual is a figure that progresses to the brink of enlightenment but does not fully enter *nirvāṇa* because such a person possesses compassion for everyone and stays within the world to teach and lead others to liberation. Thus, it is best to conceive of the *bodhisattva* as a person destined to become a Buddha (a fully enlightened being).

It is likely that the ideal of the *bodhisattva* was historically influenced by Hindu devotional movements with its emphasis on love of deity, service to others, and fervent devotion, which are elements that can also be discovered in the Buddhism of lay supporters from a formative period in Buddhist history. It is likely that Hindu devotional religion directed toward deities such as Śiva, Vishnu, Krishna, and various goddess figures provided an additional impetus to the development of the ideal of the *bodhisattva*. In comparison to the earlier history of Buddhist holy persons, the Mahāyāna school advocated the ideal of the *bodhisattva* to counter the person of the *arahant*, a fully enlightened being that teaches, and the ideal of the *pratyekabuddha*, a person enlightened by themselves who does not teach. Since the *arahant* and *pratyekabuddha* seek liberation for themselves, the Mahāyāna school depicted them as selfish and egotistical ideals because neither of them really was concerned with the spiritual condition of others. By advocating the ideal of the *bodhisattva*, the Mahāyāna school wanted to counteract the solitude, cloistered, passive, placid, and inert type of monastic life characteristic of the other types. We will see that Zen Buddhism stresses the dynamic nature of the *bodhisattva* with their teaching methods. In short, the *bodhisattva* is a person that works for her personal salvation as well as that of others. The *bodhisattva* also strives to help others find welfare and happiness within the world. Therefore, the fundamental focus of the *bodhisattva* is within the world instead of escape from the world.

If life is suffering and humans are captive within the world, is not the this-worldly focus of the *bodhisattva* misplaced? This question is best answered by the theoretical context in which the *bodhisattva* operates. As the Mādhyamika school makes clear, if everything is emptiness, this is also true of the world of rebirth and *nirvāṇa*. Since the world of rebirth is equivalent to *nirvāṇa* due to their shared emptiness, they are non-dual and without distinction. Moreover, because there is only one, non-dual reality, everything is a part of the one reality. Hence, all human beings and other creatures are tied together, interrelated, and inter-dependent parts of a single reality. Since this is the theoretical situation in which the *bodhisattva* finds herself, this forms the rationale for helping others and for being oriented toward the world rather than being motivated to flee from it.

From within the context of emptiness (although strictly speaking there is no such context) and the limitations of language to express it adequately, the *bodhisattva* demonstrates his commitment, determination, and resolve to assist others by making four fundamental vows by which she lives. The initial vow is to save all beings. Secondly, the *bodhisattva* vows to destroy evil passions, and thirdly to learn the truth and teach it to others. Finally, the *bodhisattva* promises to lead all being toward enlightenment. In addition to these four vows, the *bodhisattva* is expected to develop and practice a series of perfections (*pāramitās*).

There were originally six perfections, and four additional ones were added to this list at an undetermined historical date. A basic perfection that was integrally related to the life of a *bodhisattva* was giving or generosity (*dāna*), which could take a variety of forms from giving alms to educating a child. However, it was important that it not be practiced for selfish motives, but it was necessary to perform it in a disinterested fashion without any expectation for any type of reward. It could even involve giving oneself for the benefit of others, but any decision to sacrifice oneself must combine compassion for others with wisdom. The selfless and detached practice of this virtue led to the acquiring of merit that automatically resulted from one's actions. A natural consequence of the acquisition of merit was an eventual excessive accumulation of it. Merit was something that the *bodhisattva* could apply toward his own enlightenment, or he/she could apply it to the spiritual benefit of others.

Another perfection that the *bodhisattva* needed to develop was moral and ethical perfection (*śīla*), which is cultivated by extinguishing one's passions by developing self-control. This perfection was conceived as a proactive doing rather than a passive refraining from acting. If a reader recalls the theoretical rationale for acting in a moral and ethical manner due to the interconnection of everything and everyone, it is easier to grasp why the *bodhisattva* develops this perfection, because what one does affects others. At the top of the list of guidelines for proper behavior is nonviolence (*ahimsā*), abstention from stealing, celibacy, lying, slander, harsh speech, frivolous discourse, covetousness, malice, and heretical views. Any of these moral precepts may be violated by the *bodhisattva* when, in her judgment, a greater evil will occur. Moved by compassion for others, the *bodhisattva* transgresses the moral precepts to benefit a person or a group of people.

The third and fourth perfections are endurance (*kśānti*) and energy (*vīrya*). The former perfection represents freedom from anger and excitement, whereas the latter perfection refers to the importance of being energetic, not becoming discouraged when events unfold contrary to one's wishes, and not giving in to personal weaknesses. By keeping one's resolutions strong, enduring difficulties, and pardoning personal harm and insults, the *bodhisattva* will make good progress perfecting these aspects of the path.

The fifth and sixth perfections are connected in the sense that meditation (*dhyāna*) is a preparation for the perfection of wisdom (*prajñāpāramitā*), the highest form of perfection whose attainment equates with the achievement of *nirvāṇa*. Within the context of the Mahāyāna religious ethos, meditation does not suggest a condition of isolation, but it rather connotes reaching an awareness of the sameness of everything. Meditation includes meditating upon and cultivating the so-called four *brahma-vihāras* (divine abidings or states of mind): loving-kindness (*maitrī*), compassion (*karuṇā*), sympathetic joy (*muditā*), and equanimity (*upekkhā*). The *bodhisattva* is encouraged to extend these states of mind to others. The perfection of wisdom, which is the supreme virtue for the *bodhisattva*, means gaining an insight into reality, which involves seeing everything as empty.

To these original six virtues there were added four more that include the following: *upāya* (skillful means); *parnidhana* (vow of resolution); *bala* (power or strength); and *jñāna* (knowledge). Since two of these perfections are somewhat self-explanatory, we will only discuss two of them. Knowledge (*jñāna*) refers more to intellectual powers, whereas *prajñā* (wisdom) signifies intuition. *Upāya* (skillful means) is connected to the pedagogical function of the *bodhisattva*, who takes vows to learn the truth, teach the truth to others, and to save them. *Upāya* (skillful means) represents a myriad of ways in which one can teach others, although various methods presuppose that the truth is singular. To communicate one's message to others, it is incumbent on the teacher to access the level of understanding of one's audience and their needs. A favorite device is to resort to parables to communicate a point. A popular Mahāyāna text is the *Lotus Sūtra* in which one can find the parable of the blind man. This man is born blind, and he is convinced that there are no such things as shapes. A physician employs special medicines to restore the man's sight. Now the man born blind can truly see things as they really are.[11] It is obvious that the physician in this parable is the *bodhisattva*, whereas the blind man is suffering from ignorance. The compassion of the *bodhisattva* wants to extricate humans from their condition of ignorance and bring them to a condition of intuitive awareness and wisdom. By being sensitive to the needs of those in a state of ignorance, the *bodhisattva* may use a parable, create a fantasy, or perform a miracle to convey her point. As those in ignorance shed their condition and mature, they come to recognize the limitations and unreality of the teaching creations of the *bodhisattva*, and they gradually make progress toward enlightenment. The path of the *bodhisattva* is a way of purification, increasing insight, moral and ethical development, and self-culture that is ideally devoid of egoism and ultimately includes the welfare of others. It is precisely this ideal that a reader must remember when learning about the antics and strange teaching methods of Zen masters.

THE MAJOR CHARACTERISTICS OF ZEN

The fundamental teachings of the Buddha and the Mahāyāna tradition formed the ground from which later Buddhists schools developed like Pure Land and Chan/Zen. The Zen school presupposes aspects of the previous modes of philosophy without feeling obligated to revisit and defend various positions passed to it. At the same time, Zen developed its own philosophical positions and characteristics that contributed to defining it as a different and inimitable school.

D. T. Suzuki, who single-handedly introduced Zen to the West and thus how it was perceived by westerners in the twentieth century, presented an ideal type of Zen modeled on his understanding of the Rinzai tradition, which for him was the authentic Zen path. Suzuki was not the only writer depicting Zen in idealistic and romantic terms, because he was joined by John C. H. Wu[12] and Heinrich Dumoulin.[13] Suzuki's most glaring misstep was his neglect of any historical perspective, which was brought to the attention of readers by Hu Shih in an essay that appeared in the journal *Philosophy East and West*.[14] This essay never affected or

---

11. Watson, *Lotus Sutra*, 231.
12. Wu, *Golden Age of Zen*.
13. Dumoulin, *Zen Buddhism: A History*, vol. 1, *India and China*; and vol. 2, *Japan*.
14. Shih, "Ch'an (Zen) Buddhism in China," 3–24.

influenced Suzuki to any significant extent as he continued to publish essays and books on Zen and give lectures around the USA about his version of a pristine and primordial experiential and unhistorical religion.

Suzuki functioned basically as an apologist for Zen in addition to introducing it to a western audience. He espoused an exalted version of Zen that he claimed was unique within the context of world philosophy. Beyond this attitude toward Zen, Suzuki identified several characteristics of it. He claimed that it was irrational and inconceivable; it emphasized direct pointing to the essence of human beings; it was the art of seeing into one's own being; it pointed from bondage to freedom; it was non-intellectual; it distrusted reason and words; it was iconoclastic; it stressed what was natural, common, and concrete; it was playful and comic; it assumed a non-intentional approach to life; and it rejected conceptual categories.[15] Moreover, Suzuki thought that the essence of Zen was its pure experience or enlightenment experience (*satori*) that represented the culmination of all thought.

For these various characteristics, Suzuki provides anecdotes, episodes, statements by enlightened masters, and narratives to support his position. An unbiased reader can grant that many of his characteristics embody a grain of truth, but this is not true of all his characteristics. The non-intellectual categorization is misleading, because Zen thinkers did write accounts of their experiences and philosophy of emptiness and did study various Mahāyāna texts and quoted from these texts in their own works. Zen philosophers such as Dōgen, a Sōtō master, in the thirteenth century and Hakuin, a Rinzai master, did write with conviction and authenticity. We could also add the Kyoto School of the twentieth century. Unfortunately, Suzuki neglected some characteristics of Zen about which readers should be aware for a more well-rounded view of it.

Although Suzuki alludes to it to some degree, lineage is an important characteristic of Zen that helps to define it. The organizational model for the Chan monastery was the Chinese family kinship system, essentially creating fictive family relations among members of the monastic community. By using terms such as brother, uncle, or grandfather, family types of lineages were created. In addition to this innovation, it was suggested, since the time of Daoan (312–385), that monks and nuns should adopt the surname "Shi," a briefer transliteration of the Buddha's

---

15. Suzuki, *Essays in Zen Buddhism First Series*; *Essays in Zen Buddhism Second Series*; *Essays in Zen Buddhism Third Series*.

clan name (Śākya), which enhances the sense of being part of a family.[16] Membership into the monastic family did not occur immediately because students were expected to have mastered certain elements of doctrine and ideology. When they reached this level of competence, their teachers gave them special acknowledgment, making them members of the family and transmission lineage. This type of recognition was formalized by the inheritance certificate, which was also called the *dharma* inheritance certificate, from a master that completed the process of a monk's new status.[17] An overview of the Chan lineage dated in the Song dynasty extended from the Buddha through twenty-eight Indian patriarchs to Bodhidharma, alleged founder of Chan. Then, in China, it went through five more patriarchs to Huike (ca. 485–ca. 553), Sengan, (n.d.), Daoxin (580–651), and Hongren (601–674) and culminating with the Sixth Patriarch, Huineng. With the death of Huineng, two of his disciples, Nanyue Huainang (677–744) and Qingyuan Xingsi (d. 740), became part of the lineage. From these two disciples, the lineage branched out into numerous sub-lineages. These various families (houses) represented different styles of Chan, although they were all considered orthodox by belonging to the Huineng lineage. In the eleventh century, five traditions were recognized as valid lineages traceable to Huineng's two disciples. These traditions were the Caodong, Fayan, Guiyang, Linji, and Yunmen. During the twelfth century, a distinction is made in the Northern School that develops into the notion of the five families and seven traditions, meaning the five families plus the Huanglong branch and the Yangqi branch.

The leading figures of these various lineages were promoted by literary narratives in forms called *yulu* (records of the sayings of Chan masters that also included sermons, poetry, and encounter episodes) and *denglu* (literally meaning "Lamp Readers"). These types of narratives were basically transmission records of the various lineages. A good example of this type of literature was the *Lidai fabao ji* (*Record of the Dharma-Jewel through the Generations*). The text was produced by an obscure lineage called Bao Tang Chan, a school located in Sichuan, dating between 774–781. The work was produced by an anonymous disciple of Chan Master Wuzhu (714–774), founder of Bao Tang.[18] It is one example of several such texts that trace the lineage of patriarchs from Bodhidharma. The narratives contained in the *Transmission of the Lamp* literature also fit

16. Schlütter, *How Zen Became Zen*, 55–56.
17. Schlütter, *How Zen Became Zen*, 56, 63.
18. Adamek, *Mystique of Transmission*, 6.

into this genre. These types of narratives about leading patriarchs gave the impression that the Tang dynasty represented the "golden age of Zen," but this is a misnomer because this impression has been subverted by findings at the caves near Dunhuang, which have convinced scholars that the portraits of these patriarchs was a product of writers living during the Song dynasty (960–1279), which promoted the ideology of the Southern School that will be discussed in the next chapter.

Besides lineage, another characteristic of Zen is its emphasis on simplicity and attentiveness. Monks and nuns are allowed very few possessions, they eat simple food, they live in sparsely furnished dwellings, and these buildings are simple and unadorned. As part of their discipline, monks and nuns are instructed to be attentive to everything that they do and to their surroundings. Simplicity and attentiveness function to motivate practitioners to respect other persons and objects.

METAPHORS OF ZEN LIFE

The use of metaphors is an important aspect of any language, and they are found in all religious cultures to some degree to express what cannot be said in a direct fashion, using ordinary images to express a message that can connote several layers of significance. Metaphors do not give new information about what is real, but they can produce meaning.[19] Metaphors can be entrenched in the conceptual system of a culture. It is these primary metaphors that can create new metaphorical combinations, be used for reasoning, or link human subjective experiences and judgments to human sensory motor experience. A metaphor is appropriate to the extent that it plays a role in structuring our experience. From a practical perspective, metaphors help to define abstract concepts, functioning as a form of truth that originates in the unconscious of embodied humans.[20] The Zen use of metaphors has been a neglected aspect of the tradition.

Over the centuries, Zen Buddhism has made abundant use of visual metaphors to convey its message. Dōgen, a Sōtō sect master of the thirteenth century, claimed that human eyes are connected, for instance, to the origin of the divine light within us.[21] For Dōgen, the ability to truly see is essential for success: "If we do not see ourselves, we are not capable

---

19. See Ricoeur, *Role of Metaphor*.
20. See Lakoff and Johnson, *Philosophy in the Flesh*.
21. Dōgen, *Shōbōgenzō*, 1:105.

of seeing others—both are insufficient. If we cannot see others we cannot see ourselves."[22] Several centuries after the death of Dōgen, Hakuin, a Rinzai master, stressed again the importance of the eye and achieving the ability to genuinely see: "But if you do not have the eye to see into your own nature, you will not have the slightest chance of being responsive to the teaching."[23] The type of seeing with which these two Zen masters are concerned is an intuitive perception and not a typical subject/object type of perceptual experience. Both thinkers are not concerned too much with the physical eye as much as they are concerned with the intuitive eye. In fact, Dōgen is convinced that there is a unity between the eye, mind, entire body, and enlightenment.[24]

Prior to Dōgen, *Wumen's Gate* used the metaphor of light to illustrate its point. For example, Zhaozhou's assertion of "No" is compared to a lamp of truth that shines.[25] In another instance, the monk Longtan lit a candle for his companion Deshan late one night to help his friend find his way in the dark. As Deshan was about to take it, Longtan blew it out. At that moment, Deshan had an enlightenment experience.[26] The awakened mind is compared to lightening in the *Blue Cliff Record*.[27] Even though light is often contrasted to darkness to convey the difference between being enlightened and being benighted, light and darkness are non-dual as evident by the fact that within light there is darkness and within darkness there is light.[28]

In the *Changuan cejin* (*Whip for Spurring Students Onward through the Chan Barrier Checkpoints*), a compact Chan anthology intended to aid students that was published in 1600 by Yunqi Zhuhong (1535–1615), there are a couple of metaphorical references to light associated directly with enlightenment. Master Xueyan Qin of Yuanzhou relates to readers that when he saw an ancient cypress tree, he had an awakening experience. He expounds further that "sense objects that I had hitherto apprehended and things that were obstructions in my breast were tossed away and scattered. It was like coming out of a dark room into the bright

---

22. Dōgen, *Shōbōgenzō*, 2:96.
23. Yampolsky, *Zen Master Hakuin*, 136.
24. Dōgen, *Shōbōgenzō*, 3:134.
25. Cleary, *Wumen's Gate*, 72.
26. Cleary, *Wumen's Gate*, 92.
27. Cleary, *Blue Cliff Record*, 64, 261, 419.
28. Cleary, *Blue Cliff Record*, 380.

sunlight."[29] This experience of light provided him with absolute certainty about life and death. A second example is provided by Master Wuwen Cong, who speaks about being aware of emptiness along with brightness, light, and purity, suggesting that he had a luminous experience.[30]

Besides the importance of visual metaphors, another metaphor that is prevalent throughout Zen history is the expression that life is a journey. This is often depicted as a journey for wisdom and a liberating experience. The great *haiku* poet master Bashō was an itinerant figure during his life and composed poems while traveling that reflected common experiences. Bashō's wandering from one location to another enhanced his chances for having new experiences to write poems about and to invite his reader to join him as in the following poem: "Come / To the true flower viewing / Of the life of pilgrimage." This poem invites a reader to adopt a new attitude and lifestyle that is manifested as a life of pilgrimage to see things as they really are. In another example from his corpus of poetry, he writes the following: "This road! / With no one on it— / Autumn dusk."[31] On an autumn evening, Bashō is walking on a lonely country road during the loneliest season of the year. For him to realize his ideal, he must travel this road alone because it is the path of poetry to which he has committed his life. In another poem, her encourages a reader to "Learn from the journey / of a sorrowing wayfarer: / flies of Kiso."[32] A poem about nature reflects its own journey: "Harvest moon / wandering round the pond / all night long."[33] This poem suggests that humans should follow the path and pattern of nature as it forms a paradigm for wandering.

Just as Bashō devoted himself to his poetry, the personal decision to become a monk or a nun involves a journey from one's home to a monastic community where one's spiritual journey begins in the company of others on the same path. Of course, there are records of wandering monks often looking for the right master to guide them or a secluded cave in some mountain. An aspiring *bodhisattva* might have to wander to several masters before he finds the right one.

The Blue Cliff Record refers to a direct experience of the journey: "If you want to know the mountain road, you must be one who travels on

---

29. Broughton and Watanabe, *Chan Whip Anthology*, 91.
30. Broughton and Watanabe, *Chan Whip Anthology*, 110.
31. Barnhill, *Bashō's Haiku*, 153.
32. Barnhill, *Bashō's Haiku*, 138.
33. Barnhill, *Bashō's Haiku*, 54.

it."³⁴ The text also compares the journey to something dangerous that is expressed as being stretched "out in the tiger's mouth."³⁵ The road is compared to three roads for teaching people by Dongshan: the hidden road, the bird's path, and extending the hands. Asked by a student to explain the bird's path, Dongshan says that it is a path on which you do not meet anyone. After being asked how one can travel on the bird's path, the master replied, "Let there be no self in your footsteps."³⁶ The bird's path leaves no track or trace that is more akin to your original face. Basically, there is no way to express this path in words, although the journey returns one to one's original state.

The text *Wumen's Gate* gives readers a couple of verses that allude to the path to be followed by an aspirant:

> The Great Path, the gate of nothingness, has no gate.
> Amidst the thousand differences, there is a road.³⁷

What the writer is referring to is the gate of emptiness, but there is a road that can take you to its realization. The traveler cannot, however, use words to convey what it is like, but you can respond in other ways that are a bit more violent:

> If on the road you meet a person who has consummated the Path,
>   Don't use words or silence to reply.
>   A pinch on the cheek, a punch in the face,
> If you understand directly then you understand.³⁸

The violence advocated by these lines of poetry is typical of Chan language from the classical period. Violence is a topic that will be explored more fully in chapter 3.

The Blue Cliff Record considers the journey and where the study of scriptures and treatises fits into traveling the path. The text teaches, "Once one's cultivation of studies is completed and exhausted, one is called a non-doing free wayfarer, beyond study. When one reaches the point of ending study, only then is one near the Way."³⁹ The same text approaches the topic of the way from a different perspective that is

---

34. Barnhill, *Bashō's Haiku*, 178.
35. Barnhill, *Bashō's Haiku*, 151.
36. Barnhill, *Bashō's Haiku*, 439.
37. Cleary, *Wumen's Gate*, 70.
38. Cleary, *Wumen's Gate*, 99.
39. Cleary, *Blue Cliff Record*, 220.

illuminating about the journey of life because it is a path that goes in reverse. The goal of the way is to become an infant. The commentator explains, "A student of the Way must become again like an infant; then one cannot be moved by praise or blame, success or fame, trial, or ease. Though one sees forms, one is the same as blind; though one hears sounds, one is the same deaf."[40] The commentator is pointing to a primordial experience when he refers to becoming an infant. What makes this infantile experience so primordial is that it is an experience before conceptualization and bestowal of meaning. It is the pure experience.

With respect to the journey life, the *Record of Linji* attempts to teach readers how to walk: "There's never a thought of hoping for or seeking the fruits of Buddhahood."[41] Linji is advocating a journey on which the walker must not strive to achieve their goal. Why? To strive to attain Buddhahood creates karma (cause and effect), which is counterproductive for the walker. The traveler must forget about successfully reaching their goal. Thus, his advice is the following: Do not think about walking, rather just walk. A similar point is made in the *Bodhidharma Anthology* when it calls attention to the ease of traveling the path. This text and the *Record of Linji* are referring to selfless walking. The *Bodhidharma Anthology* states, "When walking, Dharma is walking. It is not the ego walking. It is not the ego not walking."[42] What these texts convey is embodied in the various artistic ways that will be discussed in chapters 9 and 10. The arts are conceived as paths to the goal of no-mind in Japanese Zen. Each artistic way is a pathway, a road; it is a *dō*, a term that comes from the Chinese *dao* (road, path, way) where it suggests a way of life and a cosmic reality. By following the path in Zen and Daoism, the practitioner is transformed by the experience.

The journey made by a Zen aspirant occurs within a life context of ambiguity and transience because nothing is certain, and everything is in a constant state of flux. These features of life can be illustrated by the monk Ikkyū in his work entitled *Skeletons* composed in 1457, a prose-poem that shares his own existential dissatisfaction with life. As depicted in his work, Ikkyū's journey takes him to a deserted temple far away from human habitation. He tells his reader that he falls asleep in the abandoned temple and has a dream that elicits an awareness of life and death. While he continues to dream, Ikkyū sees skeletons, figures who are both

---

40. Cleary, *Blue Cliff Record*, 353.
41. Cleary, *Record of Linji*, 18.
42. Broughton, *Bodhidharma Anthology*, 38.

dead and alive and symbolic of the transient nature of existence. At the rear of the temple, Ikkyū encounters many skeletons, and one of them speaks to him. Ikkyū learns that we are all skeletons covered by skin. Thus, from one perspective, we are presently metaphorical skeletons and will become actual skeletons after we die. Skeletons are paradoxically dead and alive just like a true monk from Ikkyū's critical perspective. The broader point that Ikkyū makes is that an unenlightened person sees another person dressed in skin, flesh, clothes, and ornaments, whereas an enlightened individual sees a person as a living corpse. For Ikkyū, skeletons have a soteriological implication because being dead means that one cannot die again and being alive means that one cannot be reborn. Thus, the skeletons symbolize an end to death and rebirth.

With respect to these various examples of a journey, play is nourished by wandering, an activity that is effortless, enjoyable, and refreshing. Play is ideally without effort to the extent of letting events happen by themselves. Play is easy when there is an absence of strain, which functions as a mode of relaxation and a way to reduce tension. It is also the case that playful wandering evokes notions associated with peace and harmony without being oriented toward some goal or following a specific path. This sense of peace and harmony is evoked by a poem of the poet-monk Ryōkan (1758–1831): "Though travels / take me to / a different stopping place each night / the dream I dream is always / that same one of home."[43] The image of being at home is undermined to some extent by another poem in which he vows his intention to be a wandering monk who never rests, carrying his water jug in high spirits.[44]

TEXTUALITY

In his characterization of the major features of Zen, Suzuki gives the impression that Zen is not tied to scriptures but is rather about direct transmission of the truth from the mind of the master to that of the disciple outside of any scriptures. Although this observation is true about the stress on direct transmission of the teaching, his assertion is misleading because texts have played an important role in the history of Zen development.

---

43. Watson, *Ryōkan*, 17.
44. Watson, *Ryōkan*, 109.

To place the issue of texts within the Chinese cultural context, it is necessary to call attention to their role in the intellectual life of the people. From ancient times, Chinese intellectuals both respected and loved books. In fact, ownership of books was related to having knowledge in the popular imagination. Books became so important that the government attempted to control their contents and distribution of them. A variety of materials were used to create books, including slips of bamboo, wood, and silk, until the invention of paper became the best medium for publishing on wooden blocks from the first century CE. And by the third century paper superseded other forms of printing material. The first extant printed book is a copy of the *Diamond Sūtra* from 868.[45]

Among Mahāyāna Buddhists in China, there developed cults focused on the book with such texts as, for instance, the *Diamond Sūtra*, *Lotus Sūtra*, and *Flower Adornment Sūtra*. For the various books given cultic treatment, the venerated book became an object of worship with flower offerings and incense made to it. More than a source of information, the cultic book became an icon to be worshiped. Certain books were believed to have holy power and could emit a strange and wonderful light. Narratives circulated about the ability of books to save their owners from calamity, such as the sword of an executioner or helping fight off demons. The sacred nature of venerated books transformed copying a Buddhist scripture into a religious service that included the burning of incense, purifying one's clothing, and fasting before commencing copying. Fanatical copiers were known to copy a sacred text with a mixture of ink and their own blood.[46] The act of copying a sacred text was considered a way to produce merit.

To discern the importance of texts in the Chan/Zen tradition, it is unnecessary to move much beyond the Sixth Patriarch Huineng. When he was a struggling, young man he overheard someone reciting the *Diamond Sūtra*, an event that triggered an awakening experience within the master that would culminate with full enlightenment later. Of course, *The Platform Sūtra of the Sixth Patriarch*, based on his life and teachings, is studied by members of the Rinzai school even today. When an old master was nearing death it was common for him to compose a verse for his disciples. These types of examples suggest that textuality has been and is important to Zen. To understand textuality in the Zen context, it

---

45. Kieschnick, *Impact of Buddhism*, 175.
46. Kieschnick, *Impact of Buddhism*, 174.

is essential to comprehend it in a non-dualistic way. There is no better example of a non-dualistic grasp of textuality than that located in the works of Dōgen.

Just like his grasp of perception, Dōgen insists that a text is not to be distinguished from the teacher: "When a teacher washes his face or drinks tea, it is an ancient sutra."[47] Since Zen texts are used as instruments to instruct others and lead them to liberation, they are constituted by any activity of a teacher. The scope of these activities is made evident by Dōgen: "When we learn the ultimate criteria, even inhaling and exhaling is a sūtra, and moving the feet is a function of the sutras. All actions are functions of the sutras—even before our parents were born, before the universe was created."[48] But these types of implications are insufficient for Dōgen, and he pushes his insights to an even more radical position.

It is possible to witness the further development of Dōgen's position in his work entitled *Sansuikyo* (*Waters and Mountain and River Sūtras*) in the larger *Shōbōgenzō* (*The Eye and Treasury of the True Law*). In this work, Dōgen asserts that mountains and rivers are *sūtras* (texts), and students should study them as texts.[49] Dōgen intends to suggest that the entire world can become a sacred text. If it is possible for the world and things within the world to become texts, it is not beyond the realm of impossibility for mountains and rivers (non-sentient beings) to become preachers of these sacred texts. This unusual type of preaching cannot be expected to be heard in the ordinary way because wordless preaching and its soundless sound cannot be heard with one's ears. Instead, the wordless form of communication must be heard with one's eyes. And just as mountains and rivers learn about themselves as mountains and rivers, we must listen and learn about them as mountains and rivers.[50]

Included within the nature of textuality for Dōgen is the element of time. What this aspect of textuality means for Dōgen is that a reader does not obtain and read a text in the past or in the present because both moments of time are "the occasion to obtain the sutras."[51] In fact, a text compresses all time because: "Within the sutras there are the letters of all the Buddhas in Parinirvana."[52] Moreover, Dōgen thinks that language

47. Dōgen, *Shōbōgenzō*, 2:111.
48. Dōgen, *Shōbōgenzō*, 2:117.
49. Dōgen, *Shōbōgenzō*, 2:117.
50. Dōgen, *Shōbōgenzō*, 4:75.
51. Dōgen, *Shōbōgenzō*, 3:81.
52. Dōgen, *Shōbōgenzō*, 3:81.

and texts are impermanent, which necessarily implies that language possesses no lasting structure, although he does give language a provisional value as a form of *upāya* (skillful means), a pedagogical method of communication and instruction. Overall, language assumes an ancillary position to experience for Dōgen.

ZEN AND PLAY

An important characteristic of Zen that is not mentioned by Suzuki is its relation to play, which is the theme of this book. After long western intellectual neglect, John Huizinga published his insightful work *Homo Ludens: A Study of the Play Element in Culture* in 1955. In this book, he identified several characteristics of play: (1) a voluntary activity that suggests freedom; (2) stands opposed to real life and gives participants an opportunity to leave the world of work and enter a realm of pretending and fun; (3) it is a disinterested, temporary activity that operates as an interlude in our lives, while also being an integral part of life that enhances one's existence; (4) it is performed within particular limits of space and time; (5) however temporary and limited, play creates order that brings participants under its spell by captivating and enchanting them with its rhythmical and harmonious natures; (6) play is risky and uncertain and thus results in a tension; (7) it eliminates doubt with its binding rules for participants; (8) it is secret in the sense that it is for a participant and not others. Huizinga concludes that without the element of play a civilization cannot endure or exist.[53]

Play is grounded in seriousness. To be serious when engaged in play renders play wholly play. Those individuals who do not take the game seriously tend to be a spoilsport. Even though a participant enters freely into play, it is important that all participants maintain seriousness with respect to their effort and interrelationship to others. Prior to engaging in some form of play, a person must decide about whether to enter into play. Although there is a level of freedom associated with such a decision, it is still limited by time, place, and human feelings. The freedom associated with deciding to enter into play implies that even work can be transformed into play.[54]

---

53. Huizinga, *Homo Ludens*.
54. Olson, "Ludic Life," 252–53.

Play is useless in the sense that it does not solve any problems within a given society, but it can function to entertain observers of those playing, which can have economic and cultural value as a social escape mechanism. The players and observers escape from the routine of daily life for a brief period. This break from the habitual pattern of everyday existence serves as an interlude that is potentially refreshing and even rejuvenating, which transforms the useless into something useful. There is also an effortless nature of play in the sense that participants allow play to happen by itself. Young children seem to be experts at allowing play to just happen without any effort. In a competitive athletic contest, the truly physically gifted players make what they do appear to be easy and natural and are admired by opponents and observers for their prowess.[55]

From a Zen perspective, play can be serious and non-serious. This implies that play is not against frolic because they are equally ways of being enchanted. "Seriousness keeps frolic from going flippant, and frolic keeps seriousness ever free and unstuck."[56] By combining seriousness and its opposite, play becomes fun. In fact, seriousness and non-seriousness need each other because they make genuine life a way of play.

Play tends to be pervasive, irrational, and repetitive. It is done for its own sake and not to an end. Those participating in play respond to each other within the context of play, making play an inter-relational and interpersonal event. Play means something to the participants and members of a particular society.

By entering play, humans create an "as if" world that represents an event with a beginning and conclusion that is structurally or temporally different than ordinary life. Thus, play is subjunctive ("as if") and replaces the indicative ("as is"). Play gives us an ability to articulate in a subjunctive fashion different ways of classifying reality.[57] The subjunctive aspect of play suggests its non-materialistic quality. Moreover, the subjunctive mood enables a person to articulate different ways of classifying reality and developing a competing view of reality because it refers to what is contingent or hypothetical action. The anthropologist Victor Turner explains, "Subjectivity is possibility. It refers to what may or might not be. It is also concerned with supposition, conjecture, and assumption within the domain of 'as-if' rather than 'as-is.'"[58] The subjunctive nature of play

55. Olson, "Ludic Life," 256–60.
56. Wu, *Butterfly as Companion*, 111.
57. Droogers, "Third Bank of the River," 81.
58. Turner, *Anthropology of Performance*, 169.

represents the inverse of the objective realm, rendering it free from external constraints. Not only does the subjunctive mood characteristic of play have a creative potential, but it is simultaneously dangerous. "Because of its subjunctiveness play by nature is subversive."[59] When humans play, for example, in religious festivals the normal social hierarchy is overturned, and customary values or forms of status are called into question. In this way, play is oxymoronic in the sense that it is dangerous harmlessness.

Finally, play possesses a liminal nature that invites inversion and experimentation. Play is liminal because it exists between rationality and madness, sacred and profane, imaginary and real. Its liminal nature makes play ambiguous because it is transient and even resists being fixed in a permanent place. Moreover, its liminal nature implies that play is located anywhere or nowhere; it can imitate anything, but can be identified with nothing in particular.[60] Being composed of a wide variety of incongruous elements that are frail and impermanent, play eludes easy taxonomic classification, although it is possible to draw a distinction between liminal and limonoid as Turner does by stating, "One works at the liminal, one plays with the limonoid."[61]

By entering play, a person takes a risk, an attractive feature of the activity, because the outcome is not predetermined and remains uncertain. By taking the risk invited by play, the player risks being injured or losing, if it is a game with mutually accepted rules. And following the path of Zen is risky business. A person can, for example, get lost, or one can suffer from Zen sickness, which the Zen master Hakuin defines as a nervous breakdown; he informs his readers that one's head becomes heated, and their lower body becomes cool. These types of symptoms can be treated by a process of deep breathing that heats the lower part of the body.[62]

It is also possible to view play as a fundamental phenomenon of human existence, which tends to lessen the marginal and contingent aspects of play, suggesting that it is not something frivolous; it is rather a spontaneous activity that transports and releases us from ordinary life.[63] By means of its activity and creativity, play gives us the present moment as it interrupts the course of life. And in Zen there is a strong emphasis on becoming aware of the present moment.

59. Droogers, "Third Bank of the River," 83.
60. Turner, *Anthropology of Performance*, 168.
61. Turner, *Ritual Process*, 55.
62. Yampolsky, *Hakuin*, 51.
63. Fink, *Play as Symbol*, 20.

Play is also a pleasurable, delightful, and imaginary activity that makes possible social existence as a subject interplay with others.[64] It is play that opens a connection between a human being and the world. In other words, play enables us to conceive of difference and an awareness that we live along with others within a world. Thus, humans are not limited within themselves because the player can ecstatically step out of and beyond themselves.[65] Play can be conceived as both actual and non-actual. In the former instance play is actual as non-serious actions that also embody a sense of non-actuality, which is indicative of its entwinement with Being and appearance.[66] In fact, play is a coming into appearance that is metaphorically like donning a mask behind which is nothing that Zen equates with emptiness.

Play is autotelic, which means an action having its own goals and purposes and duration. The purpose of play is not, however, fixed.[67] In other words, people play for the pure sake of playing that enables players to express themselves and to potentially disrupt the order of things, which suggests that play is a mode of rebellion against forms and forces within the world. As an action, play is transformative.[68] The transformative nature of play will become evident as dialogical encounters between Zen masters and novices become more evident in the following chapters.

An advantage of looking at the theme of play in Zen is that it helps us to comprehend encounter dialogues preserved by the tradition. These encounter dialogues are problematic for western scholars of Zen because they seem fabricated and false.[69] Western scholars are suspicious of these reported dialogues because they have been trained to be skeptical and critical in their approach to a subject and to access a phenomenon analytically and impartially. But it is a mistake to conclude that these encounters between enlightened masters and disciples never happened. These encounters may have been embellished by subsequent writers or even invented, but the Zen tradition itself seems to be asserting to outsiders that this is the way that we understand ourselves and how we want

---

64. Fink, *Play as Symbol*, 22–23.
65. Fink, *Play as Symbol*, 46.
66. Fink, *Play as Symbol*, 87, 92.
67. Sicart, *Play Matters*, 28.
68. Goffman, *From Analysis*, 43.
69. See for instance the following studies: McRae, *Seeing through Zen*; Faure, *Chan Insights and Oversights*, 195–204, 226–33; Faure, *Will to Orthodoxy*; Hershock, *Liberating Intimacy*.

to be known. In other words, the encounter dialogues are an example of members of the religion defining themselves. Moreover, there is a hagiographical quality to the encounter dialogues between master and disciple that is playful.

The encounter dialogues, for instance, previously mentioned briefly are an excellent example of mind games, which is arguably the highest form of play, like the opinion of the former chess world champion Bobby Fisher about his game. In a violent encounter, Linji tells an assembly of monks that his late teacher Huangbo hit him three times when he asked a question about the Buddha Dharma that many times. Linji said, "Right now I still think I deserve a beating. Who can give it to me?" When a monk volunteered to administer the blows. Linji handed the monk his staff. When the monk hesitated Linji hit him.[70] In another episode, after asking a monk where he had come from, the monk immediately shouted at Muzhou, who said that "I've been shouted at by you once." In response, the monk shouted again. Muzhou said, "After three or four shouts, then what?" The monk was speechless, so Muzhou hit him and called him a phony.[71] In a final narrative encounter example, the master Yanguan called his attendant, "Bring me the rhinoceros fan." The attendant replied, "The fan is broken." Yanguan responded, "If the fan is broken, bring the rhinoceros back to me."[72] Nonetheless, these types of playful encounter narratives will be explored further in chapter 3.

PREVIEW OF FUTURE SUBJECTS

Chapter 2 places the development of Zen into its historical context from its Indian roots to its transmission to China and its growth into an important school of Chinese Buddhism. This is following by a review of its development in Japan. Chapter 3 examines Zen teaching methods and their interconnection to violence and play. A distinction will be drawn between "realizational" and "instrumental" conceptions of Zen language and action to suggest that these various methods enable a practitioner to see one's original face and make something happen. Chapter 4 is closely associated with the subjects of chapter 3 because it will review the Zen understanding of language as it pertains to achieving enlightenment and

70. Sasaki, *Record of Linji*, 14.
71. Chung-yuan, *Original Teachings of Ch'an Buddhism*, 93.
72. Cleary, *Blue Cliff Record*, 401.

will thus involves a discussion of the Zen use of *koans*, the disruptive nature of language, meditation, and monastic life in general.

The following two chapters are representative of the two major branches of Zen, the Rinzai and Sōtō. The former chapter examines topics such as the opening of an aspirant's mind, notion of no-mind, mode of non-representational thinking, enlightenment (*satori*), and the application of enlightenment. The latter or sixth chapter looks at the philosophy of Dōgen, founder of the Sōtō school, by reviewing such topics as zazen-only, Buddha-nature, existence and time, non-thinking, and the authentic and inauthentic self.

Chapters 7 and 8 examine the interconnection between play, madness, eroticism, and humor. These chapters are comparative in spirit by comparing the eccentric Zen master Ikkyū Sojun (1394–1481) with figures from other religious traditions. With respect to the subject of eroticism, it is possible to grasp the logic of Mahāyāna Buddhism that causes its practitioners to violate sexual precepts in the name of Buddhist liberation. In chapter 8, it is indicated that Zen teaches that it is important to learn to laugh at the folly of the craving self in a state of bondage. By reviewing the relationship between the comic and humor, it is noticed that they are forms of skillful means for Zen and have commonalities with the figure of the clown.

The final two chapters examine the relationship between Japanese Zen Buddhism and Japanese culture. Chapter 9 is devoted to looking at the fine arts such as the following: haiku poetry; Nō theater; tea ceremony; landscape painting; and rock gardens. Attention is focused on the playful aspects of the artistic ways, other possible influences from other Buddhist schools, Japanese folk religion, and the indigenous religion of Shinto. Chapter 10 reviews the ways that Zen influenced martial arts like archery and swordsmanship. This final chapter also looks at problems associated with modernity by examining thinkers connected to the Kyoto School, the way that Zen leaders have engaged in intra-religious dialogue, and the spread of Zen to the West. This final chapter also briefly looks at the dark side of Zen ethos that permeated the militaristic imperialism of the Japanese government during World War II.

2

BUDDHISM IN CHINA AND JAPAN: AN OVERVIEW

FROM INDIA, BUDDHISM MADE its way to China by following the trade routes. Gradually, Chinese monks returned to India to collect and translate texts and to take them back to their homeland. The Buddhist monk Lokakṣema arrived in China between 168 to 188 CE, and he is credited with translating the *Prajñāpāramitā Sūtra in Eight Thousand Lines*. At a later period, Dharmarakṣa, a monk of Indo-Scythian heritage, arrived in China to translate works. These monks were followed eventually by even more eminent figures like Kumārajīva (344–409/413); Buddhabhadra (359–429), a famous meditation master renowned for his miraculous powers; Sengcan (384–414), a brilliant disciple of Kumārajīva; and Daoxin (ca. 360–434), another capable follower of Kumārajīva who composed commentaries on numerous Mahāyāna texts. Daoxin discussed the Buddha germ that grows in all living beings. He believed people bound to sensual desire could attain salvation, which was a controversial position for this period of Buddhist history. Daoxin's internal germ was likely influenced by a Mahāyāna text such as the *Awakening of Faith*, which has been traditionally attributed to the monk named Aśvaghoṣa, but is more likely a sixth-century Chinese apocrypha that seeks to synthesize concerns about the intrinsic nature of enlightenment and apprehensions about the source of delusion and suffering.[1] The former is identified as the *tathāgatagarbha*, the original, pure, enlightened mind that is inherent to all sentient beings and contains the store-house consciousness. The

---

1. Stone, *Original Enlightenment and the Transformation*, 5–6.

latter source of delusion is associated with not being able to realize that the original mind is identical to emptiness. The state of enlightenment enables one to realize that deluded thoughts have no reality because they are also empty.

Buddhism did not dominate Chinese culture like it did in countries such as Sri Lanka, Myanmar (Burma), Cambodia, and Thailand because China had already been shaped for centuries by Confucian and Taoist philosophies. Since Buddhism, unlike the indigenous Confucian and Taoist traditions, was a foreign religious import, it had to struggle to secure a position in Chinese culture and to ward off attacks by the predominant traditions. What complicated matters even more for the Buddhists were its internal structure and the external structure of Chinese culture. On the one hand, Buddhist monks did not feel obligated to pay homage to a ruler because the monastic community was a separate entity apart from the prevailing society. Furthermore, the monks insisted on their own laws and self-governance. These attitudes stood in potential conflict with Chinese culture where there was no recognized separation of religion and the state. In fact, any religion must be subordinate to the state bureaucracy from the traditional Chinese perspective. The Buddhists, however, adapted to their situation by integrating themselves into the structure of the state by establishing chapels, for instance, in the imperial palace where monks recited texts (*sūtras*) for the welfare and protection of the state. After subordinating themselves to the state, the monks became involved in its political fortunes. In response to this helpful attitude and subordination, the state built and financially supported national monasteries, although during the Tang Dynasty (618–906) the state even assumed control of ordination to the profession of monks and nuns that placed them further under the control of the state.

By subordinating and integrating themselves into the state apparatus, Buddhists raised the suspicions of those already entrenched in powerful and influential positions and eager to maintain their status. The Confucians leveled four general charges at the Buddhists. Firstly, the activities of Buddhism are detrimental to the authority of the government and to the stability and prosperity of the state. This political and economic argument presupposed that it was the emperor that made life possible for all his subjects by performing rituals for the benefit of the people and nation and personified himself the creative powers of nature. From the Chinese perspective, withdrawal from society as mandated by the Buddhist lifestyle was illegal, asocial, and a blasphemous act. Moreover, withdrawal from society entailed a loss to the state of tax-payers and laborers. The Buddhist offered a counter argument to the effect that monks were not disloyal, even if they are not subject to the power of the state.[2] In fact, Buddhism helps to ensure lasting peace and prosperity in the country.

The Confucians also charged that the Buddhist monastic life was useless and unproductive. The Buddhists countered this utilitarian argument by stating that monastic life was not useless because its benefits are not yielded within this world. Thirdly, the Confucians argued that Buddhism was a foreign barbarian creed that was not mentioned in the records of the past, and it made extravagant and unverifiable claims. To counter this argument based on cultural superiority, the Buddhists claimed that its foreign origin was not a good reason for rejecting it. In fact, China often borrowed things from abroad with excellent results. Moreover, Buddhists argued that their religion was not innovative, and it was mentioned by ancient authorities long before Confucius. Since China was converted to Buddhism under King Aśoka, this made Confucius and Laozi either disciples or manifestations of the Buddha, making Chinese critics shortsighted, narrow-minded, and pedestrian. Finally, the Confucians charged that Buddhism was an unnatural violation of the sacred canons of social behavior, implying that Buddhism was asocial and highly immoral because it did not practice filial piety, a fundamental Confucian virtue. The Buddhists responded to this moral argument by claiming that filial piety could also be discovered in Buddhist scriptures, and they forged a body of apocryphal literature that emphasized the virtue.

Although it did not begin as an anti-polemical attack on Buddhism, the Daoists also made anti-Buddhist charges using its *hua hu* theory. According to this theory dating to around 166 CE, Laozi preached the Buddhist doctrine after his departure to the western region to convert the barbarians, which made him either a teacher of the Buddha or the Buddha himself. Originally, the theory did not function as an anti-Buddhist stratagem. The theory allowed Daoists to incorporate Buddhist practices and institutions, and it rendered Buddhism more attractive to the Chinese people by propagating it as a foreign branch of Daoism. Around 300 CE, the theory was used for polemical purposes by the Daoists by arguing that it indicated that Buddhism was a diluted and debased foreign version of Daoism adapted to the needs of uncivilized people, whose aim was the destruction of the Chinese civilization. Therefore, the Daoists

---

2. For a fuller discussion of these interactions, see Zürcher, *Buddhist Conquest of China*.

argued that Buddhism was unfit to be introduced into China. Why did the Daoists change their attitudes toward Buddhism? Historically, there was a gradual infiltration of Hunnish and Tibetan tribes into China around 300 CE, and their conquest of northern China intensified anti-foreign sentiments. Furthermore, Buddhists undermined the power of Daoism by expanding into rural areas. And even historically earlier, Buddhism became an influential force among the gentry and higher strata of Chinese intellectual society. Again, the Buddhists did not sit idly by, and they reacted to the Daoist charge by attacking the theory on rational grounds. The Buddhists also used the Daoists' method against them by developing an apocryphal literature arguing that Laozi was either a manifestation or a disciple of the Buddha, which rendered the Daoist philosopher to an inferior position in comparison to the Buddha.

These various charges did not stop Buddhism from becoming an economic and educational force in China. Due to donations by lay people to Buddhist monasteries, they accumulated large tracts of land, which was considered an act of merit by wealthy donors. The state also granted land to monks and nuns in a procedure called the equal-field system, and monasteries purchased land. The land was cultivated by temple slaves, who were criminals freed by the state to work on the land, people attached to the land when it was donated to the monastery, and unemployed peasants who mortgaged themselves to the monastery. There was also a group of tenant farmers called pure people (*jingren*) because they farmed the land, handled gold and silver, and traded in goods, activities that spared monks from such impure actions. Buddhist monasteries were also involved in industrial enterprises by sponsoring water-power mills to produce flour, operating oil presses for oil used for cooking and fuel, and engaging in commercial goods transactions, which were called inexhaustible wealth because the goods could be used indefinitely and continuously earn interest. In addition, monasteries functioned as hostels for traveling state officials and candidates on their way to civil service exams in provincial or national capitals.[3] Functioning as educators, itinerant monks preached Buddhist texts to lay people, and there were also popular lectures that were modified versions of the texts with a mixture of prose, poetry, and fanciful embellishments.

The charges made against Buddhism by Confucians and Daoists were periodically translated into state persecution of the religion. The

---

3. See Chen, *Chinese Transformation of Buddhism*.

persecution of 845 under the impetus of Emperor Wusong (841–846), a fanatical Daoist adherent, sought to expunge Buddhism from China. The hostile measure began in 842 with the returning of monks and nuns to lay life and the confiscation of Buddhist properties. A second phase of imperial decrees in the fall of 844 attempted to destroy the religion by dissolving small monastic communities and forcing monks to pay taxes. Due to their location in the south of China and more remote areas, Chan monasteries escaped much of the harm inflicted on Buddhist institutions.[4] The Chan monasteries did a good job of remaining obscure and removed from attention of the central government.

Behind the overt persecutions of Buddhism, the court perceived the religion as a potential powerful political threat to the court's stability that needed to be controlled. In addition to the possibility that Buddhism might become an autonomous rival to the court, the ideas of the religion were considered dangerous because they promoted, for example, liberation and the natural questioning of the authority and status of political power that could potentially undermine the court.[5]

CHINESE CULTURAL INFLUENCES ON CHAN BUDDHISM

By the time Buddhism was introduced into China, the culture of the country was dominated by Confucian values. Among the important Confucian ethical virtues, there are *li* (ritual, ceremony, courtesy), *ren* (humanity), *xiao de* (filial piety and brotherly love), *yi* (righteousness), *zhong* (conscientiousness and loyalty), and *shu* (altruism and reciprocity). With respect to *li*, Confucius envisioned a society in which the gestures of each member would coordinate harmoniously with each other in an effortless and spontaneous way. Confucius thought that a smooth functioning society was analogous to a ritual dance. *Li* is in harmony with the *Dao* and acts as a restraint on a person's proclivity to act contrary to it. Thus, if everyone acts in accord with *li*, the world and society will be harmonious and peaceful, although Confucius thought that humanity (*ren*) was the penultimate virtue because its sense of person to personness involves loving others in accord with the golden rule: do not do to others what you do not want them to do to you. *Li* and *ren* can be construed as two aspects of the same virtue.

4. Dumoulin, *Zen Buddhism*, 1:212.
5. Bowring, *Religious Traditions of Japan*, 54.

Along with the predominately Confucian culture that Buddhism encountered in China and the already culturally shaped natives that Buddhist masters recruited to the monastic life, the influence of Daoism is difficult to underestimate. The Daoist influence probably began in subtle ways through the adoption and use of its terminology by Buddhist monks. Because the Sanskrit texts brought to China from India contained some very abstract notions, Chinese translators faced a difficult task finding equivalent terms in the more concrete Chinese language. Thus, translators tended to borrow terminology from Daoist philosophy as the nearest equivalents to the abstract Sanskrit notions, a practice that contributed to the transformation of Buddhist ideas and the rendering of Buddhism into a more Chinese product. A good example of this process was the Chan Buddhist conception of enlightenment as an awakening to the *Dao*, which Daoists defined as the way, the source of all things, the eternal and universal principle that is nameless, invisible, inaudible, and subtle.

Expressions used in Daoist meditation found their way into Buddhist texts. The sage Zhuangzi emphasized, for instance, sitting and forgetting everything, which implied casting away one's limbs and intelligence, becoming detached from one's body and mind, and becoming one with the *Dao*. There was also reference to "fasting of the mind," suggesting a purging of the mind and its false notions. It is helpful to know that Daoism conceived of its way as a path of reversal and unlearning bad habits and ideas rather than accumulating knowledge and progressing ahead in a temporal manner. Another important Daoist source of influence on Chan Buddhism was its notion of non-action (*wuwei*), which suggested not doing anything that was not natural or spontaneous. Thus, it was essential not to take any artificial, contrived, or thought-out, intentional action that is expressed in its classic text in this way: "No action is taken, and yet nothing is left undone."[6] Non-action involved supporting things in their natural state: "By acting without action all things will be in order."[7] The fundamental message is to let things take their own course, and this position implied that it was improper to impose one's will on the course of things or nature.

The Buddhist philosophical notion of impermanence was reinforced by the doctrine of change in Daoism and divination texts like the *Yijing* (*Book of Changes*), which became a Confucian classic and part

---

6. Ames and Hall, *Dao De Ching*, 48.
7. Ames and Hall, *Dao De Ching*, 3.

of its canon. Functioning as a diviner's manual, the text evolved from eight trigrams, a combination of broken and unbroken lines placed atop another line, which corresponded to natural phenomena such as earth, wind, fire, and water. The broken lines of the trigram represent *yin* (feminine principle), while the unbroken lines stand for the *yang* (male principle). The original eight trigrams developed into sixty-four hexagrams by placing one trigram over another. Theoretically, the trigrams portray the universe as being in a constant state of flux and transformation, whereas the term *yi* in the book's title signifies "easy." By using the book, a person can adapt to change and have a better chance for survival. Nonetheless, underlying this continuous change, there is the *Dao* that is changeless.

Besides the influence of Chinese culture, Daoism, and divination, Chan was also influenced by other Buddhism schools like Huayan and Tiantai. From the Huayan perspective, all things (*dharmas*) within the self-creating and self-maintaining cosmos are empty and thus lacking self-nature. Since things do not exist of themselves, everything exists only interdependently in the cosmos. If you examine a thing like an apple, you will discover that it possesses both a static aspect and a dynamic aspect, respectively its principle (*li*) and phenomenon (*shih*). When an apple is identical to other apples this points to its static nature, whereas its dynamic nature refers to the way that it interpenetrates with other things like other types of fruits, vegetables, people, the store where it is sold, the community in which can be found, and so forth.

By itself, the static principle is without form, while being at the same time clear, pure, perfect, and brilliant like the gold of a statue of a lion. Since the gold is devoid of form, it assumes any form that conditions assign to it. The gold is also the primary cause of the lion because it is the factor that makes the production of the lion possible. Representing the realm of things, the figure, which is a secondary and contributing cause, symbolizes the dynamic phenomenon that is represented by the work of the artisan who shapes the gold. This famous image of the golden lion was created by the founder of the school Fazang (643–712) to illustrate his philosophical point that principle and phenomenon are interfused, suggesting that all events and things of the phenomenal world arise through a combination of these two sets of causes. Moreover, each individual thing embraces all other individual things, making all phenomena mutually identical to each other. This suggests that all dynamic phenomena are manifestations of static noumenon. A good example of this interrelationship is waves of the ocean. The ocean (noumenon) is one, but its waves (phenomena) are many.

Like the Huayan school, the Tiantai school stressed the emptiness of things, the interconnectedness of all things, and the unity of the universe. In addition to these points, the Tiantai school's notion of *chikuan* (concentrated insight) influenced Chan to some extent. Concentration (*chi*) represents the process of emptying the mind of all deluded thoughts, passions, and other obstacles to clear understanding, whereas insight (*kuan*) is insight into the genuine features of reality. They form together a harmonious tension in which reality is correctly understood and Buddhahood attained, which occurs simultaneously. It is analogous to being able to see the bottom of a pond when the water is still.

Another influential notion that comes from this school and certain Mahāyāna texts is the emphasis on the absolute mind, which is defined as embracing the entire universe and all Buddhas. In fact, all things are dependent upon it for existence. Moreover, all things are manifestations of a single mind that possesses two aspects: substance and function. The former aspect is the same and undifferentiated meaning that the mind is universally the same as universal consciousness. The latter aspect means that the mind is diverse and differentiated, representing the store-house consciousness, which is non-universal consciousness that accounts for different appearances. The substance and functioning aspects of the mind help to explain why people perceive things differently. This absolute mind is equated with thusness or suchness, which means things as they really are in fact or their true state. An especially important point made by the Tiantai school for its importance to Chan is the equation of absolute mind with Buddha-nature.

This Buddha-nature is in all things that are animate and inanimate. Thus, this would include, for instance, humans, dogs, trees, grass, water, stones, and dirt. The Buddha-nature possesses three aspects: Buddhahood in potentiality, the wisdom nature of Buddha that brings enlightenment, and the activity of becoming Buddha. If this is the case, why do dogs and stones never apparently become Buddhas? In a sense, they do become enlightened because all things are identical, that is empty, and humans share the same nature as dogs and stones. Therefore, when a human becomes enlightened so do stones and dogs. What makes this possible is that all things possess the Buddha-nature. This scenario can be connected to functions of concentration (*chi*) and insight (*kuan*). The function of concentration is to achieve *nirvāṇa* by a process of realizing that all things are devoid of self-nature, are neither produced nor destroyed, have no real existence, and only appear to be real due to our illusions and imaginative creations. This type of realization terminates our erroneous thoughts. Insight is a technique of observing and examining the nature of things and to realize that things are created by the mind and have a temporary existence. By means of insight, a person can realize that things do not have real being much like the illusions of a dream. If concentration enables a person to achieve *nirvāṇa*, insight functions to return an enlightened person to the ordinary world.

EARLY PERIOD OF CHAN

With the emphasis on the family, ancestors, and lineage in Chinese culture, it is not surprising that a product of such a culture like Chan Buddhism would not also be influenced by these types of cultural values. Chan schools are conceived as families, and they trace their lineages all the way back to the historical Buddha in India. It is a Chan conviction that there has been a single transmission from the enlightened mind of the Buddha to the present. Thus, anyone achieving enlightenment today possesses the identical enlightened mind of the Buddha in ancient India. Some five major chronicles preserve traditions about his mind to mind transmission throughout the centuries that is often referred to as the "Record of the Lamp," an obvious symbolic reference to enlightenment. In these texts, one can find references to a list of twenty-eight Indian Chan patriarchs. Although it forms an essential part of the movement's self-understanding, such a list is without historical credibility or certainty.

Nonetheless, included on the list is an Indian of the Brahmin caste named Bodhidharma from southern India who allegedly reached China during the early part of the reign of Emperor Wu (502–550 CE). In the *Lidai fabao ji* (*Record of the Dharma-Jewel through the Generations*), Bodhidharma was the third son of a south Indian king. He achieved enlightenment at a young age, and sent a couple of disciples to China to discern if that country was ready for Buddhism. The disciples impressed Lord Yuan, a *Dharma* master, with their teaching. The disciples composed a work entitled *Chanmen jing* (*Scripture of the Chan Teachings*) before passing into extinction and being buried on Mount Lu. Learning that his disciples could not find anyone to believe in their teachings, Bodhidharma traveled to China where he received an audience with the Emperor Wu. By responding negatively to the emperor's question about all the merit that he thought that he had earned by his generosity toward the Buddhist religion and the futility of building up merit, Bodhidharma had an ominous premonition and decided to leave the emperor, crossing the Yangtze River on a reed.[8] He found a cave in the mountains and allegedly sat gazing at the wall for nine years, earning the title "the wall gazing Brahmin" from the populace.[9] It is unclear whether or not Bodhidharma wrote any text, although a discovery at Dunhuang early in the twentieth century in Northwest China in a cave makes scholars think that the *Two Entrances* text of the larger *Bodhidharma Anthology* can be attributed to him.[10]

Bodhidharma passed the tradition to a former student of Daoism named Huike, who failed to get the attention of the meditating master until the master took compassion on the inquirer standing in the fast falling snowstorm that reached his waist. To presumably prove his sincerity and capture Bodhidharma's attention as the master sat in meditation gazing at the wall of his cave, Huike cut off his left arm at the elbow and presented to the Bodhidharma. Huike's blood flowed out white as milk, according to the account in the *Lidai fabao ji*.[11] Now that he was convinced of the aspirant's seriousness Bodhidharma accepted him as a student and eventually a patriarch of the tradition. The fourth patriarch was Daoxin (580–651), who passed on the transmission of the mind to his disciple the fifth patriarch Hongren (6701–674), who moved his residence to the East Mountain or Mount Pingmao and marks the end of the early formative period. According to the traditional account of its history, Chan teachings were passed from the mind of one master to the next one in an orderly pattern of transmission, suggesting a homogenous tradition.

This narrative about a single line of transmission from Bodhidharma to subsequent enlightened masters represents a pious fiction. The actual historical evolution of Chan is a more ambiguous, complex, and fluid situation, according to contemporary scholars without a sectarian bias to promote. It is thus possible to discern continuity and discontinuity in the tradition. Early Chan embodies a combination of different individuals, groups, and factions. This situation is evident in the more recently discovered Dunhuang manuscripts and other records that reflect different

---

8. Adamek, *Mystique of Transmission*, 311–12.
9. Cleary, *Blue Cliff Record*, 14.
10. Broughton, *Bodhidharma Anthology*, 7.
11. Adamek, *Mystique of Transmission*, 313–14.

types of experimentation occurring within these diverse factions.[12] This diversity of often conflicting spiritual attitudes suggests a fluid situation. This historical situation stands in sharp contrast to the traditional view of an orderly transmission of the teachings. Instead of a single set of teachings that implies a single stem that branches outward historically, Chan Buddhism developed from numerous branches into a single stem.[13] From an historical perspective, Chan did not attain the status of a distinct school until the end of the eighth century.

If the diversity of the early development of Chan reflects the actual historical condition of the movement, how did the single line of transmission get started? Japanese scholars think that it was constructed by the East Mountain school that was established by Daoxin and Hongren, the fifth patriarch, and further developed by Shenxiu that was also associated with another group called the Laṅkāvatāra school that was guided by Fachong (d. ca. 665). Another important development was the advocacy of Huineng (684–758) as the sixth patriarch by Shenhui (684–758) instead of the northern master Shenxiu. According to Shenhui, the Northern School embraced a gradual path to enlightenment, whereas the Southern represented a superior sudden path to liberation, a teaching that reflected the original teaching of Bodhidharma that was embraced by the fifth patriarch and passed onward to Huineng, the sixth patriarch. Even though Chan was split into northern and southern branches, once Chan finds its identity it begins to advocate its usefulness for the protection and welfare of China, that it was superior to other Buddhist schools, that it represented authentic Buddhism, and that operated by excluding other spiritual seekers by means of its genealogical pattern.[14] This competition between the Northern and Southern Schools was just part of Chan's historical development, a process that included the evolution of other schools. Daoxin established, for example, the Dongshan school around the mid-seventh century, while other figures erected schools at different locations in China. Occasionally, historical events such as the An Lushan rebellion in 755 enabled the Dongshan school to entrench itself in the area of Luoyang, while the Baotang, Hongzhou, and Niutou schools were also opportunistic.[15]

12. McRae, *Seeing through Zen*, 17–18. McRae characterizes the lineage of Chan as a combination of Buddhist genealogy with Chinese characteristics (*Seeing through Zen*, 5).
13. Faure, *Chan Insights and Oversights*, 119.
14. McRae, *Seeing through Zen*, 5, 149.
15. For a brief historical survey, see Faure, *Will to Orthodoxy*, 4–5.

THE PROBLEMATIC NATURE OF THE SIXTH PATRIARCH

Probably more than any other single figure of the Chinese Chan tradition, the Sixth Patriarch named Huineng functions as a pivotal historical figure based on evidence from the later tradition. It would be incorrect to view him, however, as a single figure who inaugurated a new era in Chan; it is probably more accurate to view his life as a symbol for a complex historical process extending over time. The status of the Sixth Patriarch was promoted after his death by his chosen successor named Shenhui (684–758) in conjunction with the latter's attack on the Northern School of Chan and over contentions about the transmission of authority to Shenxiu (600–706) and his emphasis on gradually reaching enlightenment, whereas the Southern School stressed the suddenness of gaining enlightenment. In addition to the differences with regards to the nature of enlightenment and identity of the rightful patriarch, Shenhui also argued that the Northern School, which was founded by a disciple of Huineng named Faru (638–689), deviated from the true teachings of Bodhidharma who introduced a special method of meditation, did not ground his teachings on texts, was apolitical, critical of devotional practices, and engaged in false practices. Despite this attack and subsequent greater success historically by the Southern School, the Northern School remained a religious force for several centuries in China.[16] After Huineng and the establishment of the Southern School, Chan spread across China and gained support among peasants in a broad process of enculturation.

Although he lived a couple of centuries after the legendary Bodhidharma, Huineng is a historically important figure. His biography reflects certain Chan values and notions. According to the *Platform Sūtra of the Sixth Patriarch*, which was composed by others after his death, Huineng suffered hardship as a young boy when his father died prematurely, forcing the youngster and his mother to sell firewood to survive. On a momentous day, the young boy heard another person reciting the *Diamond Sūtra*, which occasioned the awakening of his mind toward religion and motivated him to seek a teacher. Approaching the Fifth Patriarch for instruction, Huineng was asked how he could expect to attain Buddhahood when he was nothing more than a mere barbarian. To the astonished and impressed patriarch, he replied that there was no difference between a barbarian and a civilized person in the Buddha-nature, although it was

16. Dumoulin, *Zen Buddhism*, 1:110.

possible to discern distinctions with regards to their physical bodies.[17] Thereupon, Huineng was employed as an acolyte to do menial tasks within the monastery. Desiring to find a worthy successor due to his advanced age, the Fifth Patriarch instructed his monks to return to their rooms, to examine themselves, to seek intuitive wisdom, to compose a verse based on their wisdom, and he would review the verses for proof of an enlightened state of mind. If such an enlightened person could be discovered that person would be appointed his successor and the Sixth Patriarch.

Around midnight, the head monk at the time named Shenxiu composed a verse on a wall:

> The body is the Bodhi tree
> The mind is like a clear mirror
> At all times, we must strive to polish it,
> And must not let the dust collect.[18]

If we pause to consider this verse, it is obvious that Shenxiu views the mirror-mind as something passive that remains standing and must be continuously wiped clean. Since dust is a metaphor for obscurities and passions caused by desires, images, and thoughts, meditation is a method of purification and restoring the mind to its original purity, or metaphorically becoming a spotless mirror. When the Fifth Patriarch read the verse, he thought that it was harmless, but it did not demonstrate true insight. Since Shenxiu had merely arrived at the front gate and was unable to enter it, the Fifth Patriarch told the head monk to think about his verse for a couple of days and then compose another one for his inspection.

At a later point in the narrative, the illiterate Huineng overhears another monastic acolyte reciting the verse, and he concluded that the composer had not attained enlightenment. Then, Huineng instructed the other acolyte to go with him to the southern corridor where he would recite verses to be written on the wall. These verses are revealing about the Chan enlightened state of mind, and they serve to refute the verses written by the head monk:

> Bodhi originally has no tree,
> The mirror also has no stand.
> Buddha-nature is always clean and pure;
> Where is there room for dust?
> The mind is the Bodhi tree,

---

17. Yampolsky, *Platform Sutra*, 127–29.
18. Yampolsky, *Platform Sutra*, 130.

> The body is the mirror stand.
> The mirror is originally clean and pure
> Where can it be stained by dust?[19]

After reading these verses the Fifth Patriarch knew that the writer understood the meaning of Chan. Thereupon, he called Huineng secretly to his quarters where he took that opportunity to expound on the *Diamond Sūtra*, which fully awakened Huineng. Thereupon, the Fifth Patriarch transmitted the *dharma* (teaching) and robe to his chosen successor. Due to the danger of being harmed, the Fifth Patriarch instructed Huineng to leave the monastery.

Since a comparison of the respective positions of Huineng and Shenxiu will be made in chapter 5 within the context of discussing the Zen notion of no-mind, we will conclude this discussion of the life of Huineng, which is encased within the legend of an extraordinary figure, with some later anecdotes about his life and some remarks about the distinction between sudden versus gradual enlightenment. Describing his personal enlightenment, the Sixth Patriarch allegedly said the following:

> It is like the great sea which gathers all the flowing streams, and merges together the small waters and the large waters into one. This is seeing into your own nature. [Such a person] does not abide either inside or outside; he is free to come or go.[20]

This type of unitive experience suggests that your best teacher is yourself. At the end of his life, the Sixth Patriarch was surrounded by his followers, who were crying because of his imminent demise, which motivated him to say:

> If I didn't know where I was going I wouldn't be leaving you. You're crying because you don't know where I'm going. If you knew where I was going you wouldn't be crying.[21]

The text describes the supernatural omens on the day of his death. There was a strange fragrance for several days, mountains crumbled, the earth trembled, forest trees turned white, the sun and moon ceased to shine, the wind and clouds lost their colors, and a bright light appeared at his grave. The light at his grave rose to the heaven, and it did not disappear for two days. These kinds of narrative flourishes are devices that

---

19. Yampolsky, *Platform Sutra*, 132.
20. Yampolsky, *Platform Sutra*, 150.
21. Yampolsky, *Platform Sutra*, 174.

writers use to indicate the passing of a significant person. In other words, Huineng was so important that the universe responded to his passing. After the death of the Sixth Patriarch as noted earlier, Shenhui attacked the Northern School of Shenxiu in part over the emphasis of gradual versus sudden enlightenment. Seemingly motivated by self-interest and fame, Shenhui attacked the so-called Northern School for allegedly teaching gradualism and dualism with respect to enlightenment. He argued that the true heir to Hongren, Fifth Patriarch, was Huineng, an obscure monk and founder of the Southern School. Continuing with his case, Shenhui asserted that he was the rightful successor to Huineng as the Seventh Patriarch. Shenhui's attacks distorted the teachings of the Northern School.[22] However, he was successful. In retrospect, what makes the Sixth Patriarch a problematic figure is what did not happen in the Tang dynasty and what did occur during the Song dynasty.

TANG DYNASTY PERIOD

For some scholars of Buddhism, the Tang period represented the golden age of Chan as mentioned in the previous chapter. This claim is made because of the outstanding personalities that this period produced and the idealizing of these figures. The claim that the Tang dynasty represented a golden age is misleading because, although there certainly were numerous important and influential Chan religious leaders, it was not a unified and lucidly articulated movement. Being a widely diverse movement during the Tang dynasty, Chan did not arrive at a well-defined identity until the Song period (960–1279). What the Tang period did have was a series of contending lineages vying for leadership and acceptance of its own claims of authority and authenticity. It is more accurate to view the Tang period as a beginning of a process that was completed in the Song period.[23] Other schools of Mahāyāna Buddhism like Huayan, Tiantai, and Pure Land reached maturity and became fully sinicized by its culture and simultaneously transformed Chinese culture, even though the historical reality was a long process of development along uneven trajectories in the north and south of the country.[24] In contrast to Chan during this historical period, there was a revival of Confucianism associated with

---

22. Schlütter, *How Zen Became Zen*, 19.
23. Gregory, "Vitality of Buddhism in the Sung," 4.
24. Gregory and Ebrey, "Religious and Historical Landscape," 18.

the establishment of a strong centralized state, although this revival did nothing to hamper the growth by 739 of a total of three thousand monasteries and two thousand nunneries.

Representing the third generation after the life of the Sixth Patriarch Huineng, the Tang period witnessed several teachers of great stature like Mazu, Baizhang, Huangbo (d. 850), and Linji (d. 866), sharing the single feature that they were all eccentric teachers. The historical period also witnessed the birth of families or houses of Chan associated with these and other figures. These lineages represented a kind of internal sectarianism that served as regional versions of Chan that manifested significant differences of emphasis and teaching style. Although there was a rivalry between the houses, there did not appear to be any genuine animosity. But before we review the various houses, it is wise to consider the important lineage of Mazu Daoyi (709–788), whose name *ma* means horse.

Mazu was ordained a monk at an early age, and the tradition has preserved a dialogue that allegedly occurred early in his career. While residing in a monastery constantly absorbed in meditation, his master Nanyue, who was cognizant of Mazu's spiritual gifts, asked him why he was sitting in meditation. Mazu responded that he wanted to become a Buddha. Thereupon, the master picked up a title and started rubbing it on a stone in front of the hermitage. After Mazu asked him what he was doing, the master replied that he was attempting to make a mirror. When Mazu inquired about how he could create a mirror by rubbing a title, the master countered with his own question about how it was possible to become a Buddha by sitting in meditation.[25] The point of the master's action was to convey to Mazu that enlightenment was not a passive condition; it was rather active. Moreover, a person cannot purify or polish themselves to create a Buddha (an enlightened being), if the Buddha-nature is not there from the very start. Later in his career, Mazu refined the trigger mechanism for sudden enlightenment by pioneering several unusual teaching methods.

Mazu was the first master to ask a novice an unanswerable question. While a novice would struggle for an answer, Mazu would shout at him something like "Ho!" to jolt the student into a non-dualistic state of mind. Mazu also used physical violence, and he encouraged a spirit of violence and fearlessness in his students. We will examine these methods more fully in chapters 3 and 4. He combined the use of such unusual methods

25. Whitfield, *Records of the Transmission of the Lamp*, 2:115; hereafter cited as Whitfield, *Lamp*.

with a simplifying of the notion of enlightenment that he defined as seeing into one's own nature. This involves understanding intuitively who you are and what you are.

But to gain enlightenment, one must master self-control that he often referred to as herding an ox, a metaphor for the uncontrollable aspects of human nature. The herding of the ox did not involve making value judgments or following rules; it did mean to see what is most rewarding to a person at a particular moment. An anecdote about Mazu and a disciple doing kitchen duty illustrates the point when the master asked his disciple what he was doing. The disciple replied that he was herding an ox. The master inquired further about the method of the disciple to which the disciple explained how he pulls it by its nostrils when it begins to overindulge itself. The master was obviously well pleased because he made a remark about retiring. This narrative contains nothing abstract or metaphysical because simple physical action is victorious in this anecdote that emphasizes naturalness and simplicity. This kind of simplicity turned against Mazu when he learned that one can never go home to one's native village. When he arrived for a temporary visit he was warmly welcomed by the villagers except for an old woman who was his next-door neighbor while he was young. She came to see what all the commotion was about, and was disappointed to discover that it was nothing more than the son of the garbage cleaner.

When Mazu was about to pass away he was asked late in the day by the head monk about the condition of his health. Mazu replied, "Sun-face Buddha (and) moon-face Buddha."[26] This cryptic response reflects his invoking the names of two scriptural Buddhas, namely Sun-face and Moon-face. The Sun-face Buddha is expected to live 1,800 years, whereas the Moon-face Buddha can anticipate a life span of one day and one night. By invoking these figures, Mazu intends to suggest something about the relative nature of time.

Among the important disciples of Mazu was Baizhang Huikai (ca. 720–814), who was credited with founding the first wholly Chan monastery by combining monastic discipline with spontaneity and naturalness. Among the changes that he initiated in the monastery was the importance of being self-supporting and rejecting begging as the primary means of support. His major principle was: "A day of no work is a day without

---

26. Poceski, *Record of Mazu*, 233.

eating."²⁷ Thus the necessity of physical labor was integrated with meditation and worship, and it was obligatory for all monks. Even as an old man, Baizhang continued to live according to his own rules by working in the fields. When his disciples took away his tools because of concerns for his health he refused to eat until his tools were returned to him.

Another significant disciple of Mazu was Nanquan Puyuan (748–835), a founder of his own monastery in 795 on Mount Nanquan. He was famous for emphasizing the irrational in sharp contrast to the rational concerns of Confucian philosophy. Before taking a journey with two of his disciples to visit an eminent teacher, he drew a circle on the road and asked his disciple to give him the right answer before they began their journey. Thereupon, one monk sat down inside the circle and the other bowed in the manner of a woman. Nanquan concluded by their responses that it was not necessary to go.²⁸ Nanquan demonstrated a concern about the relationship of doubt and the enlightenment experience, and he argued that the person having an awakening experience does not have any doubts about what they are experiencing and its reality. Nonetheless, the enlightenment experience cannot be proven or disproved by objective standards, although a master could test another person's enlightenment by comparing the claimant's illogic with his own.

A famous disciple of Nanquan was Zhaozhou Congshen (778–897), who was noted for his itinerant style of life. He emphasized the need to be spontaneous, creative, and inventive. He was also concerned to manifest the inadequacy of language to express reality. Arguably, his most famous encounter came with a monk who asked him, "Does a dog have the Buddha nature or not?" And he replied, "Wu" ("no, nothingness").²⁹ This encounter dialogue became a famous *kōan*, an enigmatic statement made by a master, which was subsequently meditated on by many aspiring monks attempting to gain enlightenment. Moreover, he was convinced that enlightenment derived from doing the ordinary activities of life and not something special. A novice monk begged, for example, Zhaozhou for his instructions. The master asked the monk if he had eaten anything yet to which the novice confessed that he had eaten. Thereupon, Zhaozhou said, "Then go wash the bowl," giving the aspirant an insight.³⁰

27. Ichimura, *Baizhang Zen Monastic Regulations*, 300.
28. Whitfield, *Lamp*, 2:216.
29. Cleary, *Wumen's Gate*, 71.
30. Cleary, *Wumen's Gate*, 77.

In contrast, Huangbo (d. ca. 850), who took his name from a mountain, studied with the master Baizhang, having arrived too late after the death of Mazu to study with that master. Huangbo was concerned in his adult life with the transmission of intuitive insight. He became convinced that communication must be wordless and free from the trap of either logical assertion or negation. An excellent example of his concern was embodied in dialogue with Baizhang, who asked his disciple where he had been that day. The disciple replied that he had been picking mushrooms at the foot of the Taishan Mountain. Asked by Baizhang if he had seen any tigers, Huangbo immediately roared like a tiger. Baizhang picked up an axe to kill the tiger, but his tiger imitating disciple suddenly slapped his face. Responding with a good laugh, the master returned to the temple to inform others that there is in fact a tiger at the foot of the mountain, and everyone should be warned because he has already been bitten that day.[31] This tale is a good example of freedom from words or silence and the role of play in Chan. This attitude toward language suggests that Chan could not be taught, and it could only be gained by an intuitive insight. Moreover, this is an experience that cannot be conceptualized because concepts are related to sense experience, which obscure wisdom. It is important for an aspirant to learn to be unreceptive to one's sensations and not to be attentive to distinctions, which purge one respectively of receptivity to external stimuli and vain discriminations. It is essential that the transition of intuitive insight be directly from mind to mind. How did one get around words? Baizhang advocated the unusual methods of Mazu by utilizing shouts, violence, silence, calling a disciple's name unexpectedly, or continually contradicting a student until one realized that language represented obscuring concepts.

MAJOR FAMILIES OF CHAN

The Great Persecution of 845 did not crush the spirit of Chan Buddhism because in its aftermath Chan became a dominant religious force in China and evolved into several so-called houses, which were examples of its adaptation to Chinese culture and helped to contribute to its success. These organizations are good examples of Chan identifying itself as Chinese and not something suspicious from a foreign country.[32] The

---

31. Cleary, *Blue Cliff Record*, 128.
32. Bowring, *Religious Traditions of Japan*, 299.

Guizong House was founded by Guizong (771–853), who was formerly a disciple of Baizhang. The story of his enlightenment is revealing about the spirit of Chan. While waiting upon his master Baizhang one day, the master asked the disciple to poke the stove to see if there was any fire left in it. Guizong poked but he discovered no spark. Thereupon, Baizhang rose to poke it himself, and he succeeded in discovering a little spark. He showed his discovery to his disciple, and he asked whether this was fire. At that moment, the disciple became enlightened.[33]

An important distinction made by this house was between Tathāgata and Patriarch Chan. The former is representative of faith, meditation, asceticism, and is dependent on scriptures, whereas Patriarch (meaning traditional) Chan expressed a spontaneous and direct insight into a person's true self devoid of any conceptual, rational, or ethical elements. This school affirms sudden enlightenment, but it insists on the necessity of gradual cultivation with one's progress dependent upon the individual and what that student needs from the master. A disciple of Guishan named Yangshan compared his teaching methods to a shop that sells all kinds of merchandise: "In my shop I handle all kinds of wares. When a man comes to me for rat excrement he will get it; when he wants genuine gold, I will hand that to him."[34] In other words, the master is attuned to the needs of his disciples and responds with methods that will bring the desired results, which tended to prefer action and silence over words.

The second major house was the Yunmen House named for Yunmen Wenyan (862/4–949) that was called "The Barrier of a Single Word." Yunmen was famous for his one-word answers. For example, to the question, What is the right *dharma*-eye? he responded, "All-comprehensive." In response to the question: What is Dao? he replied "Go!" Yunmen's reply was "Echo" to the following question: How do you look at the wonderful coincidence between the chick tapping inside its hell and the hen's pecking from the outside? In one final example, a monk asked Yunmen: "What is the teaching that transcends the Buddha and patriarchs?" To which he responded, "A sesame bun."[35] His answers represented spontaneous reactions to questions, and they were not thought-out or artificially contrived. His answers were based on what was on his mind at the precise moment of the question. Therefore, responses like all-comprehensive, go,

---

33. Whitfield, *Lamp*, 2:253.
34. Chung-yuan, *Original Teachings of Ch'an Buddhism*, 212.
35. Chung-yuan, "Ch'an Teachings of Yun-men School," 21.

echo, and sesame bun reflected his state of mind when the question was first raised and thus served as the response in a very spontaneous, immediate, and natural way. Moreover, the answers were directed to the spiritual condition of the questioner, and they had no bearing on the personal nature of the questioner. From the examples presented, the answers were not a logical response to the questions. Yunmen's objective was not to allow the questioner any opportunity to reason, to avoid rational entanglements, and to escape confusion, enabling the mind to become open to the truth.

Breaking with his single word answers to a question, Yunmen responded more fully in one anecdote to the following question: "How is one to grasp Chan?" He replied that it was important not to let others deceive or control you. He cautioned about relying on the words of a master and immediately swallowing them "like a group of flies on top of manure struggling to gobble up the dirt." His point is that a person that seeks the truth should cast aside such words and "get support from your own backbone."[36] This type of advice to rely upon oneself was also tied to his radical iconoclasm. After relating the legend that the Buddha, for instance, immediately after his birth, with one hand pointing to heaven and the other pointing to earth, walked seven steps, looked at the four quarters, and declared, "Above heaven and below heaven, I alone am the Honored One," Yunmen said: "Had I seen him then, I would have struck him dead with one blow and fed him to the dogs, so that there might be peace in the world."[37]

During a historical period that witnessed several remarkable leaders, Linji Yixuan (d. 866) deserves a place of the highest honor in both China and Japan because the Linji House in China became the Rinzai sect in Japan, and he made important contributions to Chan thought. Linji's name is derived from a little temple called "Overlooking the Ford." In an interesting story of the transmission of authority from his master to Linji, the monks were proceeding to the fields to work with Linji following his master Huangbo, who noticed that his disciple was not carrying a hoe. After listening to a feeble excuse about why Linji did not have a hoe with which to work, the master called the disciple nearer, and Huangbo threw his hoe on the ground and challenged Linji to pick it up. After Linji responded by picking up the hoe, Huangbo admitted that with the

---

36. Chung-yuan, "Ch'an Teachings of Yun-men School," 23.
37. Cleary, *Blue Cliff Record*, 97.

additional help it was not necessary for him to help in the fields, and he returned to the temple leaving Linji holding his hoe and the authority of the master.[38]

Although his methods will be explored more fully in the next chapter, his method of teaching was strict and harsh because he used beatings and shouting to great effect. He thought that teachers must not teach or explain anything, but they must rather force students to experience truth for themselves. This pedagogical emphasis was consistent with his emphasis on wordless teaching. He also stressed naturalness in his method, which included the elements of no concern and no seeking. By being overly concerned about it or seeking diligently for the truth, this merely took an aspirant further astray and was unnatural.

Although Linji might not have characterized it this way, there was an egalitarian spirit embodied in his thought that was especially evident with his notion of a true human being, which for him meant someone without rank or title. Of course, this was a radical position to take in a society in which social rank was extremely important. The true human being was a person freed of all fetters. Such a person existed concretely in the here and now. The true human being was thus not some vague concept, not an isolated, or an absolutized person because such a person was lively, dynamic, attuned to nature, and dependent on nothing. Even though this person was grounded in the transcendent, such a person was ordinary, simple, natural, and direct, a concrete being that revealed the Buddha-nature. Like the Daoist notion from which it was derived, the true human is without face, a solitary and independent figure freely following the way, indefinable, not clinging to motion or its opposite, and a marginal figure on the fringes of society. This marginal figure must be willing to destroy all obstacles to liberation. Linji defined these obstacles in terms of committing the five great sins: killing one's father, killing one's mother, killing the Buddha, destroying the harmony of the monastic community, and burning the scriptures.[39] If a reader considers the initial two sins seriously, it is not difficult to imagine how radical this would sound in a cultural milieu like China in which the family is the foundation of the state and its society.

In contrast to the Linji lineage, another house was founded jointly by Tungshan Liangjian (807–869) and his disciple Cao Penji (840–901)

---

38. Cleary, *Recorded Sayings of Linji*, 58.
39. Cleary, *Recorded Sayings of Linji*, 43.

named the Caodong House after a mountain, which later became the Sōtō school in Japan. The tradition preserved a story about the enlightenment of Tungshan after he asked his master Yunmen a question about what he should say about his master's true face after his death if someone asked him. After a period of silence, the master replied, "Just this one is." Tungshan was puzzled by this reply, and he went on a journey musing over the words of his master. While crossing a stream, he looked to see his own reflection in the water, and he was awakened to the real meaning of his master's words.[40] The master was attempting to convey to his disciple that his true face was right there in front of him all the time. Tungshan preferred an indirect teaching method. When performing an annual memorial service, for instance, for his master Yunmen a monk asked Tungshan about the type of teaching he received from his master, to which he replied that his master did not teach him anything. The monk was puzzled about why he would conduct a memorial service for a master who taught him nothing. Tungshan replied that he respected his master because he never taught him anything openly.[41] In practical terms this penchant for indirect teaching led him to prefer metaphor to concrete examples, but it motivated him to avoid being deliberately illogical.

The Fayuan House was the last house to be established by Fayuan Wenyi (885–958), and it enjoyed a rather short historical existence. Its name was derived from a posthumous title given to its founder by a friend and patron of the royalty. While wandering past a monastery, Fayuan was caught in a snowstorm, and he sought refuge in the monastery. As he was warming himself by the stove, the abbot asked him a question regarding his destination to which the traveler replied that he was a mere pilgrim. Inquiring about the significance of his pilgrimage, Fayuan told the abbot that he did not know the answer to his question. In response, the abbot made a cryptic remark about the intimacy of unknowing, which apparently did not make much of an impression on the traveler. When the snow stopped the two men went to the door and, looking at the courtyard, the abbot asked Fayuan the following question: "Now tell me, is that stone out there in the courtyard within your mind or outside of your mind?" After the traveler responded that it was within his mind, the abbot lamented that he was traveling with a stone on his mind. Being disturbed at such a question, Fayuan decided to stay to have his doubts

40. Chung-yuan, *Original Teachings of Ch'an Buddhism*, 167.
41. Chung-yuan, *Original Teachings of Ch'an Buddhism*, 289.

resolved, but he was unsuccessful after a month and admitted he had exhausted all his energy. The abbot replied, "As regards the Buddha-nature, everything is a present reality." These precise words caused Fayuan to become enlightened.[42] The point that the abbot was attempting to get the pilgrim to grasp was that reality was right there before him, and it can only be perceived by a direct intuition.

Fayuan was famous for his pedagogical method of using repetition to awaken a student. When asked, for instance, by a monk, "Does the void contain the six phenomena?" Fayuan immediately responded, "Void."[43] The repetitive nature of the reply functions like an echo. And no intellectual pursuit is possible. Fayuan also used abrupt negation as a method. When he was asked, for instance, about the nature of the first principle he responded with, "If I should tell, it would become the second principle."[44] Such a method was intended to eradicate all intellectual approaches to a question. A third method used by Fayuan was the approach of opposites. In response to a question about the nature of the moon Fayuan replied, "Finger." In response to a question about the nature of finger he replied, "Moon."[45] Again, this type of method leaves a questioner no opportunity to reason. Fayuan disdained the use of violence as a method of teaching.

Another house begun during the Tang period was the Ox-head School that appeared south of Nanking around the mid-eighth century and was named for a mountain in the area. The school had a brief period of activity in the south, and it was significant for its historical contribution to the form of Chinese Chan during the post-Huineng era. This school did not become embroiled in the conflict between the Northern and Southern Schools, and it attempted to devise an alternative perspective. It attempted to steer a middle way between relying on Mahāyāna scriptures and rejecting them.[46] The school developed a teaching pattern that included a beginning question, intermediate hesitation, and final attainment, a pattern that resembles the three truths: absolute, relative, and middle way.

---

42. Chung-yuan, *Original Teachings of Ch'an Buddhism*, 236.
43. Chung-yuan, *Original Teachings of Ch'an Buddhism*, 231.
44. Chung-yuan, *Original Teachings of Ch'an Buddhism*, 246.
45. Chung-yuan, *Original Teachings of Ch'an Buddhism*, 242.
46. Dumoulin, *Zen Buddhism*, 1:116.

SONG DYNASTY PERIOD

The religiosity of Chinese culture during the Tang and Song periods was characterized by the centrality of the ancestor cult with its basic assumption of a continuity between the living and the dead that also implied that the two parties can affect each other. The gods of the Chinese pantheon became more bureaucratized and Confucianized, and they resembled scholars and government officials that could be promoted or demoted depending on their performance. Heaven was a moral force that operated within history, and the emperor as the son of heaven played the role of a mediator between heaven and earth, whose sacrifice on behalf of the people and his virtue ensured a cosmic harmony. The self-generating, self-sustaining, and self-regulating universe was an organism in which each part was interrelated through a process that included the inter-working of *yin* and *yang*, the five elements (water, fire, wood, metal, and earth), and *qi* (energy), a medium for the interacting of the five elements.[47] Within this cultural context, Chan continued to develop and take root in China.

The Song Dynasty was a period divided into two parts, called the Northern Song (960–1126) and the Southern Song (1127–1279), representing a renaissance for Chinese culture with a flowering of literature, art, and the rise of Neo-Confucianism as the predominant intellectual movement, whereas the later phase of this period was marked by social and cultural decay. Important welfare projects were established during this time that included the building of hospitals for the indigent, public graveyards, and a national school system. During this period, Chan Buddhism was involved in political affairs like other Buddhist schools and formed a focal point for social and cultural life in China, although there were no new traditions of Buddhism that developed during the Song. It was mostly a time of continued evolution of the Buddhist schools as Song era writers shaped the image of Chan into an elite form of Buddhist monasticism. They also constructed a sacred history of Tang era Chan that served to legitimize the Song Chan school and its claim to represent a unique transmission of the teachings outside of Buddhist scriptures.[48]

The Song conception of Chan lineage was shaped by the efforts of Zongmi (780–841), who created an inclusive portrait of Buddhism. He was the first person to recognize and identify the different Chan groups as extended clans with their roots in Bodhidharma. And he did not

---

47. See Needham, *Science and Civilization of China*, vol. 2, ch. 13.
48. Schlütter, *How Zen Became Zen*, 15.

accept the opinion that the Buddhism of Bodhidharma represented a different form of Buddhism from that of the Mahāyāna *sūtras*.[49] Even though different traditions of Chan placed importance on diverse principles, Zongmi wanted to reconcile the different traditions. His synthetic method viewed the various traditions as wrong in making their respective positions absolute, but the whole of the various traditions was valid.[50] Zongmi also had a hidden agenda to promote the Heze lineage, which represented an example of the superior interpretation of Chan. In his work the *Chan Chart*, Zongmi recognized other lineages of Chan, but argued for the superiority of Heze Chan of which he was a member as representing the most authentic rendition of the tradition, especially the Hongzhou lineage that he fervently opposed.[51] What Zongmi created were lineages that descended from a single ancestor, namely Huineng, back to Bodhidharma and finally the Buddha.

Zongmi's work can be construed as an attempt by the various Chan schools to differentiate themselves from each other, to define themselves, and to decide what was orthodox. Zongmi portrayed Chan as unique among Buddhist movements with multiple branches, a multifaceted nature, and a common core, even though he wrote from the perspective of a sectarian agenda to define his school as the most authentic version of the Chan tradition. The case advanced by Shenhui and the hierarchy of schools advocated by Zongmi are excellent examples of a religious tradition attempting to define its identity by deciding what is orthodox and what is not, which is what the Chan scholar Faure calls the "will to orthodoxy."[52] It is ironic that by determining what is orthodox from your school's perspective you are separating your school from the others, a process leading to increasing sectarianism.

From a historical perspective, Zongmi became implicated in the "Sweet Dew Incident" of 835, an abortive attempt to oust the palace eunuchs from power. Having become army supervisors, in control of the royal treasury and the transmission of official documents, the eunuchs represented a powerful group at the top of the government. A plan was devised to ambush and massacre the eunuchs, but the plot failed after being exposed. Zongmi was implicated in the plot along with others, but he saved his life by claiming that as a Buddhist he was committed to saving

49. Foulk, "Sung Controversies," 224–35.
50. Gregory, *Tsung-mi and the Sinification*, 229–30.
51. Welter, *Monks, Rulers, and Literati*, 34–37.
52. See Faure, *Will to Orthodoxy*.

all lives. Along with this argument and an apparent willingness to give up his own life, he was pardoned by eunuch generals.[53]

JAPANESE RELIGIOUS CONTEXT PRIOR TO BUDDHISM

Before the arrival of Buddhism into Japan, it was known as the "land of the *kami*," which were spirits of various aspects of nature such as a rock, a spring, a river, a mountain, or a tree. There were also examples of malevolent *kami* associated with epidemics, diseases, floods, and drought that could be triggered by human transgressions against the spirits. These types of natural phenomena occurred within the cultural context of a belief that the Japanese islands were created by supernatural *kami* when they dipped their spears into the primordial waters and gathered up mud that fell off their spears and formed the islands. This place of the *kami* was also called the "way of the *kami*" in order to identify a way of life. Japan's native deities or *kami* were referred to by the synonym Shinto, although it did not refer to an indigenous religion at an early historical period. Actually, it was not until Yoshida Kanetomo (1435–1511) and after the arrival of Buddhism that the term Shinto connoted a coherent or independent religious system.[54] Shinto, a synonym for *kami*, assumed a sectarian identity during the medieval period in reaction to the introduction of Buddhism into the country.

Because of the prevalence of *kami*, Shinto belief reflects a sensitivity, respect, mutual sympathy, and awe toward nature. Moreover, the *kami* are interdependent and interwoven into a sacred totality. When a *kami* enters, for instance, a natural object it infuses that object with spiritual power (*tama*). A major implication of this type of occurrence is that the relation between the spiritual and material can be external, internal, or both.[55] This also implies that the material is always to some degree related to the spiritual. This type of belief suggests a cosmic orientation in which no object or human act has autonomous value because a person is always an integral part of the cosmos and shares in the sacred *kami* nature, suggesting a deep kinship between humans and nature that demands cooperation and flowing with the rhythms of nature.[56] But any relation

---

53. Gregory, *Tsung-mi and the Sinification*, 85–88.
54. Nauman, "State Cult of the Nara," 64; Teeuwen, "From Jindō to Shinto," 233–63.
55. Kasulis, *Shinto*, 16.
56. Kitagawa, *Religion in Japanese History*, 16.

to a *kami* presupposes and demands that a human must be in a pure condition that is attained by purifying oneself with water, salt, or fire. In comparison to Buddhism, Shinto is world-affirming and celebrates life.

Besides its intimate relation and sensitivity to nature, Shinto embodies a strong folk element, an emphasis on simplicity, a value that derives from it naturalism, stress on maintaining purity, and a commitment to social solidarity. The folk elements include practices such as divination, use of magical instruments such as amulets to protect oneself, and embrace of shamanistic expertise. Shamanism has existed from ancient times in Japan. A primary feature of the shaman is his or her ability to enter into a trance state in order to converse with supernatural spirits, and to travel to unimagined locations to find lost souls, retrieve them, restore them to the body of the afflicted person suffering from soul loss, and thus to heal them.

Some shamans were associated with the royal court in Japanese history, including a class called *miko* (female shaman), with others living in villages. There is also a more magical tradition and an ascetic figure who is mostly a healer with the power to leave their body and to banish malevolent spirits.[57] The ascetic type of shaman has the power to heal by means of an innate power and does not have to rely necessarily on the aid of spirits. The shaman can also use a drum to induce a trance state, summon spirits, or function as a charm against spirits, whereas Ainu shamans of Sakhalin, Japan, use a catalpa bow, a single hempen-stringed instrument, to summon spirits.[58] Successful shamans have a clairvoyant vision that enables them to see which spiritual beings are responsible for a particular illness and to take remedial measures to counteract them. The shamanistic and Shinto traditions continue alongside of Buddhism in Japan to the present.

ZEN TRANSMISSION TO JAPAN

It took a few centuries for Chan, which became Zen, to take root in Japan as an independent school. The first known contact with Buddhism in Japan occurred by way of Korea in 552 when the first image of the Buddha reached the imperial court during the reign of Emperor Kinmei. The prince-regent Shōtoku Taishi (577–621) played an important political

---

57. Hori, *Folk Religion in Japan*, 182–83; Blacker, *Catalpa Bow*, 22.
58. Ohnuki-Tierney, *Illness and Healing*, 75.

and religious role during this time by introducing the *tennō* (emperor) state and being a strong advocate of Buddhism, which he believed would be an effective means of building a solid moral foundation for the nation and produce a better quality of life for the lay people.[59]

There were also some contacts with Zen Buddhism by Japanese citizens. During a trip to China in 653, the monk Dōshō (628–670) learned Zen from the Indian pilgrim Xuanzang, and he studied with a disciple of the second Chinese patriarch Huike. Dōshō established the Hossō school, basing it on Yogācāra philosophy. It is recorded that in the next century the first Chinese Chan master, named Daoxuan (702–760), arrived in Japan, and he taught meditation techniques to the monk Gyōhyō (722–797), who in turn was to instruct Saichō (767–822), founder of the Japanese Tendai sect of Buddhism. At the invitation of the empress Tachibana Kachiko, another Chinese monk named Yikuang visited Japan, but there was nothing substantial that developed from his visit. For the most part, Zen was a non-factor in Japanese Buddhism for about three centuries, while the Tendai and Shingon schools dominated the culture in addition to the indigenous Shinto religion. What existed of Zen was incorporated into and subordinate to the Tendai tradition.

Everything began to change during the Kamakura Period (1185–1333), a time of Buddhist renewal with the rise of new sects, a period of social and political upheaval, and the rise of regional military powers. In 1185, the era was ushered into existence with the defeat of the Taira clan by the Minamoto clan that was called the Genpei War (1180–1185). The Minamoto leadership established the *bakufu* (tent government) at the town of Kamakura, which functioned as a second center of political power that rivaled the court in the city of Kyoto. During the Kamakura period, the populace endured drought, famine, and an earthquake in 1257 that destroyed most of Kamakura. The country was also threatened by external political powers with two attempts, in 1274 and 1281, of invasion by the Mongols. Pure Land Buddhism flourished during this time under the inspiration of such leaders as Hōnen (1133–1212) and Shinran (1173–1262) and their faith-centered message for the lay people, even though it suffered periods of persecution. These persecutions only served to reinforce the movement's conviction about the approaching last age and the decline of the Buddhist law when people must rely for salvation on the power of Amida Buddha. The broad appeal of the Pure Land

---

59. Dumoulin, *Zen Buddhism*, 2:5.

message did not eclipse the powerful Shingon and Tendai schools, but it did motivate them to respond to the criticism of Pure Land leaders and use its political influence to persecute the devotional movement.

The greatest non-religious impetus was given to the budding Zen movement by the rise of the class of ruling knights (samurai) and their early patronage of Zen. These warriors were impressed by the character of the Zen monks, their mental alertness, learning, physical vigor, strict discipline, broad intellectual horizons, and Zen's political utility as a counterbalance to the established and politically connected Buddhist sects. Moreover, the samurai viewed Zen as a means to acquire cultural credentials and status appropriate to their new gained military and political power. Nonetheless, the Japanese monks traveling to China for instruction were primarily from the Tendai tradition, which necessitated an incongruous coexistence of Song Zen with the more esoteric Tendai school. A good example of this tendency was someone like Dainichi Nōnin (n.d.), who established the Daruma School by using Tendai meditation practices, synthesizing Zen with the teachings of the Mahāyāna texts, and incorporating esoteric Tendai practices.

Another such example was Myōan Eisai, who was educated as a Tendai monk and whom the tradition has given credit for founding Zen in Japan. He made two trips to China, retrieving Tendai scriptures on the initial visit in 1168, and was exposed to Zen on his second voyage in 1187, becoming convinced that it would contribute to curing the ills of Japanese society. Eisai identified himself as a member of the Huanglong branch of the Linji (Rinzai) school. Besides insisting on Zen's independence, he argued Zen would be a useful religion that would protect the state. In 1198, he composed a treatise for the emperor in which he also drew a connection between enlightenment and morality. In his work *A Treatise on Letting Zen Flourish to Protect the State*, Eisai composed a series of ten gates that quotes extensively from Mahāyāna literature to support his position that Zen can protect the state. In his treatise, he informs its reader about the lineage of the Zen school.[60] In gate six, Eisai also defines Zen and what makes it unique from his perspective:

> The principle of this Zen school does not set up any words out of which to make dogma. It has been specially transmitted outside of scriptural teachings. It does not cling to passages taught; it only transmits the seal of the mind. It is free from letters, being

---

60. Eisai, *Treatise on Letting Zen*, 131–33.

without words. Through directly pointing to the source of the mind, it has one attain awakening.[61]

A reader should notice the attitude toward the limits of language, the lack of dogmatic assertions, the stress on mind to mind transmission of the truth, and the direct pointing to the foundation of the mind. These are features that readers will encounter again.

Being officially authorized to establish the Rinzai tradition in Japan, Eisai encountered resistance from the pre-existing hierarchy of the Tendai school, but he was protected by the shōgun Minamoto Yoritomo, enabling him to establish a monastery in Hakata in 1195, although Zen was practiced along with esoteric ritual typical of other schools. Slowly, Zen would establish its own identity distinct from the domination of the Tendai tradition. Therefore, Eisai did not establish a genuine and independent Japanese Rinzai school because he never extricated himself from his original ties to Tendai and his tendency to attempt to harmonize disparate religious traditions.

In contrast to Eisai's tendency to include a strong Tendai influence on Zen, Enni Ben'en (1201–1280) proved to be a significant figure because he reflected a more undiluted Zen that moved it closer toward an independent position. As a young man, he studied in Tendai and Shingon schools before visiting China in 1235, and received the mark of recognition (inka-shōmei) from his master. Becoming abbot of Tōfuku-ji in Kyoto on his return to Japan in 1242, he expressed a willingness to utilize Tendai and Shingon rituals, although he was convinced that Zen was the authentic way as evident by his claim that Zen represented the Buddha mind. He identified three foundations of Zen that issue from the Buddha mind that included the following: moral precepts as its outward means; the teachings as its explanatory means; and invocations (nembutsu) are its effective means.

Shinchi Kakushin (1207–1298) was a contemporary of Enni, whose fame was due to his bringing the kōan collection called the Mumonkan in Japanese to the island nation from China, an event that suggests his instrumental role establishing kōan practice as an essential practice in the Rinzai school. Shinchi started his religious career as a member of the Shingon school and its esoteric practices. After taking monastic vows with Dōgen, he trained with the Fuke school, which replaced textual recitation with the playing of flutes. While in China his master gave him the

---

61. Eisai, *Treatise on Letting Zen*, 137.

seal of recognition (*inka-shōmei*) and made him a *dharma* successor. On his return to Japan in 1254, he founded the Saihō-ji.

But the most historically significant figure during the thirteenth century was Dōgen Kigen (1200–1253), who established the Sōtō school in Japan after a successful sojourn to China and composed important works on Zen discipline and philosophy, especially the seventy-five volumes of the *Shōbōgenzō* composed late in his life after having attained enlightenment. We will look more closely at this remarkable monk's thought in chapter 6. Dōgen did advocate a pure Zen devoid of elements of esoteric Buddhism, namely Shingon. He also demonstrated a sincere concern for monastic rules and regulations, and he opened the monastic community to everyone regardless of intelligence, social status, gender, or profession. Moreover, he abolished the separation between laity and monks. Dōgen accepted scriptures because he did not think that they deceived a person because it was persons who deceived themselves. An enlightened mind was free to elucidate and appropriate the scriptures. He adopted only the Mahāyāna precepts as necessary, accorded a secondary importance to *kōans*, although he did not reject them, and he made *zazen* (seated meditation) the primary mode of practice. There is a genuine sense of urgency in his writings in the sense that humans have had the good fortune to be born with a human body, and it is foolish to waste this lifetime. He puts it more metaphorically: "Our bodies are like dew on the grass, and our lives like a flash of lightning, vanishing in a moment."[62]

After Dōgen's death he was succeeded by Koun Ejo (1198–1280), and several of his works were edited by Sen'e (n.d.), who also composed a commentary on the *Shōbōgenzō*, whereas Koun Ejō compiled Dōgen's *Shōbōgenzō zuimonki*. Dōgen's third successor, Tettsū Gikai (1217–1300), founded the Higo (or Kyushu) branch of Sōtō Zen, but was forced to resign after he had introduced Shingon rituals into the liturgies and gotten involved in building projects that veered away from the emphasis on simplicity and poverty introduced by its founder. A final noteworthy monk of this period was Keizan Jōkin (1268–1325) for his authorship of the *Zazen yōjinki*, a manual on Zen practice, which is still used today. Keizan strayed from Dōgen's quest for a pure tradition more akin to mountain asceticism by espousing beliefs in Japanese *kami* spirits and Buddhist divinities, thereby blending Zen practice with a belief in spiritual beings and infusing the use of astrology, geomancy, and the power

---

62. Yokoi and Daizen, *Zen Master Dogen*, 47.

of worship into his brand of Zen.⁶³ In order to illustrate how intertwined these spirits became in the Sōtō school, it is informative to note that some temples performed ordination rites for *kami*, and each monastery had its own local protective spirit (*ryūten*). This engagement with local beliefs, encouragement of eclecticism, and functioning as a source for local elites contributed to the success of Sōtō Zen in Japan.⁶⁴

In the early fourteenth century, Japanese disciples of Chinese masters began to assume the leadership of Zen monasteries, and they began to develop a system of official monasteries that became known as the Five Mountains or *gozan* system, which was a hierarchical network of monasteries based on the Five Mountain system of Chan monasteries in Song China. The three-tiered system included the following structure: Five Mountains (*gozan*), Ten Temples (*jissetsu*) and several larger temples (*shozan*). This list was revised periodically during its early history. It began with the Zen temples of Kyoto, whereas the second tier represented temples in cities and rural areas with political influence. Another system that developed later was the *rinka* monasteries that were separate from the *gozan* system and located in rural areas. An excellent example of a *rinka* monastery is the famous Daitoku-ji, which in 1331 was raised to the rank of first monastery of the country by the Emperor Go-Daigo and given the power to select its own abbots for its generational line of disciples. The entire *gozan* system was state controlled and supervised by a bureaucracy, although not all Zen temples became a part of this system. Some of these temples were said "to be below the grove," while those within the system were "in the grove."⁶⁵ This system declined when the fortunes of the Ashikaga shogunate fell and secularization of the Zen monasteries increased.⁶⁶ The decline of the system was accelerated by the destructive Ōnin War (1467–77) and its struggle over succession to the shogunate.

The fourteenth century was a period when several historically significant monks made important contributions to the development of Zen. Musō Soseki (1275–1351) was highly honored during his lifetime with the title National Teacher given to him. Originally a Shingon monk for ten years, a liberating dream about a Shingon monk and an incarnation of Bodhidharma drew him to Zen. He combined academic learning (*richi*) with the direct *kōan* method of sudden experience. Another

63. Bodiford, *Sōtō Zen in Medieval Japan*, 88, 91.
64. Bowring, *Religious Traditions of Japan*, 406.
65. Bowring, *Religious Traditions of Japan*, 404.
66. Dumoulin, *Zen Buddhism*, 2:152.

significant figure was Shūdō Myōchō (1282–1338), who was also called Daitō Kokushi and co-founder of the Daitoku-ji temple. The name Shūdō Myōchō means "Wondrous Transcendence" with Myōchō being the initial name (*imina*) given to him by his teacher. According to legend, Shūdō resided with beggars on the Gojō bridge in Kyoto until the Emperor Hanazono decided to discover the identity of the strange beggar for himself. Knowing Shūdō's fondness for melons, the emperor brought a basket of them to the bridge, and informed the beggars that he would give the fruit to anyone who could step forward without the help of his feet. Challenging the emperor to a more difficult test, Shūdō asked that a melon be given to a beggar who could do so without using his hands. Thereupon, exposing himself to the emperor by his cleverness, Shūdō was escorted to the imperial palace where he conversed with the emperor and received new robes.

Eventually, the Emperor Hanazono bestowed the honorary title Daitō ("Great Lamp") on Shūdō, whose enlightenment represented the foundation for his original mind, which is the most important aspect of religious life and only criterion of authentic Zen.[67] The unenlightened not only are destined to suffer individually, but they also put at risk the transmission of the tradition.

An even more unusual figure was Ikkyū Sōjun (1394–1481), a disciple of Kasō Sōdon (1352–1428), who was known for his iconoclasm, poetry, and risqué lifestyle. Ikkyū was allegedly the illegitimate child of Emperor Gokomatsu. His mother, a member of the Fujiwara clan, was a favorite concubine of the emperor, but she was banished before the birth of Ikkyū to a lower-class dwelling in Kyoto because a jealous empress slandered her by accusing her of sympathizing with the rival, southern court.[68] Early in his life Ikkyū studied Chinese poems, and he began to exhibit promise as a poet himself. At seventeen years of age, Ikkyū studied with Kenō, his first Zen master, for four years until the master died, which caused the young man considerable grief. Ikkyū's inconsolable loss prompted him to pray at the Ishiyama temple. Unable to console himself, he resolved to commit suicide at Lake Biwa, but he encountered a servant of his sick mother who persuaded him to visit his mother.[69] Eventually Ikkyū found a new teacher, Kasō Sōdon, who was a strict and demanding disciplinarian. After some years of arduous effort,

67. Kraft, *Eloquent Zen*, 117.
68. Arntzen, *Ikkyū Sōjun*, 15.
69. Arntzen, *Ikkyū Sōjun*, 15.

Ikkyū finally attained full enlightenment in 1420, while he was adrift in a boat and heard the sudden cry of a crow, which triggered his awakening experience and marked a turning point in his life and the beginning of his erratic personal behavior. Sometime between 1426–32, he probably left the religious life, became a layman, married, and fathered a son.[70] Although it was not unusual for a monk to leave the Zen order, Ikkyū returned to the Zen fold in the 1430s to become famous for his wild style of Zen, as will become evident in chapter 7. He is famous for his poetry and its unusual topics as well as a work entitled *Skeletons*.

By developing national unity, intellectual and cultural progress, and secularization, Oda Nobunaga (1534–1582), Toyotomi Hideyoshi (1536–1598) and Tokugawa Ieyasu (1542–1616) led Japan into the Tokugawa era (1600–1868) and they selected the village of Edo as their headquarters, where Ieyasu built Edo Castle. This village was to grow into the renamed city of Tokyo and the capital of the Japanese empire during the Meiji period (1868–1912). The Tokugawa rulers favored Confucianism as the official ideology, and they exerted an oppressive and highly centralized government that allowed some local autonomy. The Japanese society was divided into four classes of samurai, farmers, workers, and merchants. The nation closed itself to all foreigners and their influence, which led to the expulsion of foreigners already present within the country and the persecution of Christians, an import religion. All religious groups were subjected to strict state organization and pressured to contribute to the general welfare of the nation. During this period, Buddhism lost power and influence. The decline of Buddhism was hastened, for instance, by an order from Nobunaga to burn down all the Tendai temples on Mount Hiei. In contrast, Zen remained unscathed by the persecution. In fact, Nobunaga granted it special privileges, and Hideyoshi felt indebted to Zen for raising the cultural status of the country,[71] by inspiring a period of artistic creativity that could be witnessed in decorative prints and wood cravings, Kabuki theater, puppet plays, Zen-influenced gardens, ink landscape drawings, Nō drama, and tea ceremony, which are some cultural phenomena that will be discussed in chapter 9.

A major event of the Tokugawa period was the government-issued edict that every citizen had to register and be an active member of a Buddhist temple within the overall context of a national hierarchy of temples

---

70. Sanford, *Zen-Man Ikkyū*, 32.
71. Dumoulin, *Zen Buddhism*, 2:261.

and a need for state control of religion. This move contributed to the creation of national sectarian institutions.[72] This development led to an unprecedented expansion of Buddhist institutions. Because the Sōtō school operated more than seventeen thousand temples in countless villages around the country, it could capitalize on the situation and exert more political influence.[73] This arrangement also had ritual benefits especially at the end of a life, and was a way that one could legally certify that one was a non-Christian, during a period when Christians were persecuted for their faith and foreign powers were excluded from Japan.

Besides these political and cultural developments during the Tokugawa period, there were several important figures in Zen. One such person was Takuan Sōhō (1573–1645) with his vision for a new lifestyle for Zen that combined academic study and monastic discipline, with the latter taking second place in importance to the study of Buddhist scriptures and Chinese thought. He desired to reconcile Zen with neo-Confucian thought, which can be illustrated by his work *Record of the Marvelous Power of Immovable Wisdom* that will be discussed in the final chapter.

Tetsugen Dōkō (1630–1682) was the most famous figure within the ōbaku school, which arose amid political turmoil and represented a revivalist movement contrasting sharply with conservative politics. During the latter half of the seventeenth century, the ōbaku school was established by a group of Chinese Zen teachers and their disciples of Japanese descent. After a brief period of growth in which it established thirty-two temples in Nagasaki, the school came to a halt. Before it declined, the ōbaku school incorporated elements of Pure Land Buddhism into its practices and beliefs by adopting such features as chanting the name of Amida Buddha, features that caused people to call it "Nembutsu Zen" because it copied the practice of chanting from Pure Land practice. Ōbaku also retained Chinese style of dress, liturgical language, and customs, resulting in a feeling of community and self-identity.[74] The adoption of these types of devotional practices placed the school in tension and disagreement with the Rinzai school. Within the confines of their monasteries, monks wore Chinese-style robes and shoes, chanted texts in Chinese, and adopted musical instruments.[75]

72. Williams, *Other Side of Zen*, 7.
73. Williams, *Other Side of Zen*, 20.
74. Baroni, *Obaku Zen*, 21.
75. Baroni, *Iron Eyes*, 6.

Arguably, the most eminent member of the ōbaku school was Tetsugen Dōkō, an advocate of the *Śūramgama Sūtra* as the primary teaching text for the sect. His most significant accomplishment was his role raising money to produce the first complete wood block printing of the Chinese Buddhist scriptures in Japan. Even though the school adopted some Chinese cultural elements and Pure Land practices, Dōkō rejected the doctrine of *mappo* that concerns the basic presupposition of the Pure Land school that during the present decline of the *dharma* (law) it was impossible to perform an ethical act. In contrast to the Pure Land position, Dōkō insisted that it was important for a person to keep and practice the Buddhist precepts.[76]

Although born into a Confucian family in the seventeenth century, Bankei Yōtaku (1622–1693) became a Zen monk and is credited with founding three monasteries. While residing in a hut, ill, and unable to eat in 1647, he spit out a dark ball of phlegm that he ejected against the wall, an event that cured his illness and that prompted an awakening experience that enabled him to realize that he possessed the truth all the time. Bankei emphasized what he called the Unborn, which represented both harmony and what lies beyond the unborn and undying. The Unborn also represents the Buddha mind that is innate in everyone. Bankei taught others to "abide in the Unborn," a reality that was intrinsic, original, and uncreated. His instruction to "abide in the Unborn" did not mean that it was a state that must be reached; it was rather something already present. Bankei equated the Unborn with the Buddha-Mind that are both intrinsically empty and thus non-dual. By following his advice about abiding in the Unborn, he thought that there was no chance that one would violate the ethical precepts of the religion.[77] From Bankei's perspective, an aspirant did not have to adopt some unique method to realize the truth. He advocated being oneself and being natural and spontaneous.

A former samurai warrior taught something very similar to Bankei. Remaining exterior to official schools of Zen, Suzuki Shōsan (1579–1655) demonstrated an interest in religious practice and living Buddhism concretely in the world. For him all activities and occupations were meaningful and could lead to spiritual progress after retiring to a monastery. He taught that all human beings are endowed with the Buddha-nature. Thus, they lack nothing.

76. Baroni, *Iron Eyes*, 25–30.
77. Haskel, *Bankei Zen*, 7.

A poet monk of the Sōtō school was Daigu Ryōkan (1758–1831). His master gave him a Chinese name that means good (*ryo*) and abundant (*kan*), while the other part of his name means "big fool" (*daigu*) for his unusual antics and his penchant for playing games with village children.[78] During the fall, he let children bury him under fallen leaves. He composed some poems about his play with children:

> Long spring days
> When mists rise—
> Hitting the handball
> Along with the children
> I've passed this one too.[79]

When he was sixty-nine, he began to write poems to Teishin, a twenty-nine-year old nun, who had been married to a young man who died prematurely. At the end of his life, she nursed Ryōkan, and she collected his poems after his death into an anthology called *Drew-drops on a Lotus Leaf*.

Another important poet was Matsuo Bashō (1644–1694), who was born into a lower-class samurai family. He was to become the greatest *haiku* poet and teacher. He opened a school and gathered a group of students around him in Edo in 1672 to perpetuate this art of poetry of seventeen syllables, which will be discussed more fully in chapter 9. Late in life Bashō became an itinerant figure and enjoyed a very creative and productive period of his career. He often expressed in his brief poems a temporary enlightenment into the life of things as he painted things with words. He also expressed being in unity with the world around him and a truth of Zen that the transient is merely a part of the eternal. Thus, it was not usual to find transient elements like the chirps of insects, songs of birds, and scents of blossoms intermixed with eternal elements expressed by water, wind, sunshine, and the four seasons in his poems. Many of his *haiku* poems evoked notions like selflessness, loneliness, wordlessness, non-intentionality, freedom, simplicity, and humor.

The classical period of Zen Buddhism ends with Hakuin (1685–1768), a product of the samurai class. Although he was an intellectually gifted child, he was physically frail and mischievous when he sadistically practiced the torture and destruction of insects and birds. At a formative age, he was upset by a sermon on hell, and became a monk to escape what

78. Dumoulin, *Zen Buddhism*, 2:344.
79. Watson, *Ryōkan*, 36.

he perceived to be his destiny for his cruelty. He became famous for a *kōan* that he devised: We all know what the sound of two hands clapping sounds like. But what is the sound of one hand clapping?[80] He often wrote personally of his quest for enlightenment and his identification of what he called Zen sickness, which was akin to a nervous breakdown. He reported that his head became heated and his lower body became cool. He recovered by heating his lower body with deep breathing exercises.[81] He defined the essentials of Buddhism as the precepts, meditation, and wisdom.

Hakuin lived during a period when Pure Land Buddhism and adherence to the *Lotus Sūtra* were very popular. In a letter to a nun and devotee of the *Lotus Sūtra*, he wrote, "Outside the mind there is no *Lotus Sūtra* and outside the *Lotus Sūtra* there is no mind."[82] Here he was advocating a non-dualistic position in which the mind included the all. For Hakuin, a text like the *Lotus Sūtra* possessed utility as a meditation device, even though it was essentially a devotional text. In response to those within devotional Buddhism who believed that it was impossible to achieve enlightenment during this final degenerate age, his response was a resounding affirmation.[83] In fact, all Buddhist sects were ultimately one. But this did not mean that one can practice both Zen and Pure Land at the same time. For Hakuin, the true Pure Land was within oneself.[84] It was, however, possible to recite the name of the Buddha with success to lead one to salvation in the sense that it helped a person to concentrate, a feature that it possessed in common with the *kōan*.[85] The final chapter will have more to say about Zen in the twentieth century.

---

80. Yampolsky, *Zen Master Hakuin*, 164–65; hereafter cited as Yampolsky, *Hakuin*.
81. Yampolsky, *Hakuin*, 51.
82. Yampolsky, *Hakuin*, 87.
83. Yampolsky, *Hakuin*, 97.
84. Yampolsky, *Hakuin*, 136.
85. Yampolsky, *Hakuin*, 127, 130.

3

GETTING THE GOOSE OUT OF THE BOTTLE

LET US SUPPOSE THAT you have been given the following assignment by your teacher: How do you extricate a goose from the interior of a long-stemmed bottle without breaking the bottle or killing the goose? Admittedly, this is a very difficult assignment because you cannot simply grasp the head or neck of the goose and pull it through without harming the bird or breaking the glass bottle. Lubrications of various sorts would not appear to do the trick because of the wide size of the lower half of the goose in comparison to the small circumference of the stem of the bottle. This assignment represents in a metaphorical way the fundamental problem for a Zen student, because to find the solution to this problem is equivalent to becoming enlightened. The resolution of the problem is not an intellectual solution, because it is more an issue of intuitive insight. Once you have the insight, the resolution of the problem occurs simultaneously. How does a person arrive at that moment? Classical Zen Buddhism proposes a regimented lifestyle, discipline, and methods. As noted in chapter 3, various Zen masters used a variety of methods related to language that manifested one-word responses to questions, repetition, shouts, silence, and *kōans* (enigmatic statements or dialogues between student and master). Therefore, getting the goose out of the bottle is also a problem of language. This chapter will review the Zen understanding of language as it pertains to achieving enlightenment, the nature of *kōans*, and some of the more unique features of Zen monastic life.

LANGUAGE IN ZEN

Zen monks use language within a context that is communal and focused to achieve the specific goal of enlightenment (*satori*). Within the confines of this community, monks are bonded together by their common language and the ways that this shared language is utilized in the pursuit of their goal. Language is more than simply a means of communication in Zen or expressing oneself. Zen monks use language to break out of the confines of ordinary discourse to free people from constraints imposed by conventional modes of language. Ironically, language has no power of its own because it is devoid of inherent self-nature, substance, or significance.

Zen attempts to use language in both a non-dualistic way and a non-representational manner. In the former case, the Zen master, for instance, uses language in such a way that what the master teaches his students is also what he is living. Thus, there is no distinction between the language used to teach, its message, and the messenger. Therefore, to grasp the nature of Zen, it is necessary to understand its language. This point is illustrated nicely about an incident related to the nature of herding an ox. One day when he was at work in the kitchen, Mazu asked the master: "What are you doing?" The master replied: "Herding the ox." Mazu asked: "Herding?" The master responded: "As soon as he runs back to the grass, I pull him out by his nostrils." Mazu concluded: "You really herd the ox."[1] In other words, the master really does know what he is doing because what he says he is doing in fact is precisely what he is doing. This suggests that there is no duality between speech and action. Moreover, in this example, the metaphor of herding an ox is often used to refer to taming the egotistical and desiring self in a sequence of drawings. The ox herding episode is recalled every time the ox herding pictures are used as a pedagogical device for a novice. The pictures move from seeing traces of the ox, to finding it, to taming it, to riding it home, and finally to a drawing of a circle signifying emptiness.

By the notion of representational language, Zen Buddhists understand a language that conveys an image or representation of the word expressed. For instance, the word *cow* evokes the image of a four-legged animal with a tail that feeds on grass. The Zen use of language attempts to avoid representational modes of language because the enlightenment experience and mode of thinking that it is attempting to develop is

---

1. Whitfield, *Lamp*, 157.

without concepts or representations. A good illustration of the non-representational mode of language is the following example from the early Zen tradition: There once was a monk who drew four lines in front of Mazu. The upper line was longer than the three shorter lines beneath it. The monk said: "Without arguing that one line is longer, and three lines are shorter, leaving aside the four assertions and the hundred negations, may I ask your reverence to answer me." Thereupon, Mazu drew one line on the ground and said: "Without arguing about long and short, there is your answer."[2] Mazu refused to get caught in the language game being played by the monk. His response was a non-verbal gesture that avoided any entanglement in language or representational discourse.

The Zen awakening experience does not occur in a sphere devoid of language, but it rather occurs within the midst of language, and it can even be evoked by language, although the enlightenment experience itself cannot be expressed in words. Mazu shows that he understands this point when Baizhang asked: "What is the essence of Buddhism?" Mazu replied: "It is precisely where you let go of your life."[3] There is no argument that occurs in this dialogue. Rather the dialogue between these two functions demonstrates that enlightenment cannot be put into words. Nonetheless, the intended point is made by showing it rather than arguing for it by means of a rational dialogue.

As noted in the previous chapter, beatings, shouts, and gestures are forms of language that are intended to make something happen. Thus, the Zen use of language can cause results just as it can transform a person's experience. The performative aspect of the Zen use of language often is dependent on a "turning word," a crucial point on which an encounter changes. A turning word fits into a context but can also open the context in a revealing manner not previously witnessed.[4] The "turning word" exposes the situation and calls attention to the present moment.

Paradoxically, silence can also make something happen in the sense of disrupting a dialogue, terminating a conversation, or evoking an awakening experience, and it also serves as a symbol of awakening. Within the Zen context, silence is much more than the absence of sound, because it potentially functions to bring language to our awareness by offering a different perspective on language. Instead of speaking, an aspirant can communicate by performing an action. Along with Puhua,

2. Whitfield, *Lamp*, 144.
3. Whitfield, *Lamp*, 143.
4. Wright, *Philosophical Meditations*, 103.

Linji attended, for example, a vegetarian feast at a donor's home. Linji asked Puhua, "A single hair swallows the giant ocean, and a mustard seed contains Mt. Sumeru. Is this the wondrous function of spiritual powers, or is it fundamentally in essence so?" In response, Puhua kicked over the table with the food. Linji said, "Too crude." Puhua said, "What place is this to talk of crude or fine?"[5] While in the capital to sell fish, Shanhui is recommended by Master Zhi in another episode to come and expound on the *Diamond Sūtra* to the emperor, who invites Shanhui to the inner palace. After mounting the lecturing seat, he immediately proceeds to shake the lectern and gets down.[6] Silence operates in this case by transcending words, sentences, and mere stillness. Silence does not suggest that speech is completely rejected, but rather leaves words behind when they reach the limit of conceptualization.[7] Silence possesses the ability to express a correspondence between the inner harmony of a meditator and ultimate emptiness.

Besides the importance of the "turning word" and silence to understanding the Zen notion of language, there is also a distinction made between words and no words. In the second chapter, the method of Yunmen was mentioned and his usage of single word answers. For example, as a response to the question: "What is Tao?" he replied, "Go!" In another instance, a monk asked, "When you kill your parents, you repent before the Buddha; when you kill the Buddha, where do you turn to repent?" Yunmen said, "Exposed." Another monk asked, "What is the treasury of the eye of the true Dharma?" Yunmen said, "Universal."[8] These single word answers are spontaneous reactions to a question without taking one's time to think about a proper response, to devise a rational answer or a contrived reaction. The single word is a mere sign that lacks any substantial nature. It is like the names Buddha or Bodhidharma that are mere labels without any substance. This point is illustrated nicely by a humorous dialogue:

> The master asked a monk: "What is your name?"
> "I," answered the monk.
> "What, then, is the Acarya's host?" asked the master.
> "Just who you see answering," replied the monk.

---

5. Sasaki, *Record of Linji*, 48.
6. Cleary, *Blue Cliff Record*, 307.
7. Heine, *Zen Skin, Zen Marrow*, 25.
8. Cleary, *Blue Cliff Record*, 42.

The master said, "How sad, how sad. The like of people today is all just like this monk. They can only see themselves as the horse behind the donkey. That is to make the Buddha Dharma common. They still don't even understand the guest's view of the host. How could they perceive the host from the point of view of the host?"[9]

Like the horse walking behind a donkey, humans only see the backside of a donkey, which suggests that they have a very limited and distorted perspective on life. Moreover, the response of the master possesses no connection to the original question. The name of the person did not really matter because it lacks any essence, functioning as a mere supplement to an aggregate of ever-changing parts. In other words, the name Buddha is merely a proper nature added to a skeleton covered by muscle, skin, and clothing that possesses the ability to speak, think, perceive, and walk. To overcome the supplemental nature of a name or word advocates the usefulness of no words. An example of the spirit of no words comes from the *Linji lu*:

> When Linji reached Cuifeng's place, Cuifeng asked:
> "Where did you come from?"
> "I came from Huangbo," said Linji.
> "What words does Huangbo use to instruct people?" asked Cuifeng.
> "Huangbo has no words," said Linji.
> "Why not?" asked Cuifeng.
> "Even if he had any, I wouldn't know how to state them," answered Linji.
> "Come on, try and tell me," said Cuifeng.
> "The arrow has flown off to the Western Heaven," said Linji.[10]

The message embodied in this dialogue is suggestive about the inherent limitations of names and words, and it implies that a person should not place too much value or rely on them too much. At the same time, this suggestion does not mean that words lack any utility, because it is possible to observe the usefulness of words in the basic distinction made between live words and dead words.

By the latter type of words, Zen masters classify ordinary discourse, explanations, or analytical terms, which do not contribute to the awakening and freeing of a person from everyday language. However, in contrast

---

9. Chang, *Treasury of Mahāyāna Sūtras*, 69.
10. Sasaki, *Record of Linji*, 49.

to dead words, live words function to overturn and disrupt our normal way of using language. Moreover, live words embody an ability to open the mind to new and previously unexplored possibilities. Live words are equated with turning words, which possess a transformative power, whereas dead words are simply dualistic and are totally devoid of any ability to transform anything. In contrast to dead words, live words are non-dualistic because a speaker does not intend to use language to dominate or control a situation, and utterance of non-dual words does not attempt to control a dialogue, for instance, by being willing to flow with the words regardless of the direction they may take. Since words possess no inherent power and lack innate meaning, the context of an utterance is significant because it gives words their power to open the context in some new and revealing way.[11] In short, live words give us insight into a situation and transform us. These comments are reinforced by the sage advice of Master Yantou in *The Blue Cliff Record*, "Study the living word, not the dead word. If you understand at the dead word, you will be unable to save yourself."[12]

LIVE WORDS OF THE *KŌAN*

The most obvious example of live words to be discovered in the Zen tradition are *kōans*, a statement (often brief) uttered by an old master, or an answer given to a question by a master. For example, a monk asked Zhaozhou, "Myriad things return to one—where does the one return?" Zhaozhou said, "When I was in Qingzhou I made a cloth shirt. It weighed seven pounds."[13] In another example, a monk asked Zhaozhou, "What is the meaning of the patriarch coming from the West?" Zhaozhou said, "The cypress tree in the garden."[14] In one final example of many, a monk asked Dongshan, "What is the Buddha?" Dongshan said, "Three pounds of hemp."[15] What these examples indicate is that the enlightened master responded immediately to the question by verbally expressing what was on their minds at that precise moment, which happened to be a shirt of seven pounds, a cypress tree, and three pounds of hemp. These examples

---

11. Wright, *Philosophical Meditations*, 103.
12. Cleary, *Blue Cliff Record*, 202.
13. Cleary, *Blue Cliff Record*, 224.
14. Cleary, *Wumen's Gate*, 99.
15. Cleary, *Wumen's Gate*, 85.

are useful, but they do not fully convey the meaning or significance of the term for which a reader must probe the historical roots of the term. *The Blue Cliff Record* contains a useful insightful hint for anyone who grapples with a *kōan* with their entire being: "The question is in the answer, the answer is in the question."[16] Everyone who enters the game of the *kōan* should remember this non-dualistic way of looking at a *kōan* and take solace that the answer is right there in front of you.

Prior to the twelfth century when *kōan* usage became popular as a method, the term referred to a passage from the patriarchal records on which scholars would compose commentaries that came to be called old cases (*ku-tse*, literally ancient precedents). The procedure involved a question being raised by a disciple or someone from an assembly of monks to a master about a passage from the patriarchal records. It was not unusual for a master to raise a question of his audience to elicit responses on which he might pass judgment or serve as a preparation for his own comments. This practice had a twofold purpose related to clarifying insights of the ancient patriarchs and serving to manifest the status and authority of the current master.[17] This practice is historically related to a gradual shift from apophatic language to kataphatic discourse in Buddhism during the Tang dynasty, a movement from negative to positive forms of language.[18]

If we investigate the historical origins of the term *kōan*, we find that it is connected to the Chinese term *kung-an* (case record), suggesting a case in accord with the Buddha and Patriarchs of the tradition. Originating in Chinese jurisprudence, the *kung-an* evoked the image of a table or bench of a magistrate or judge, implying a written brief on the judge's table, or it could be the record of a judicated legal decision. Outside the context of Chan Buddhism, the term is associated with Chinese jurisprudence by implying a table or bench of a legal authority. In addition, it embodies the connotation of something public and unbiased. These types of connotations were embraced by a Zen master when he compared himself to a legal magistrate with the power to legally bind and to dispense necessary punishment for the guilty. Within the Chan context, as suggested by the previous chapter on teaching methods, a guilty person was in a state of ignorance, whereas an innocent person was equivalent to

---

16. Cleary, *Blue Cliff Record*, 62.
17. Foulk, "Form and Function of Kōan Literature," 17.
18. Gimello, "Apophatic and Kataphatic Discourse," 116–36.

an awakened person.[19] The term *kung-an* also embodies the meaning of something "public," emphasizing the public nature of a *kōan* that stands opposed to private understanding.

Building on the legal origins of the term, Zen masters used the term *kōan* to refer to a statement made by an old master, or an answer given to a question by a master. These statements or answers were invariably brief and made no logical sense. For instance, a favorite *kōan* often began "What was the meaning of Bodhidharma coming from the West?" A wide variety of responses were made to this question. Among them was the response by Tung-shan, "It is as big as a rhinoceros whose horn often frightens chickens."[20]

From this kind of example, it becomes apparent that the answers given by masters have absolutely no connection to the question. The lack of a connection between the question and the answer is purposeful, because the *kōan* is intended to terminate ordinary understanding and to disrupt a questioner from his normal mode of consciousness. The purpose of the *kōan* is to disrupt a person's normal mode of thinking and to get them to see, understand, and think in a completely new way. The disruption is caused to a person's normal mode of thinking because the *kōan* possesses no meaningful significance. It is preferable to grasp the *kōan* as an instrument that erases meaning. It also functions to disrupt rationality by forming an obstacle that is impossible for it to overcome. The spirit of this type of language obstacle is captured in the following dialogical exchange: A monk asked Yunmen, "When it's not the present potential and not the present situation, what is it?" Yunmen said, "An upside-down statement."[21] The words of the *kōan* are what can be described as live words because they are non-dualistic, they can open the mind to new modes of awareness, and they possess a power to transform a person. Moreover, the words of the *kōan* are instructive in the sense that they suggest that words are empty of inherent meaning by themselves. In the *Recorded Sayings of Linji*, words are characterized as "illusory transformations."[22]

Just as the response to a question within the context of a *kōan* is nonsensical with respect to the actual question, the question/answer format itself of a *kōan* does not necessarily have to be verbal because any type of

19. Foulk, "Form and Function of Kōan Literature," 18–20.
20. Chang, *Treasury of Mahāyāna Sūtras*, 63.
21. Cleary, *Blue Cliff Record*, 89.
22. Cleary, *Recorded Sayings of Linji*, 39.

non-verbal action can meet the intention of a master. When master Guishan and Yangshan were picking tea leaves, the master said, "All day I have heard your voice as we picked tea leaves, but I have not seen you yourself. Show me your real self." Immediately, Yangshan responded by shaking the tea tree.[23] By non-verbally directly pointing toward awakening, this direct and spontaneous rhetorical act communicates spontaneity devoid of reflection. If this communication does not occur immediately, it does not communicate anything at all.

By giving a student a *kōan* on which to meditate, the master possesses a method by which he can examine the mind of the novice and maintain standards related to spiritual progress. When a person is transformed from a benighted individual into an enlightened individual, that person's response to a *kōan* on which they have been meditating to a master will indicate such a transformation. By using a novice's response to a *kōan*, the master can examine and, in a sense, read the mind of the novice to discern their status. This means that the master always possesses a metaphorical gauge by which to measure the student. Throughout the examination process, the content of the *kōan* is not all that important because it is the intended result that is important, although the tradition catalogued them according to perceived levels of difficulty as we will note shortly. It is simpler to think of the *kōan* as an unsolvable problem that the master gives to a student to fix his concentration on a single point. The student exerts his entire being, mind, and body into its solution. Yet the incongruous problem does not have a common-sense answer. It is only by arduously struggling with and working on the *kōan* in the process of meditation that a person will reach a point at which one realizes that all intellectual attempts to solve the *kōan* and simultaneously reach enlightenment are totally futile. By recognizing that it can only go so far, the intellect is forced by the impenetrable nature of the *kōan* to discover a new direction around its unsolvable problem. To find this new direction is the achievement of enlightenment (*satori*). For someone attaining enlightenment by means of the *kōan* method, it is a standard practice to compose a capping verse or phrase and attach it to the *kōan* on which a person meditated. Those judged famous would be attached to the *kōan* within a collection, and they were regarded as possessing "the identical power of disclosure for those who might meditate on them."[24]

23. Whitfield, *Lamp*, 256.
24. Wright, "Kōan History," 202.

A person reading a *kōan* will never be able to learn the price of stocks or rice, because it does not give any information. It does not argue for a philosophical position, and it is neither true nor false. Like the sound of one hand clapping, the dog with or without the Buddha-nature, or the appearance of your face before your parents were born, the *kōan* refers to an ontological absurdity, which cannot be experienced or conceived. Like the examples of a pregnant virgin or a square circle, the *kōan* is paradoxical. It is this paradoxical nature of the *kōan* that gives rise to the ball of doubt and destroys a person's ordinary understanding of the world. If one does not retreat from the paradoxical nature of the *kōan*, and if one grapples with it with all one's being and energy, an intuitive understanding of a transcendental realm of reality is unveiled. With this shift to another realm of reality, the paradoxical nature of the *kōan* is resolved, although it is not truly solved in a rational way or dissolved by explaining its incongruity. In a sense, the resolution occurs by clarifying the paradoxicality of the paradox. This means that an enlightened person intuitively understands why the language of the *kōan* is paradoxical; it reflects the nature of enlightenment itself.[25] In other words, the incongruity of the paradox remains, although enlightenment comes by grasping the nature of the paradox and not by mastering the paradox.

From a historical perspective, the sense of the paradoxical nature of *kōans* was encouraged by using contemplations (*kuan*) for Chinese meditators even before *kōan* practice became common. Around the twelfth century, the *kōan* was absorbed into seated meditation (*zazen*), which sought to be as non-conceptual as possible. This movement toward non-conceptuality was also applied to the *kōan* itself. To eliminate any kind of thinking, which would only cause confusion, the original narrative structure of the *kōan* was eliminated to focus on a single point. This was called the critical phrase (*huatou*), which was even stated to be without meaning.[26]

MEDITATING ON THE *KŌAN*

A novice is given a *kōan* on which to meditate by the *roshi* (teacher, master). This is especially true of the Rinzai sect in Japan because the Sōtō sect places much less emphasis on *kōan* use and more on quiet sitting in meditation. To learn about what is at stake with regard to meditating

---

25. Cheng, "On Zen (Ch'an) Language," 77–102.
26. Wright, "Kōan History," 207.

on a *kōan*, we will review the thoughts on this subject by a great Rinzai sect reformer named Hakuin. This historically important figure identifies several features that occur when a person investigates a *kōan*. According to Hakuin, when a person investigates a *kōan* with every fiber of energy with one's body the mind dies, the will is destroyed, one faces death, one is suddenly one with the *kōan*, body and mind are cast off, one finds oneself beyond distinctions, and one realizes true reality. It is important to unpack this sequence to arrive at a fuller understanding about *kōan* meditation. But before we do this unpacking, it is necessary to look at his understanding of the root problem of life.

According to Hakuin, the root problem of life is ignorance which prevents a person from seeing into their own natures. There is a person, for example, in Chinese Chan literature who witnesses a rabbit collide with a tree stump and die. After taking the rabbit for food, the man waited by the stump hoping that it would obtain another rabbit for him. This represents the universal plight of all humans who ignorantly stand waiting for an inert tree stump to provide them with a meal. The fact of ignorance can be reduced to a single concept: the self is real. Hakuin expounds that "because of this view that the self exists, we have birth and death, Nirvana, the passions, enlightenment. Although a person does not possess a permanent self, a person is, however, endowed with the wisdom and form of the Buddha."[27] Therefore, a person lacks nothing because they possess the Buddha-nature, which is eternal and unchanging, and metaphorically like a hidden jewel in a person's clothing.

Due to the existential fact that a person is sunk in the mire of ignorance, a way must be found to extricate a person from this dilemma. The mechanical winch used to pull a person out of the muck of ignorance is the *kōan*, an enigmatic statement of a Zen master, which operates by creating doubt. What Hakuin advocates is inducing doubt in a creative way to serve as a bridge to liberation. This is very dangerous because doubt can lead a person to feelings of insecurity, anxiety, and despair. However, the risk that a person can become totally shipwrecked must be taken, if a person is to achieve total certainty. The risk involved is like trying to ride a tiger, or like the dangerous chance that one takes by entering a tiger's den; unless a person enters the tiger's den, they will never capture the tiger cub.[28]

---

27. Yampolsky, *Hakuin*, 134.
28. Cleary, *Blue Cliff Record*, 93.

Before a person even begins meditation on a *kōan*, there are certain qualities that a student must possess from Hakuin's perspective. All students of Zen must have three basic qualities: overriding faith, great doubt when facing the *kōan*, and strong aspiration and perseverance.[29] Possessing these qualities, a student can begin the method of introspection called *naikan* that consists of contemplating the region below the navel to the soles of one's feet, an area associated with one's original face.[30] This method is not limited to seated meditation, but it is also part of a person's waking consciousness. Moreover, it forms the nucleus around which the Great Death coalesces, which we will discuss shortly. Within the context of *kōan* practice, the ordinary bifurcation between body and mind dissolves.

As part of his analysis of *kōan* practice, Hakuin examines the Mu *kōan*, which involves the following question and response: "Does a dog have the Buddha-nature?" To which the master replies "*Mu!*" or in translation "nothingness." What is the significance of this *kōan*? Hakuin informs us that it is neither a concept nor something physical. Instead, it represents the source of a person. More precisely, it is pre-reflective non-thinking. From this primordial type of non-thinking, all experiences and differentiations arise. Fully practicing the *Mu kōan*, for instance, is to enter the consciousness of *Mu* (nothingness). This is equivalent to the state of no-mind (*mushin*) of which we will have more to say in the next chapter.

As a person is working on a *kōan*, this practice intensifies the Great Doubt in three ways. Firstly, it concentrates seated meditation (*zazen*) by deconstructing conceptual distinctions between body and mind that we normally make. The whole person becomes Mu (nothingness). Thirdly, the *kōan* is not resolvable by either thinking or un-thinking because it is fundamentally paradoxical. This realization leads to a search for another approach. In fact, it leads to the discovery of non-thinking, which is exemplified by the master who obstructs all responses from a student that does not arise from non-thinking.

As the student continues to work on the *kōan*, it creates the Great Doubt, which represents a not-thinking that is restricted until there is nothing left to deny. It is this doubt that a person must resolve. The resolution of the Great Doubt entails discarding emotions, concepts, and thoughts. By investigating the *kōan* single-mindedly, the ball of doubt

---

29. Yampolsky, *Hakuin*, 144.
30. Yampolsky, *Hakuin*, 38.

will enable one to advance: "It must be understood that this ball of doubt is like a pair of wings that advances you along the way."[31] What is finally significant is that the resolution of doubt leads to awakening: "At the bottom of great doubt lies great awakening. If you doubt fully you will awaken fully."[32]

But before this awakening occurs, the *kōan* leads a person to a place where reason is exhausted and words end. An important result of this process is the termination of the karmic root of birth and death. In other words, it stops the cycle of rebirth. Furthermore, it breaks down ignorance: "At this time the basis of mind, consciousness, and emotion is suddenly shattered; the realm of illusion with its endless sinking in the cycle of birth and death is overturned."[33] Referring to the *kōan* about the sound of one hand clapping that he devised, Hakuin states that when a person hears a single hand clapping a person experiences the Great Death.

In fact, *kōan* practice leads directly to the Great Death. What Hakuin means by the Great Death is that before a person can become enlightened or reborn one must die to one's former condition. Hakuin describes in metaphorical language the Great Death and being born again: "Thus you will attain to a peace in which the phoenix has left the golden net and the crane has been set free of the basket. At this time, the basis of the mind, consciousness, and emotion is suddenly shattered; the realm of illusion with its endless sinking in the cycle of birth and death is overturned."[34] What Hakuin means in less metaphorical language is that a person's mind dies and their will is destroyed. There is a dilemma that illustrates Hakuin's point:

> Supposing a man should find himself in some desolate area where no man has ever walked before. Below him are the perpendicular walls of a bottomless chasm. His feet rest precariously on a patch of slippery moss, and there is no spot of earth on which he can steady himself. He can neither advance nor retreat; he faces only death. The only things he has on which to depend are a vine that he grasps by the left hand and a creeper that he holds with his right. His life hangs as if from a dangling thread. If he were suddenly to let go his dried bones would not even be left.[35]

31. Yampolsky, *Hakuin*, 146.
32. Yampolsky, *Hakuin*, 144.
33. Yampolsky, *Hakuin*, 164.
34. Yampolsky, *Hakuin*, 164.
35. Yampolsky, *Hakuin*, 135.

What this dilemma suggests is that a person must be prepared to let go. Moreover, a person must be prepared to die and to return to life. What he means is something radical because when a person is in unity with the *kōan* their body and mind are cast off or die. This scenario does not mean that a person should relax and take their time turning their attention to working on a *kōan*. In fact, time is short for everyone. There is thus an urgency built into the message of Hakuin.[36]

THE PLACE OF MEDITATION

During its development, Zen monks kept the metaphor of journey alive, but they tended to organize themselves into more permanent religious structures where they could form communities apart from ordinary society, study, live an arduous life, and meditate. Rules, modes of behavior, daily procedures, and administrative structure were provided in writing in such works as *The Baizhang Zen Monastic Regulations in China* and Dōgen's *Pure Standards* (*Eihei Shingi*), representing the two major schools in Japan—Rinzai and Sōtō. Both texts have a political slant. Baizhang begins his text, for example, by reminding monks that imperial court has exempted them from paying taxes for which they should be grateful. For this exemption and other reasons, the state and monastery are interconnected with the monastery being subordinate to the state.

The emperor is the linchpin of the relationship between the state and monastery. Besides annually celebrating the imperial birthday and placing an imperial portrait on the Buddha's altar within the monastery, the importance of the emperor is expressed in the following way by the text: "Each emperor is said to govern the realm of heaven and earth as an incarnate Buddha body (*nirmāṇakāya*), and upon completing his task of transforming the realm returns to the state of Buddhahood."[37] This statement represents a Buddhist reinterpretation of the Confucian vision of the emperor as the son of god. Baizhang claims that the emperor is an incarnation of the Buddha and will return to his Buddha status after he dies. Whether from a Buddhist or Confucian perspective, the emperor is a divine being. The monastic obligation is not simply to honor and revere the emperor, but it is also to protect the state from external enemies, demonic beings, and natural disasters and to foster general prosperity for the citizens.

36. See Yampolsky, *Hakuin*, 168–69.
37. Ichimura, *Baizhang Zen Monastic Regulations*, 23.

Baizhang explains the role of sounds, physical acts, and the use of incense during services. The striking of bells and gongs mark, for instance, the arrival of the abbot at the Buddha hall where a metal gong is struck three times, or when the abbot returns from visiting other temples a monk tolls a large bell. Baizhang explains the purpose of sounds when he states that they are intended as a "warning against confusion and idleness, encouraging compliance with the teachings and regulations, giving guidance for those who abide in dark subhuman states, and pleasing of gods and humans."[38] Physical actions of prostrations and bowings punctuate various encounters with superiors, before various religious actions, and prior to daily events such as eating. Baizhang provides as rationale for the use of incense: "It perfumes the senses of seeing, hearing, and so on and transforms them into ultimate quiescence."[39] This statement suggests a connection between incense and a goal of meditation.

Baizhang's discussion of the duties of various temple officials and the prevailing regulations and precepts make it obvious that the monastery is hierarchically ordered, and it is important for everyone to know their place in this structure. For those that break the regulations, there are punitive consequences. To cite only the transgressing of a grave offense as an example, the offender's robe and alms bowl are burned, and he is expelled by the temple side gate.[40] This punishment is diabolical because it represents the symbolic destruction of his status as a religious figure.

Much like Baizhang's text, Dōgen's *Pure Standards* stresses harmony, order, and the proper time for events, which are announced by ringing bells or clapping together wooden blocks. Throughout his text, Dōgen retells old Chinese narratives to function as models for current behavior. Dōgen covers many of the topics discussed by Baizhang, although there are two topics that he interestingly goes into greater depth compared with Baizhang's text that relate to eating and sleeping.

According to Dōgen's description of the activities surrounding eating, the preparation of the food and action of eating it are ritualized. While the chief cook (*tenzo*) prepares the rice and vegetables, his attendants chant, for example, a *sūtra* (text) and dedicate this action to the guardian god of the oven. Before the food is served, the chief cook dons the *okesa* (robe), unfolds the *zagu* (bowing cloth), and, while facing the *sōdō* (monk's hall where they eat, sleep, and meditate), offers incense and

38. Ichimura, *Baizhang Zen Monastic Regulations*, 410.
39. Ichimura, *Baizhang Zen Monastic Regulations*, 230.
40. Ichimura, *Baizhang Zen Monastic Regulations*, 87.

does nine prostrations.[41] Dōgen goes into detail about the proper way to eat by instructing monks to focus their attention on their bowls while eating, not making noise while chewing your food, not licking your lips, and not sticking out your tongue while eating.[42] Prior to eating, a monk should take care to remove small bugs from the rice, which reflects the spirit of nonviolence. And the water used to wash rice should not be wasted by being reused with the rice gruel.[43] Dōgen envisions eating, a daily activity that the vast majority of people take for granted, as a non-dual activity. At first, he affirms that *dharma* is food and food is *dharma*. Then, he states, "If the dharma is suchness, food is also suchness."[44] Thus, just as the *dharma* is empty so also is food, making them non-dual.

Besides instructions for eating, Dōgen informs monks that their heads must face the direction of the Buddha. This instruction is followed by a series of restrictions: do not look at the Buddha while lying down; do not stretch out your legs together; do not eat lying down on your back or stomach; do not raise your knees while lying down; do not remove your robe to sleep; do not sleep naked; and sleep on your right side and not the left.[45] With respect to this last restriction, the right side of the human body is the positive, male, or yang side of the body while the left side is the exact opposite. Sleeping flat on one's back is considered the dead man's position. Dōgen relates sleeping to meditation when he instructs aspirants that it is best to meditate with your eyes open, otherwise you risk inducing drowsiness and falling asleep.[46]

The life of a Zen monk is focused on meditation, but it also includes related activities like labor and maintaining a state of poverty, which necessitates the practice of begging, a practice that dates to the time of the historical Buddha, although some monasteries from the time of Eisai's ten provisions have ceased requiring monks to perform manual labor, arguing that these activities interfere with meditation practice.[47] Zen monks are allowed some meager possessions that include a set of robes, razor for shaving a monk's face and head, some money to be used for

---

41. Leighton and Okumura, *Dōgen's Pure Standards*, 36, 39.
42. Leighton and Okumura, *Dōgen's Pure Standards*, 94.
43. Leighton and Okumura, *Dōgen's Pure Standards*, 35–36.
44. Leighton and Okumura, *Dōgen's Pure Standards*, 83–84.
45. Leighton and Okumura, *Dōgen's Pure Standards*, 65.
46. Leighton and Okumura, *Dōgen's Pure Standards*, 66.
47. Welter, "Buddhist Rituals for Protecting," 123.

one's burial in the instances of an unexpected death, a book or two, and a set of bowls for eating meals and begging.

The practice of begging possesses a dual purpose: to teach the beggar (monk or nun) humility and to offer a donor an opportunity to gain merit that would improve a giver's chances for a more favorable rebirth. Although it is possible for monks to beg individually, they often canvassed a village or neighborhood in small groups. In Japan, the monks often wear broad-rimmed hats that cut the vision of the wearer. When standing before a donor and tilting one's head forward with the hat on one's head an individual monk can obliterate the face of the donor, making begging and giving an impersonal process. From another perspective, the donor is not giving to a monk, but she is giving to the entire monastic institution. It is also important that the charity of people not lead to the development of more personal relationships because social ties are viewed as an additional burden to be overcome by the monk.

The emphasis on labor dates to the rule instituted by Baizhang (749–814) that a day without working is a day without eating. Monks are not simply expected to live on the generosity of their patrons. The Zen monastery embodies a democratic spirit with regard to work, because everyone does some type of useful work that involves duties from cleaning latrines to teaching. Duties are often rotated to maintain their democratic spirit. It is important that work be performed in the right spirit and not performed with a negative attitude or with the thought of personal reward. As the Zen master Hakuin taught, a person can transform everything that they do into a true form of meditation. By this, he specified making everything that one does into a single *kōan*.[48] The goal of requiring manual labor for monks was to make the monastery a self-sustaining entity, but by the medieval period in Japan this was not considered as important as seated meditation as noted previously with the teachings of Eisai. Even during the classical period in China, it is possible to find differences of opinion about monk labor. On a visit to the master Linji, a layman asked him if monks read texts and study Zen, to which Linji replied negatively. The layman pressed the master further about what monks really do. Linji said, "We're making them all into buddhas and patriarchs."[49]

---

48. Yampolsky, *Hakuin*, 58.
49. Cleary, *Blue Cliff Record*, 51.

Before a person can begin this life of poverty, labor and meditation, a novice must present themselves for ordination. The novice is initially refused by the *roshi* (master). This initial refusal recalls the reluctance of Bodhidharma to accept Huike as a student, and it tests the sincerity and determination of the student. At a Zen monastery, this is considered a probation period during which the student must wait two to three days or even a week before being admitted to the *Zendo* (meditation hall). Due to the physical location of the novice and their marginal status outside the meditation hall, this period is called occupying the entrance court. When the novice is finally admitted to the *Zendo* (meditation hall), the male monk dons a *kesa*, a formal ceremonial robe, and he pays his respect to Mañjuśrī, a *bodhisattva* who embodies wisdom, enshrined typically at the entrance to many meditation halls. The newly admitted novice spreads his *zagu*, a square piece of silk, on the floor, and he prostrates himself three times before the image. Thereafter, he is escorted to his seat where he meditates, eats his meals, and sleeps. Then, the ushering monk announces the admission of a new member into the brotherhood. Oftentimes, a tea ceremony follows the announcement. A few days later, the novice is introduced to the master. The novice offers incense to the *roshi* (master), which is a pledge that the novice takes the master as his instructor. Approaching the threshold of the master's room, the novice spreads his *zagu* (seat-cloth) and bows on it three times. Then, a tea ceremony and interview take place. The interview is brief and confined to the master asking the novice the following questions: his name, place of origin, and education.

At the end of a probationary period, full ordination occurs with a monk agreeing to adhere to 250 precepts. More specifically, a new monk vows to observe the following: the three refuges (Buddha, *dharma*, and *sangha*), five basic precepts (nonviolence, no stealing, chastity, no lying, and no consumption of alcohol), the ten precepts of a novice (includes five basic precepts along with an additional five of avoiding eating after noon, sleeping on luxurious beds, viewing theater or listening to music, using perfume or cosmetics, and handling money or other valuables). If one places these vows in conjunction with begging, labor, and meditation, it is an understatement to affirm that Zen monks live a very austere lifestyle. The basic rationale for this lifestyle is related to keeping a person's focus on the goal of enlightenment. Thus, all potential distractions are avoided to keep a person focused on the goal of awakening. In medieval China, final ordination involved receiving identifying scars that were created by small cones of incense being placed horizontally in lines of three between the forehead and the crown of the head. As the incense cones burned the scalp, the monk chanted sacred verses to take his mind off the pain.

In medieval Chinese monasteries, the tonsure ceremony, which involves shaving of the head, functioned as a ritual expression of renouncing ordinary life. As other monks witness the ceremony, the new disciple follows his master into the hall, offers incense at the main altar, kneels at a side altar while the master delivers a brief sermon recalling the renunciation of the historical Buddha, makes a final kowtow to his parents, is sprinkled with holy water by the master, offers his master a razor, shampoos his own head, master shaves his head, disciple stands and offers incense, and finally recites and accepts the threefold refuge in the three jewels (e.g., Buddha, *dharma*, and *sangha*).[50] The novice also renounces his family by giving up his family surname and adopting a new religious name. He uses the surname Shi, which is the initial syllable of Śākyamuni, signifying that he is now a son of the Buddha. Thereupon, he chooses two personal names by which he would be known with the first name being called the tonsure name, which places him in the same generation of members of the same tonsure family. The novice was also given a style name by the master, which represented his name to outsiders and his equals or juniors within his tonsure group. This rendered the novice part of a lineage.

This entire scenario means that a novice joins a new family rather than falling into a social vacuum. The master becomes his father, his fellow monks are his brothers, and he performs the ancestral rites for his master just as he would for his biological father. Moreover, he inherits his master's temple just as he would stand to inherit from his biological father, if he remained within the world. The novice accepted a paradoxical kind of freedom. On the one hand, the novice freed himself from ordinary family and state obligations by joining the monastic community, and he gained material security and more leisure time to devote to study and personal cultivation. On the other hand, he surrendered himself to the cultural institution of the monastery and to those that operated it and possessed authority within it. Although his new religious family made demands on him and regimented his life, this submission to authority should not be construed as antithetical to freedom, because what the

---

50. Faure, *Power of Denial*, 44.

novice relinquished was considered a prerequisite for the possibility of ultimate freedom that was far superior to any surrendered freedoms. It is true that the monks did not have freedom of autonomy, but they did have freedom within certain constraints with the possibility of achieving absolute freedom.[51]

Under normal circumstances, the life of meditation is conducted within the confines of a monastery that is often conceived as a mountain retreat, which is the reason for finding the name of a mountain in the formal title of a monastery. From a cross-cultural perspective, a mountain is often symbolically connected to transcendence.[52] From a more practical perspective, it is a place set apart from society and an ideal place for the solitude necessary for a life of meditation. This mountain retreat is also anthropomorphic in the sense that it is modeled on a cosmic person with its body hierarchically ordered. The left leg of this person is represented by the latrine, the right leg is the bath house, and the mountain gate is symbolically equivalent to a person's private parts. These are, of course, the symbolically lower part of the human body and are associated with dirt and its removal. The left and right arms are represented respectively by the meditation hall and the storehouse. The heart of the cosmic person is symbolized by the Buddha Hall, whereas the head is equivalent to the Dharma Hall.

The symbolism of the center plays an important function because it is connected to the locus of spiritual energy that the Zen tradition believes is in the abdomen. It is also appropriate that the Buddha Hall represents the heart and the teaching of the *dharma* (doctrine), which transcends Buddhism. As a person enters the entrance hall, they are symbolically purged of desires and attachments, impurities of the body and mind. The meditation hall and storehouse provide support for the process of reaching enlightenment, and they give monks the physical (e.g., food and sleep) requisites necessary of success. The Buddha Hall, which is symbolically the heart of the cosmic person, houses an image of the Buddha that is set on a pedestal on an altar platform that is symbolic of Mount Sumeru, center of the Buddhist cosmos. The Dharma Hall functions as a lecture hall and place where dialogical exchanges can take place.

Monks live a communal lifestyle in a single open hall where they sleep, eat meals, and meditate. The *Zendo* (meditation hall) contains

---

51. Faure, *Power of Denial*, 45.
52. See Eliade, *Sacred and the Profane*, 37–40.

raised platforms called *tan* that are located along the walls where the monks reside. When seated in meditation the monks of the Rinzai school sit facing each other on either side of the hall, whereas the monks of the Sōtō school sit with their backs turned against those of the other raised platform (*tan*). The platforms are about knee-high in height and the nearby walls contain cupboards to hold bedding, robes, and a razor for shaving. In between the raised platforms, the attendant paces with a large staff called a *keisaku* that is rounded at one end—its handle—and flat on the other end, like an English cricket bat. This is the stick of warning or admonition that is used to strike monks who fall asleep during meditation or assume an incorrect meditation posture. It is also possible that a monk, for instance suffering from back soreness or muscle cramping, will request that the attendant hit him with the stick.

At the margins of the monastery are its gates that are symbolically important. The gate represents more than just the entrance to the monastery. The term for gate is *sanmon*, which can be translated as either mountain or the number three. By symbolizing a mountain and reinforcing the name of the monastery and its association with a mountain, the gate signifies the Buddhist search for truth and liberation, which is suggested by the symbolism of ascent. The three doors of the gate are symbolic of the promise of liberation from the bondage to illusion and suffering in the three worlds of the Buddhist cosmos. The three gates are symbolic of three forms of realization. These modes of realization are: the non-substantiality of self and *dharma*, the non-existence of phenomena, and non-existence of desire. The background of these three modes of realization is shaped by the philosophy of emptiness and the fact that everything lacks self-nature. In a sense, the three gates are symbolic of the realization of emptiness (*śūnyatā*). In addition, the three gates represent the symbolic boundaries between attachment and liberation, the outside world and an interior realm, and they serve as a bulwark against moral-ethical pollution.

In addition to this symbolic structure, the typical medieval Japanese monastery needed a bureaucracy to keep it functioning. Without going into great depth, the monastery was led by the abbot (*jūji* or *chōrō*) appointed to seniority from among qualified candidates occupying the chief seat (*shuso*) by emperors, retired emperors, and shōguns. The abbot served as a spiritual guide for the community and provided administrative direction for the community. Next in rank were the officers referred to as the eastern and western rank, depending on their positions in the

Dharma Hall, whereas the prefects assisted the abbot in meditation training, discipline, study of texts, and monastic ceremonies. The name of the chief seat was derived from this person's place next to the abbot on the meditation platforms where this individual led meditation. The monastic official responsible for official documents was the scribe, while the *sūtra* prefect was responsible for the acquisition and preservation of texts. The titles of other prefects reflected closely their responsibilities: guest prefect, bath prefect, hall prefect. The monastery employed several stewards to look after economic affairs, a prior to supervise the comptroller, a registrar for new arrivals, a bursar to supervise the stewards, a labor supervisor, acolytes with various duties, private secretary of the abbot, postulants, and novices. The final two categories have not taken full vows, but they will become fully ordained monks.

A LIFE OF MEDITATION

Zazen is the Zen Japanese term for seated meditation. It involves the mastery and control of the breath, body, and mind with the goal of reaching *samādhi* (concentration), self-mastery, and awakening (*satori*). If this is the general path that one wants to follow, why is it necessary to begin with *zazen* (seated meditation) and put oneself through plenty of difficult physically and mentally exhausting work? It is important to grasp a basic Zen presupposition: an ordinary person is confused. The reason for this primordial confusion rests with the fact that one is caught in a maze of ideas, theories, reflections, prejudices, feelings, erroneous notions, and emotions that tend to normally give us segments of experience. In other words, we catch a glimpse of reality here and there, but we never arrive at anything substantial or enduring. Generally, we do not experience reality itself because we tend to experience a network of ideas, notions, feelings, or whatever about reality. It is as if reality existed behind a veil through which we cannot see clearly because our direct vision is obscured. Thus, there is always something standing between a person and reality. *Zazen* is intended to remove the barriers or mediating network. In conjunction with the basic presupposition about confusion, there is a conviction that our mind is normally scattered in many different directions, which renders concentration very difficult or even impossible. If the mind is unified, it becomes free of all distractions. This process of unification begins with control of the body and breath.

The bodily posture of a meditator is extremely important because to attempt to meditate with incorrect or asymmetrical posture is counterproductive. The ideal posture is the full-lotus position with the right foot on the left thigh and the left foot on the right thigh. The meditator places their hands on their lap with the right hand under the left hand and the palms facing upward. The thumbs may touch forming a circle. If this position is too difficult, a meditator may adopt the half-lotus position with the right foot under the left thigh and the left foot resting on the right thigh. Whatever posture one uses, what is important is for one's spinal column to be gently curved and not simply straight. It is also important to have the waist and lower abdomen correctly positioned with the waist pushed forward for the weight of the body to be concentrated in the lower abdomen and navel, which represents the center of stress, a region called the *tandem*. The Zen reformer Hakuin locates the *tandem* as being two inches below the navel with the center of breathing (*kikai*) located an inch and a half below the navel.[53] The *kikai* and *tandem* form a unity, and they represent the center of the body. The meditator's face should be turned slightly downward, and the neck should be slanted forward and kept motionless, whereas the chest and shoulders should be lowered. The purpose of these suggestions is to relieve tension in the shoulders, neck, and pit of the stomach. In summary, the perfect posture resembles an isosceles triangle with the legs and backbone forming a ninety-degree angle.

Once the correct posture is mastered, a meditator is prepared to begin to control the breath. This can be done by counting both inhalations and exhalations. A meditator can also count only exhalations or only inhalations. A meditator can count to ten and then repeat the counting. Breath control is important because unrhythmic breathing interferes with one's consciousness, and it obstructs any attempt to concentrate on one's flow of consciousness. This can be illustrated by a process called working on *mu* (nothingness). At the initial stage of this process, the meditator breathes with the mouth slightly open and forces the breath out through the narrow gap between the lips. Then, the meditator checks the first thought that arises in one's consciousness, which is done to arrest wandering thoughts. In the second step, the mouth is closed, and the tongue is pressed firmly against the palate and upper jaw, and the meditator breathes through the nostrils. It is now possible to experience the falling away of body and mind. Slowly, all awareness of wakefulness and

---

53. Yampolsky, *Hakuin*, 43.

the feeling of the body's painful pressure will dissipate. In the third stage, breathing becomes softer and gentler, and one reaches a point at which breathing almost stops. Without a thought to stir one's mind, *samādhi* (concentration) begins. There is a *samādhi* whose locus is the world of conscious activity, and there is another absolute *samādhi* that transcends consciousness, forming the foundation for all *zazen* (seated meditation) practice. At this point, there is no reflecting action of consciousness. The quality of *samādhi* is described in Japanese as *jishu-zammai*. The unpacking of this terminology is instructive. *Jishu* means self-mastery and *zammai* is Japanese for *samādhi*, which suggests concentrating on a single thing. Within the Rinzai Zen context, the point of concentration is focused on the *kōan*.

A meditator recites the *kōan* to oneself, exerts one's mind on it, and deconstructs it by taking it apart syllable by syllable and word by word. The meditator should say it with all one's attention focused on it and dwell on each word. This concentration can be coordinated with one's breathing by giving a new stress to the respiratory muscles of the abdomen with each change of sound. This process is called *karna*, working on the *kōan* in *zazen* (seated meditation). More literally, *karna* means viewing (*kar*) the topic (*na*), which can be rendered as seeing into the topic. Of course, the meditator wants to eventually reach the *satori* (enlightenment experience) that is also called *kenshō*.

The progress to awakening can be made more lucid by examining the three phases of consciousness. In the first phase, consciousness is directed outwardly toward the phenomena of the world. At the second phase, consciousness illuminates and recognizes the preceding phase. This is akin to being aware of consciousness observing, which represents a reflecting action of consciousness. During the third phase, consciousness illuminates all the preceding thought impulses and integrates them into a stream of consciousness. Now, a meditator becomes aware that they know that they have been thinking. This represents absolute *samādhi* when all phases of consciousness disappear. This is the instant of pure awareness and existence. There is no time, no space, and no causation. There is only the present moment in which one discovers the oneness of all things and one's true nature. These points will be developed more fully in the next chapter.

After a meditator works on their *kōan* for a time and feels that they are ready to give an answer to it, the meditator meets with the master for a *sanzen* session (consultation period). Normally, this occurs twice each day. During the day, a *roshi* (master) will give a lecture or discourse (*teisho* or *kōza*) on a Buddhist text, with the intention of elucidating the inner meaning of the text, for about an hour. During a week-long meditation period that occurs each month between April to August and October to February, there occurs *sesshin* periods, which are intense periods of meditation when monks are exempted from work. The monks practice *zazen* (seated meditation) from early morning (3:30 a.m.) until evening (9:30 p.m.), a lecture (*teisho*) is given each day, and *sanzen* (consultations) with the *roshi* occur four or five times a day. These more intense *sesshin* periods also include periods for eating, exercising, and relaxation. Consultations with the *roshi* take place in his room. The monk announces his arrival by striking a bell, bows at the entrance, and gives a response to the *kōan* on which he has been working.

It is possible to better understand the role of the *roshi* (master) in the process of meditation by comparing him to a midwife. Since the enlightenment experience is personal and existential, this means that it is not something that can be imposed on a person or transmitted from the outside. Therefore, the *roshi* must allow the meditator to awaken. The crucial turning point is called *sokutokuroki*. The unpacking of this term is instructive for the role being played by the *roshi*, a method that harkens back to the *Blue Cliff Record*.[54] The term *soku* connotes the image of a mother hen picking at the shell of her egg. The term *taku* refers to the picking of the baby chick from the inside of the egg shell. If the inside and outside picking is performed in a coordinated manner, the baby chick (read enlightened being) will be hatched. Thus, the role of the *roshi*, as suggested by the metaphor of the egg, hen, and chick, is to allow birth (enlightenment) to occur naturally and not to impose his will on the meditator.

The life of meditation is intended to permeate a monk's everyday life. This includes one's duties within the monastic community, performing simple things like brushing one's teeth or going to the latrine, or eating a meal. Within the context of a Zen monastery, meals are not convivial affairs. They are solemn activities that are akin to an active meditation. After a simple breakfast of possibly rice gruel and pickles, the best meal (*saiza* or *otoki*) of the day occurs around ten o'clock, which may consist of rice mixed with barley, *miso* soup, and pickles, while dinner consists of leftovers of the previous meal, which is referred to as medicinal food because monks are supposed to eat only twice a day. During a main meal,

---

54. Cleary, *Blue Cliff Record*, 95.

a monk might recite a text, the names of *bodhisattvas*, or a prayer to share the meal with all sentient beings. The five subjects of meditation may be repeated and followed by the three vows: to destroy evil, to practice deeds of goodness, and to save all beings. There is no idle conversation during the meals. A meal ends when the head monk claps together two wooden blocks. Then, the monks proceed to wash their bowls with another opportunity for meditation concluded.

BY-PRODUCTS OF MEDITATION

While on the way to Mount Tiantai, a master met a monk, and they talked, laughed, and enjoyed each other's company like longtime companions. They traveled together until they encountered a swollen valley stream. The master planted his staff, took off his hat, and stopped there. The other monk volunteered to take the master across the stream, but the master told him to cross over himself. Gathering his things together the monk walked upon the waves like he was walking on ordinary ground. Looking back, he beckoned the master to follow him, whereupon the master upbraided him and told him that he would have broken his legs if he had known that the monk would perform wonders. The other sighed in admiration at the comments by the master, and he acknowledged that the master was a genuine representative of the Buddhist way.[55] As his words ended, he disappeared. This narrative is more than just an entertaining tale of an encounter of two monks because it reflects an important by-product of practicing the path of meditation. This narrative reflects one type of extraordinary power. The Zen tradition testifies to many other types of powers.

As a monk meditates and makes spiritual progress, he can acquire certain powers as a by-product of his efforts. This is true of all types of yogic practice long before the advent of Zen.[56] A monk may acquire, for instance, the six super knowledges (Sanskrit: *abhijñā*; Chinese: *shentong*). In his work *Visuddhimagga* (*The Path of Purification*) Buddhaghoṣa (fifth century) identifies several mental powers: divine ear; read the minds of others; recollection of past lives; divine eye; knowledge of the future; and knowledge of the future according to karma. In addition to these

---

55. Cleary, *Blue Cliff Record*, 70.

56. For a fuller discussion of the nature of power and asceticism, see Olson, *Indian Asceticism*.

types of mental powers, Buddhaghoṣa identifies other powers: having become one, one becomes many; possessing the divine ear; penetrating knowledge of other minds; knowing one's past lives and those of others; knowing about passing away and rebirth of beings.[57]

Another group of powers gained by meditators are certain physical and mental powers (*siddhis*, *ṛdhis*). These powers allow a person to fly, to pass through obstacles like doors and walls, to become ubiquitous, to tame wild animals, and to perform many different types of magical transformations. Another kind of power is called the heavenly eye (*divya-cakṣus*), which enables one to see the death and rebirth of all beings, whereas the heavenly ear allows a person to hear all the sounds in the universe. The Rinzai sect reformer Hakuin refers to being able to see all worlds.[58] Additional powers include the ability to read the minds of others, to remember one's own previous modes of life and those of other people, and knowledge of the destruction of defilements.

Advanced monks became wonder workers in the sense that they could control natural phenomena, predict the future, and perform miracles. Master Huangbo met a monk, for example, on the way to Mount Tiantai, and they traveled together until reaching a swollen valley stream. While Huangbo stood and watched, the other monk walked across the deep stream. After the master upbraided him, the water traversing monk disappeared.[59] In the ninth century, Huangbo was reported to have restored a prime minster to life.[60] In a final example, Sengchou (480–560) was credited with taming two tigers and getting a well to appear.[61]

Monks with extraordinary powers and those that became Patriarchs of the tradition became icons during their lives. This reverence for them formed the foundation of a cult of relics after their death. Why did it occur? There was a belief that the power of certain special monks passed into their relics after their death, obliterating any distinction between the person and the relics. The relics served as by-products of meditation and the powers that it made possible as well as proofs of enlightenment. The most cherished relics were crystalline fragments left after the cremation of the body. Other types of bodily relics included hair, nail clippings, ashes, and bones. What could be called contact relics because of their intimate

57. Warren, *Visuddhimagga*, 12.2.
58. Yampolsky, *Hakuin*, 165.
59. Cleary, *Blue Cliff Record*, 33.
60. Faure, *Rhetoric of Immediacy*, 182.
61. Faure, *Rhetoric of Immediacy*, 99.

association with the deceased included items like a begging bowl, staff, robe, or text. The relics were important because they served as a channel through which supernatural power was made available for ordinary life.

This power was made available to ordinary people through the construction of a *stūpa* (a memorial mount) for housing the relics. This mount-shaped structure represented an *axis mundus* (center of the world), which was a place at which heaven and earth communicated through the remains of the deceased holy person. By means of his relics, the deceased person is perceived as a living presence and power. The relics function to mediate between this world and the other world. They render death closer to the world of the living, and they assure the continuity of life into death as well as the regeneration of life through death.

Another form of relic was the so-called flesh bodies by means of a process of self-mummification. After the deceased entered final *samādhi* and died, the body was lacquered. The deceased continued to exist in a sense alive as a paradoxical dead master. In such a case, the corpse becomes an icon, a representation of the living dead. Finally, there were the portraits created of masters called a *chinso*. These portraits became animate because they contained the presence of relics within them. This thus rendered these portraits alive, and they represented an embodiment of the *dharma* (teaching) master after his death. These portraits often included a verse by the master that served as a mechanism of pointing to the message of the master, representing a proof of transmission. There is a strange kind of irony here because relics and icons reintroduce presence and mediation into the world of Zen, whereas the philosophy of Zen stresses emptiness and selflessness.[62]

RITUAL AND POLITICS

Before the advent of Chan Buddhism in China, ritual played a central role in Confucian thought, the most dominant ancient philosophy. The term used for ritual (*li*) was a Confucian virtue that the philosopher wanted to have implemented into social relations to create a harmonious and peaceful society. In the *Book of Rites* (*Li ji*), music is conceived as the harmony of heaven and earth, whereas ritual represented the order of heaven and earth.[63] The emperor is the primary performer of rites for the

---

62. Faure, *Rhetoric of Immediacy*, 178.
63. Legge, *Li Chi*, 2:100–101.

welfare of the state and his own reign. Confucius envisioned a parallel between human action and the moral realm. The virtue of *li* (ritual) acts to restrain attempts by humans to act contrary to it. It is essential for human actions to follow the already established patterns of *li* so that the social gestures of everyone are in harmony. However, the outward display of *li* is insufficient without the feelings of sincerity and reverence. Any Chinese citizen becoming a Buddhist monk would bring these types of convictions with them to the monastery, making them predisposed to accepting ritual as an essential activity. This Confucian influence also permeated Japan and made them similarly inclined about the importance of ritual.

Throughout Zen history, rituals have been intertwined with politics to secure its cultural position within the state. Despite those that downplayed the importance of ritual performance in the classical tradition, Zen monks have performed a variety of rituals for the benefit of themselves, their patrons, and the state. On a personal level, seated meditation (*zazen*) is the most common daily ritual performed by a monk, who also performs chanting of scriptures, synchronized bowing, initiation, and going to the master for interviews during *sanzen* sessions. Monks perform funeral rites for their patrons and recite prayers for the welfare of the state and the emperor, which are basically indistinguishable and an approved way to ingratiate the monastery to the state. Monks would, for instance, commemorate the emperor's birthday by reading scriptures daily for thirty days until the actual birthday. Monks could spread imperial virtue by chanting texts and repay the kindness of the emperor. Besides rituals directed at the emperor or state, monks performed rituals for a wide variety of reasons that included enlisting *kami* for a Buddhist cause, annual commemorations of the Buddha's birthday, enlightenment, death, and his relics. They made offerings for creatures of water and land. Another example of ritual activity was Guanyin repentance rites that were based on Tendai devotional observances. There was the ritualized scene during personal interviews within the abbot's quarters, recitation of precepts and confession of violations, and common meals with their observance of silence, bowing, setting aside grains of rice for hungry ghosts, and cleaning their bowls.[64] In conclusion, the Zen monk's life was highly regimented and ritualized. Thus, even though classical Chan debunked it, monks still practiced various types of ritual that differed according to region and monastery, indicating that they did not share any universal

---

64. Welter, "Buddhist Rituals for Protecting," 123–30.

agreement about ritual practices.[65] Sometimes, a ritual could have deep roots in Buddhist history extending before the birth of the Buddha into ancient Indian culture. In Japan, on New Year's Eve, parishioners would visit the local temple at midnight for the ringing of the large outdoor bell, which was rung 108 times. For Zen Buddhists, the number symbolized purification from the 108 afflictions that cause suffering.[66] If one goes back to the ancient Vedic period of Indian culture, the number 108 is a sacred number that is sometimes associated with the total number of gods in the pantheon, the number of Upaniṣadic texts, the number of beads on a prayer counter in Tibet, and so forth.

An extremely important Zen ritual occurs with the transmission of the *dharma* from the master to his successor, a rite performed in private that involved a document testifying to the transmission. Some transmission documents were written in blood from the tongues of the two participants. Why chose to cut the tongue? The tongue was associated with the oral teaching of the *dharma*. From the Zen perspective, it is essential for a master to secure an heir, otherwise the master would be guilty of cutting off the Buddha seed.[67] The appointment of a successor is often associated with the practice of a master leaving death verses as he lay dying. The death verses represented an opportunity for a master to leave his disciples and designated successor a final lucid rendition of his teaching; the verses testify to the master's level of enlightenment, a verification of his age, and testimony of his detachment from his impending death.[68]

Just as prestigious as the transmission of the *dharma*, there was the granting of the purple robe, a garment that confers royal authority on a monk. The purple color was an imperial color of the utmost distinction. The receiving of a purple robe was not only a personal honor but was also a mark of recognition for the lineage of the monk.[69] To receive such a robe confirms that a special consecration or ordination has occurred. From this body of evidence, it is evident that Zen did not reject ritual practices. It is also evident that Chan monasteries in China and Zen institutions in Japan adopted elements that came from other Buddhism movements, Confucianism, Daoism, Shinto, and folk religion and synthesized them

---

65. Wright, "Introduction," 4, 8.
66. Foulk, "Ritual in Japanese Zen Buddhism," 80.
67. Bodiford, "Dharma Transmission in Theory and Practice," 265.
68. Faure, *Rhetoric of Immediacy*, 187.
69. Faure, *Rhetoric of Immediacy*, 265.

into a meaningful whole, suggesting that a pristine Zen free of these borrowings and accretions never existed in East Asian history.

In fact, the performance of ritual services was a way for Zen monasteries to involve themselves in the political machinations of the country. In fact, numerous recent scholars have attempted to correct the historical record by calling attention to the political aspects of Zen and the fact that it was not so ardently iconoclastic. In chapter 2, we saw that the development of Chan was a complex process that combined the interplay of public support, political patronage, and an urge to define the meaning of orthodoxy.

Not only did Chan/Zen leaders play political roles, but they also engaged in playful activity with respect to ritual. In ritual, practitioners act in the ritual "as if" things were different than they seem. Whether during ritual, seated meditation, or working on a *kōan*, a monk becomes absorbed within a subjunctive ("as if") mood, which enables the monk to find different ways to classify reality; it is what can be. The absorption in the subjunctive mood is the inverse of the objective world and frees the absorbed person from external constraints. Although it is potentially creative, the subjunctive mood represents a danger because this aspect of play can be subversive in the sense of overturning social hierarchy and common social values.

ROLE OF NUNS

In ancient Indian culture, the predominate patriarchal conception about the status of women was simply that they were inferior to men and should have a subordinate social role compared to that of men. In contrast to this common cultural view, Buddhism was more favorable to women because they were viewed more positively during the formative period of Buddhism. Some women were poets, teachers, preachers, and generous donors to the movement. The beginning of the order of nuns can be traced to Mahāpajapati's request to the Buddha to start an order for women. After the Buddha refused his aunt, Ananda interceded for the Buddha's aunt and pressed the Buddha to admit that women could attain enlightenment. Thus, the Buddha reluctantly agreed to allow an order for women. Sometime before the appearance of Buddhist scriptures, the status of women began to decline because they were denigrated and negatively stereotyped by monk scholars, who made a concerted effort to keep women, who were viewed as sources of temptation and a threat to male monastic purity, subordinate to them, and constructed monastic rules to ensure the subservient status of women.[70] Thus, the monastic code was formed to make women totally dependent on men by including injunctions such as never instructing or admonishing a monk, the necessity of receiving instructions from a monk periodically, and not residing in a retreat place without a monk being present.

If the lives of people are characterized by suffering according to the first noble truth of the Buddha, women are generally comprehended as assuming a greater share of suffering because there are five additional forms of suffering that they endured by virtue of their gender. These extra forms of suffering for women include the following: menstruation, pregnancy, childbirth, having to serve males, and being subjected to the authority of in-laws. These additional feminine forms of suffering are connected to a woman's biology and social status as a subordinate person.

In Japan, women also encountered gender prejudice and were considered inferior to men, although a thinker like Dōgen asserted that there were no sexual differences in the Buddha-nature. The chance to choose to become a nun, however, gave Japanese women an alternative lifestyle to the traditional role of motherhood. Women opting for a monastic life gained a measure of freedom and autonomy from common social obligations and social roles. Japanese women were not simply passive actors within patriarchal Buddhism, because there is evidence that they resisted the prevailing attitudes espoused by monks.

Despite the disadvantages of being female in a patriarchal culture, Japanese nuns managed to make a gallant effort to empower and legitimize themselves through ritual. The initial such ritual example is the *Anan Kōshiki*, a rite that includes doing a formal procession, three prostrations, offering of incense, and making a circle with each of three nuns respectively carrying an incense burner, purified water, and the third nun scattering lotus petals. The background and motivation for this rite is to highlight the actions of Ananda who interceded with the Buddha on behalf of women to allow them to become nuns, which is considered an act of wisdom because it is declared that all women can attain enlightenment.[71]

---

70. Falk, "Image of Woman," 105.
71. Arai, "Women and Dōgen," 196–98.

The second important rite is the *Jizō Nagashi*, a memorial rite intended to help people coping with loss that functions as a healing rite. The names of those who have died are given posthumous Buddhist names (*kaimyō*) written on a wooden tablet. Each nun receives a stack of the tablets and raises one at a time to her head, a gesture of respect for the presence of the Buddha. The nuns proceed to a large boat and go to the center of the lake where they release the slips of rice paper bearing an image of the *bodhisattva* Jizō into the lake after touching them to their foreheads.[72]

There were also rites that pertained to both nuns and monks. The practice of bestowing a *kaimyō* (precept name), for example, on a deceased person by an abbot to someone at their funeral was common in Japanese Zen, creating a socioeconomic connection between the temple priest and family of the deceased. The giving of this posthumous name was intended to guarantee a favorable situation for the deceased in the afterlife.[73] Another common practice after death was to give the deceased a lineage chart that connected a person to Zen masters all the way back to the Buddha. It ensured a favorable rebirth and served as a talismanic power that protected a person from evil. It was not uncommon to sell these posthumous names, which was a major source of revenue for a temple.[74]

CONCLUDING REMARKS

The encounter dialogues discussed in this chapter demonstrate Zen masters using language in a playful way. The resort to silence is also often executed in a playful manner. From one perspective, the encounter dialogue is a contest between at least two minds. The encounters exhibit a new type of play that represents anti-structural behavior; it is a game that cuts across the grain of polite social behavior because to shout nonsense at someone, to slap someone, to give someone the finger, to hit someone with a staff, or to simply threaten violence are unacceptable forms of social behavior. These various methods cause social disjunction and mental distress, which is precisely what they are intended to do. Social and personal convention are subverted by the dialogical encounter. A reader does not know where the questions raised or the answers provided

72. Arai, "Women and Dōgen," 201–2.
73. Williams, *Other Side of Zen*, 26–27.
74. Williams, *Other Side of Zen*, 42–43.

are going except to say toward some type of mind to mind crash. The encounter evokes images of two humongous rugby or football players running at top speed and crashing into each other. But in the dialogues, it is not human bodies that go flying, it is words, which can be aptly described in this way: "Words intersect with no words, structure with antistructure, to place personal realization rather than ideas as the highest truth."[75] This type of scenario makes the establishment of doctrine very difficult, if not impossible. It reminds one of Linji's insightful statement, "There are no fixed doctrine to give to people, only methods to cure diseases and release bonds."[76] Linji's statement seems to support the observation about the difficulty of creating a viable doctrine.

By means of the rigors of their lifestyle, Zen monks are like professional athletes. The discipline of training the breath, body, and mind by a Zen monk finds many parallels with a professionally trained athlete. The single-minded focus necessary for success also finds a place in both types of athleticism. The potential for the close association between Zen meditation training and athletic preparation is certainly evident in activities like the art of swordsmanship and archery, which have historically served as important martial arts in Japan. We will have more to say about those activities in a later chapter.

The spiritual athletic training of a Zen monk takes place within a structure that is designed like an unusual playing field. It is on this spiritual playing field that a monk plays his game with the *kōan*, for example, by means of the discipline of seated meditation. The aspirant is both an individual performer and a member of a team of monks or nuns. In this spiritual game of enlightenment, it is true that the individual aspirant who achieves enlightenment wins, but this is also true of the entire monk brotherhood because the enlightenment of a single monk or nun affects everyone, just as the Sōtō master Dōgen makes clear when he states that a single enlightenment is universal.

By successfully focusing and meditating on the *kōan*, the Zen practitioner learns how to get the goose out of the bottle without breaking it or harming the goose. It suddenly dawns on the meditator that in fact the goose is simply out. Nothing more need be said. Such a situation suggests the joy of play.

75. Heine, *Zen Skin, Zen Marrow*, 62.
76. Cleary, *Recorded Sayings of Linji*, 33.

4

VIOLENCE, BEATINGS, SHOUTS, AND FINGER RAISING

When the Chan master Linji was a novice he lived with his master Huangbo for three years without ever speaking to the master. A leading monk of the monastic community prompted Linji to approach the master. With his new-found courage, Linji asked the master about the essence of the Buddha-law; he was sent away after being beaten by the master. Undaunted, the novice approached the master twice more with the same results. Confused, forlorn, and dejected, Linji bid farewell to his master, and he went to Dayu to receive the right guidance. When Linji told Dayu what had happened to him, the master replied that Huangbo had treated him with consummate kindness. Thereupon, Linji was suddenly awakened, and he said, "There's nothing special about Huangbo's Buddha-law." After Dayu struck him for mocking his former teacher, Linji countered with three blows to Dayu's ribs.[1] Based on the subsequent life and teaching methods of Linji, this story probably has an historical basis because throughout his life Linji utilized various forms of violence as part of his teaching method. To an outsider, subjecting students to physical abuse seems at the very least rather odd behavior by a teacher and at worst very cruel treatment. Nonetheless, Linji and other Zen masters had noble intentions behind their unusual methods. By means of his choice of teaching methods, Linji made Zen into a contact sport that combined violence and play.

---

1. Sasaki, *Record of Linji*, 316.

The use of physical violence is like shouting and other gestures of the master, such as raising a single finger or a whisk. The purpose of this chapter is to examine these Zen teaching methods to discern what they have in common and to attempt to understand these phenomena as a form of language. In short, this chapter will try to make sense out of these phenomena from both a Buddhist and a western philosophical perspective. This will involve placing these phenomena within the context of Buddhist history and utilizing the philosophical insights into language of J. L. Austin in the second way. We will also pause to consider the violence associated with some of these methods and its relationship to play.

As a point of clarification, the use of violence by Zen masters is not confined simply to physical violence. The encounters between eager students and masters, who had reputations for using violence, suggest a preliminary threat of violence on the minds of the novices. This threat of violence is directly related to the mental anticipation of violence that might be potentially inflicted by masters, giving rise into mental stress and tension prior to an encounter with a master, a kind of anticipatory violence that is hidden for the most part from others. In other words, the threat of violence embodied in the reputation of a given master often preceded meeting him.

A number of Zen scholars have questioned the historical authenticity of these violent encounters and suggested that they were fictions from monks with creative imaginations. Since many scholars believe that Song dynasty figures such as Zongmi created a romanticized portrait of Chan during the Tang dynasty, transforming the earlier period into a golden age of the religion, they conclude that we cannot trust the accuracy of the accounts. Whether the accounts of encounters are truthful ones of actual encounters between aspirants and enlightened masters, it seems reasonable to conclude that the narratives represent a discourse that Chan leaders thought represented their ethos, and how they wanted to be depicted within the historical context of attempting to define themselves to outsiders. If these violent encounters possessed even a modicum of truth or reflect the intentional spirit of the encounter dialogues, the narratives of these encounter dialogues are attempting to convey a message to a reader. An element of this message is that violence can be put to a positive purpose—awakening to the truth. Thus, this chapter proposes to examine Zen violent methods and discourse without attempting to determine whether or not the narratives are absolutely true, an endeavor that seems impossible anyway. Moreover, the encounter dialogues are a form of game similar to a game such as chess during which players move pieces according to already established rules. When players agree to play the game they must adhere to the rules beforehand. In comparison to a game of chess played on a pre-established board and rules, the Chan masters perform more intuitively and spontaneously. Thus these encounter dialogues should be studied seriously and not quickly dismissed as imaginative fiction.

Certainly, these encounter dialogues manifest a hagiographical quality. Nonetheless, hagiography can be construed as a form of truth, embodying a rhetorical strategy that combines mythical, fictional, legendary, and historical elements that appeal to popular piety. Hagiographical narratives are intended to preserve the memory of the subject, to operate as a mediator between the subject and followers, and to function as a recruitment tool. These narratives operate to not only preserve the life of the subject but to also record the reactions and experiences of other players. Encounter narratives are also a didactic device that refers to both the past and the present.

VIOLENCE, SHOUTS, AND FINGER RAISING

In Zen writings, the use of physical abuse appears to be meaningless at times. For example, after an old woman refused to answer his question by walking away, Linji beat her.[2] Xuansong asked Huangbo, "What's the use of paying respect?" Huangbo replied immediately by slapping him. Xuansong said, "Too coarse." Huangbo said, "What is this to talk of coarse and fine?" and slapped him again.[3] Yunmen once asked a monk, "Where did you come from?" The monk replied, "Xichan." Yunmen asked, "What words and phrases are there at Xichan these days?" The monk extended both hands, and Yunmen slapped him once. The monk replied, "I'm still talking." Yunmen then extended his two hands, a gesture that repeated the earlier one of the monk's. The monk was speechless, thereupon Yunmen hit him.[4] The replies of the old woman, Xuansong, and the anonymous monk are either nonexistent or too literal. They did not give a Zen response. In other words, their responses are not indicative of an enlightened state of mind. Therefore, their answers are inadequate.

2. Sasaki, *Record of Linji*, 60.
3. Cleary, *Blue Cliff Record*, 76.
4. Cleary, *Blue Cliff Record*, 259–60.

The understanding that the masters were trying to elicit is beyond mere words or a discourteous gesture. The master attempts to get the right, or Zen, response by engaging in a game that is often violent yet playful by manifesting a to-and-fro movement typical of play.

There are episodes in which the person beaten is transformed into a beater by certain circumstances. One day, for instance, Huangbo ordered all the monks of the temple to work in the tea garden. He was the last to arrive. Linji greeted him but stood there with his hands resting on his hoe. "Are you tired?" asked Huangbo. Linji replied, "I just started working; how can you say that I am tired?" Huangbo immediately lifted his stick and struck Linji, who then seized the stick, and with a push, made his master fall to the ground. Huangbo called the supervisor to help him up. After doing so, the supervisor asked, "Master, how can you let such a madman insult you like that?" Huangbo picked up the stick and struck the supervisor. Linji, digging by himself, made this remark: "Let all other places use cremation; here I will bury you alive."[5] This type of scenario is reminiscent of the old Three Stooges comedy act with Moe, Larry, and Curly taking turns hitting one another in ridiculous ways. Whereas the antics of the Three Stooges comedy act is intended to elicit laughter, the purpose of the Zen antics is very different because they are trying to trigger a breakthrough to a new level of awareness.

A final example is offered by Linji when he addressed an assembly of monks with the following words: "Listen all of you! He who wants to learn Dharma must never worry about the loss of his own life. When I was with Master Huangbo I asked three times for the real meaning of Buddhism, and three times I was struck as if tall reeds whipped me in the wind. I want those blows again, but who can give them to me now?" A monk came forth from the crowd, answering: "I can give them to you!" Linji picked up a stick and handed it to him. When the monk tried to grab it, the master struck the monk instead.[6] The Zen tradition contains an example of a nun matching wits with Linji when he asked a nun, "Do you come from good or from evil?" The nun shouted. Linji picked up his staff and said, "Say more, say more." The nun shouted again, so Linji hit her.[7] The monk who volunteered to give Linji blows and the anonymous nun reacted too literally or artificially to their respective situations and thus failed. Their responses were too contrived and not spontaneous.

5. Sasaki, *Record of Linji*, 317.
6. Cleary, *Recorded Sayings of Linji*, 13–14.
7. Cleary, *Recorded Sayings of Linji*, 53.

Besides beatings, Zen masters frequently resorted to shouts or simply raising a finger. Mazu (707–786) was probably the first master to use shouting as a teaching technique, whereas Judi was famous for his one finger Zen, because whenever he was asked anything he would just raise one finger. On the surface, a nonsensical shout or the raising of a finger appear to be meaningless. Master Linji asked Luopu, for instance, "From the early days on some taught by means of the stick; other through 'Ho!' Which of the two means do you prefer?" "I prefer neither," replied Luopu. "What is wrong with having a preference?" retorted the master. Luopu immediately exclaimed, "Ho!" and master Linji struck him.[8]

What does a master do if the shout fails? It is possible to try the stick. For example, the master took the high seat in the hall. A monk asked, "What about the cardinal principle of the Buddha-dharma?" The master raised his whisk. The monk shouted. The master struck him. Then, another asked, "What about the cardinal principle of the Buddha-dharma?" Again, the master raised his whisk. The monk shouted. The master also shouted. The monk faltered; the master struck him.[9]

There are episodes when a series of combined methods are used. The master asked a monk, for instance, "Where do you come from?" The monk shouted. The master saluted him and motioned him to sit down. The monk hesitated. The master hit him. Seeing another monk coming, the master raised his whisk. The monk bowed low. The master responded by hitting him. Spying still another monk coming, the master again raised his whisk. The monk paid no attention. The master hit him too.[10]

From a superficial perspective, beatings, shouts, and raising a whisk or a finger seem to be nonsensical. To grasp the significance of these actions, a person must penetrate beyond the surface manifestation of these actions to their underlying meaning. Firstly, they are intended to shock and awaken.[11] Secondly, these actions leave the uninitiated no chance to reason. Thirdly, by cutting off a person's reasoning process, they enable one to avoid rational entanglements and confusion. Fourthly, shouts are also a manifestation of what is in a person's mind.[12] Therefore, the shout seems meaningless because the truth cannot be captured in words. Moreover, the shout is merely attempting to point to the truth that can only

8. Sasaki, *Lin-chi Hui-chao*, 46.
9. Sasaki, *Lin-chi Hui-chao*, 4.
10. Sasaki, *Lin-chi Hui-chao*, 41.
11. Dumoulin, *Zen Enlightenment*, 62.
12. Chung-yuan, *Original Teachings of Ch'an Buddhism*, 132.

be captured in silence by a lone person. Fifthly, the finger points beyond itself. Thus, it is a manifestation of one's ignorance to view the finger as a finger. It is absolutely necessary to penetrate to the marrow of the finger and see it in its essence. To what does the finger point? What is the shout attempting to convey? What is the purpose of the beatings? The purpose and objective of these methods are enlightenment. In other words, beatings, shouting, and finger raising have a single intention. Therefore, one should not view them as the sadism of the teacher or the masochism of the student.[13] Although they may appear to be crude or a form of punishment, they are intended as an incentive and practical means for comprehending reality.[14] The Zen literature testifies to the success of these methods.

Xuefeng, for instance, had an insight into reality after his master struck him.[15] After being slapped and pushed round by Linji, the elder Ding was suddenly enlightened, as he stood motionless, when a monk asked him why he did not bow after receiving such rough treatment.[16] There is the famous story of Yunmen's enlightenment occurring after he had been continually rebuffed by his teacher Muzhou. Unable to respond to his teacher's command to speak, Yunmen was pushed out the door. As the master closed the door, Yunmen's foot was caught in it, and he was suddenly awakened to the truth by the pain in his foot.[17] While away from Judi's hermitage, a servant related to another that his master taught by simply raising one finger. Recounting this episode to the master upon his return, Judi took a knife and cut off the youth's finger; as he ran out screaming, Judi called to him. When the servant looked back, the master raised his finger, and the servant attained understanding at that moment.[18] If you see a finger as a raised finger, you are missing the message of the teacher. The author of the *Blue Cliff Record* informs his reader that "it is necessary to pierce the bone, penetrate the marrow, and see all the way through."[19] In his text on monastic regulations, Baizhang explains the significance of the finger:

13. Blyth, *Zen and Zen Classics*, 3:154.
14. Dumoulin, *History of Zen Buddhism*, 101.
15. Cleary, *Blue Cliff Record*, 32.
16. Cleary, *Blue Cliff Record*, 202.
17. Cleary, *Blue Cliff Record*, 37–38.
18. Cleary, *Wumen's Gate*, 74.
19. Cleary, *Blue Cliff Record*, 111.

The use of a finger is meant to exemplify the truth that it is not the finger [but what it points to], and thus this finger also ceases to be [merely a finger] simultaneously with its being [that which it points to]. While it resembles emptiness (śūnyatā) and contains it within, it is yet juxtaposed with emptiness, and thus emptiness [and form] are reciprocal.[20]

At the end of his life, Judi said that he had used the one finger all his life without exhausting it, and asked those present if they wanted to understand. Then, he raised one finger and died.[21] Other numerous examples could be recounted for shouts. However, the important thing is to let the beatings, senseless shouts, and one finger speak to you. Ask yourself what they are saying, and then penetrate beyond them to the truth.

THE ROLE OF VIOLENCE

A theme that runs throughout the episodes about beatings, shouts, and finger raising is violence, which can be defined as an action that injures or destroys anything or anyone to which is it applied or directed.[22] Many of the examples used demonstrate Zen masters committing violence and violating a fundamental Buddhist precept, nonviolence (ahimsā). Even out of compassion, a Buddhist monk should refrain from encouraging others to harm themselves or others.[23] The Pāli Buddhist tradition traces the roots of violence to greed, hatred, and delusion.[24] In some Pāli texts it is stated that sense-pleasures lead to desire for more such pleasures that then lead to conflict.[25] Or it is possible for a speculative perspective or a fixed view on an issue to lead to conflict.[26] When a person is a victim of violence an even greater harm arises when that person responds with anger or violence because the law of karma (cause and effect) brings negative consequences, according to the Pāli commentator Buddhaghoṣa.[27] Another Pāli text makes it clear that becoming prey to anger brings negative results, which is another passage that must be grasped within the overall

20. Ichimura, *Baizhang Zen Monastic Regulations*, 375.
21. Cleary, *Blue Cliff Record*, 111.
22. Blackburn, *Oxford Dictionary of Philosophy*, 394.
23. Horner, *Book of Discipline*, 3:71–74, 76.
24. Davids, *Dialogues of the Buddha*, 2:276–77; 3:182.
25. Horner, *Middle Length Sayings*, 1:86–87.
26. Davids and Woodward, *Book of the Kindred Sayings*, 2:766–975.
27. Warren, *Visuddhimagga*, 300.

context of causation.²⁸ Giving into anger and violence is like throwing dust into a strong wind; it will be swept back into the thrower's face.

In Mahāyāna Buddhism, the *bodhisattva* makes a series of vows that includes saving other beings. Although nonviolence is the norm of behavior, it is permissible for a *bodhisattva* to commit a violent deed and suffer the negative karmic consequences for his violent action, if the violence prevents a greater misdeed. In a Mahāyāna text from the *Mahāratnakūta Sūtras*, the Buddha tells a story about himself in a former birth as a leader of a band of 500 traders. Among the 500 traders seeking wealth in foreign lands, there is an evil, greedy, violent person who is desirous of the wealth acquired by the others. Thus, he plots how he can kill all of them and steal their treasures. Meanwhile, the *bodhisattva* receives a vision in a dream informing him about the intention of this evil trader, and he thinks that the evil man will suffer for countless ages in hell after he commits the transgression. The *bodhisattva* is instructed to devise a skillful means to prevent the mass murders, and he decides that the best course of action is to kill the evil trader regardless of the consequences for his own karmic destiny. He also decides not to inform the other traders because they might become angry with the evil person and give rise to negative karmic consequences for themselves. He dispatches the evil man with a spear, and the other traders can make it home safely without being aware that their lives were in danger or that they were saved by the selfless and compassionate actions of the *bodhisattva*.²⁹ It is within this religious context that the actions of the Zen masters must be placed to enable us to understand them.

In sharp contrast to the Buddhist position, René Girard develops a theory of violence as central to the nature of religion with the victim receiving the thrust of the violence as a substitute for the entire community. Since the community is essentially violent, sacrifice is a social invention that serves to protect the community from its violent nature and channels violence to a victim, thereby saving the community from destroying itself.³⁰ Girard sees a cycle of violence given impetus by the desire for revenge, which means that it is incumbent that "religion invariably strives to subdue violence, to keep it from running wild."³¹

---

28. Woodward, *Book of the Gradual Sayings*, 4:94.
29. Chang, *Treasury of Mahāyāna Sūtras*, 456–57.
30. Girard, *Violence and the Sacred*, 8.
31. Girard, *Violence and the Sacred*, 20.

Mahāyāna Buddhists go beyond Girard and perceive the possibility that violence can be terminated. In another narrative from the *Mahāratnakūta Sūtra*, there is a tale about a butcher named Horrible, who is described as ferocious, bloodthirsty, irritable, and merciless, trying to kill a cow that escapes and runs into the forest in the direction of a *bodhisattva* named Tathāgata Born Victorious only to fall into a deep pit. With his knife in hand, the butcher jumps into the pit with the moaning and bellowing cow anticipating its death just as the *bodhisattva* was giving a sermon about causation within hearing distance of the butcher. Upon hearing the sermon, the butcher Horrible attains an awakening experience that terminates his intention to kill the terrified cow. The narrative ends with the butcher becoming a monk and repenting of his former lifestyle of violence.[32] Despite the spirit embodied in this narrative and its conviction that violence can be terminated by turning to Buddhism and thereby contradicting Girard's contention about the never-ending nature of the cycle of violence, the behavior of the Zen masters seems to oppose the spirit of their own tradition and tends to support the theory of Girard.

This possibility gives rise to several questions. Are Zen masters eliminating differences as Girard claims in his theory? Are they putting an end to the cycle of violence? Are they humanizing violence as Girard claims? Zen masters that resort to violence view it as a dynamic method with the intention of making something positive happen. And their method is not motivated by desire as violence is for Girard.[33]

For the Zen masters, violence is a means to an end, an attempt to trigger an awakening experience in an aspirant. Their use of violence also does not mean that it is divine in a way as it is for Girard. Writing about the possibility of the end of violence, Girard states, "Violence will come to an end only after it has had the last word and that word has been accepted as divine."[34] Later Girard writes about violence becoming appeased and subsiding, being expelled from society, and becoming part of the divine substance. Since it becomes totally indistinguishable from the divine, it initially manifests itself as god.[35] With the strong iconoclastic spirit in Zen, there is no chance of violence becoming deified in any sense. Girard's claim that the choice of a victim is always an arbitrary act stands in sharp contradiction to the Zen use of violence where the master

---

32. Chang, *Treasury of Mahāyāna Sūtras*, 159–60.
33. Girard, *Violence and the Sacred*, 145.
34. Girard *Violence and the Sacred*, 134.
35. Girard, *Violence and the Sacred*, 265–66.

using violence directs it at an aspirant that might be ripe for the violence to cause an awakening.

There is a dramatic episode from the Zen tradition of lore that seems to be totally contrary to Girard's position. According to this narrative, some monks in a monastery were quarreling over the possession of a cat. Nanquan seized the cat, saying to the monks, "If you can speak, I won't kill it." As no one answered, he ruthlessly cut the cat in half. When Zhaozhou returned in the evening, the master told him about the whole incident. Zhaozhou did not say anything, but, removing his sandals from his feet and putting them on his head he walked out. The master said, "If you had been here, you would have saved the cat!"[36] This fascinating episode would seem to confirm some of Girard's theory. But from the Zen perspective, the action of killing the feline in this incident was intended to shock the monks out of their attachment to the cat. To be a genuine monk means that a monk must cut all ties. From the perspective of the master, it is only through ruthless violence that one can get started on the road to freedom. If we examine Zhaozhou's action of placing his sandals on his head, it appears to be an entirely arbitrary act. But it is totally spontaneous. Moreover, it is intended to indicate that in the realm of true reality, the values of this world are turned upside down. In response to the act of killing the cat, the commentator of the text states from his Chan perspective, "The fact is that he really did not kill. The story is not in killing or not killing."[37] The violent act is beyond the distinction between good and evil.

THE BUDDHIST CONTEXT

If we place beatings, shouts, and finger raising within the context of Mahāyāna Buddhist religious history, they can be viewed as forms of *upāya* (skillful means). The various forms of *upāya* are pedagogical devices, gimmicks, or tricks. Before an instructor decides what type of device to use, he surveys the needs and level of understanding of his students. The instructor may, for examples, create a magic city or, like a father trying to lure his children out of a burning house, promise them fine toys as evident by the parable of the burning house in the *Lotus Sūtra*.[38]

36. Cleary, *Blue Cliff Record*, 292–93.
37. Cleary, *Blue Cliff Record*, 293.
38. Watson, *Lotus Sutra*, 56.

Thus teachings are relative to the capacities of the student to understand. As D. T. Suzuki aptly observes concerning the teaching of method of a *bodhisattva*, "When he perceives his fellow-beings drowning in the ocean of birth and death because of their ignorance and passionate clinging to a world of particulars, he awakens his great heart of love and compassion for them and contrives all kinds of means to save them, to enlighten them, to mature their consciousness for the reception of the ultimate truth."³⁹ The practice of *upāya* is grounded in the superior knowledge (*prajñā*) of the *bodhisattva* and grows out of his compassion (*karuṇā*) for all beings. Therefore, beating, shouting, and finger raising are legitimate forms of teaching. Once the aspirant, like the blind person who has never seen forms, has their sight restored, he can see things as they really are. Moreover, skillful means (*upāya*) is a fundamental perfection that all *bodhisattvas* are obligated to develop and employ, even though violence itself is not specifically advocated.

The use of the fly whisk is another example of the creative use of skillful means (*upāya*) by masters that transforms a common object into something educational and playful. From its original use in China as an instrument to chase away mosquitoes and other annoying insects, the whisk became a ceremonial object in Chinese monasteries used in ceremonies or during sermons.⁴⁰ It can be grasped as an objective toy utilized to signal to or hit someone within the context of playing a game of enlightenment. The whisk or finger are indicative of the transformational power of play in the sense of altering the forms or patterns of the world.⁴¹ As a style of subjective expression, the Zen master's play is more transformative rather than conformative. The Zen master's use of the whisk is also, for instance, a form of mimicry, which reflects continual invention that makes the game unique and fascinates any spectators.⁴²

From another Buddhist perspective, beatings, shouting, and finger or whisk raising are forms of meditation. This assertion is supported by the seventeenth-century master named Hakuin who writes, "What is this true meditation? It is to make everything: coughing, swallowing, waving the arms, motion, stillness, words, action, the evils and the good, prosperity and shame, gain and loss, right and wrong, into one single koan."⁴³ Just

39. Suzuki, *Essays in Zen Buddhism Third Series*, 290.
40. Poceski, *Record of Mazu*, 235.
41. Henricks, *Play Reconsidered*, 185.
42. Caillois, *Man, Play, and Games*, 123.
43. Yampolsky, *Hakuin*, 58.

as a *kōan* is used to block our rational thought process, beatings, shouts, and raising a finger form a barrier that a person must overcome. They enable us to experience the "Great Death" that Hakuin feels is so important to our spiritual rebirth. Creatively describing this process, Hakuin states, "Thus you will attain to a peace in which the phoenix has left the golden net and the crane has been set free of the basket. At this time, the basis of mind, consciousness, and emotion is suddenly shattered; the realm of illusion with its endless sinking in the cycle of birth and death is overturned."[44] These unusual teaching methods help a person to realize the futility of all intellectual attempts to reach enlightenment. They stimulate a person to move in another direction. On the one hand, these various methods enable a person to kill one's false self, to terminate a person's rational way of thinking and clinging to false views. On the other hand, these methods give life to the truth.

To the unenlightened person, raising a finger is a meaningless gesture, a shout is senseless noise, and a beating is merely punitive cruelty. However, an enlightened individual sees the entire universe in a single finger, he hears the eternal in a shout, and recognizes the emptiness of the stick that he is being beaten with. Thus, there is emptiness, beating emptiness, emptiness shouting emptiness, and an empty finger pointing toward emptiness. All this finally dawns on the aspiring monk. However, the beatings, shouts, and finger raising must not be thought-out or contrived. They must be spontaneous and free, meaningless and intentionless. In short, they must be natural and unrehearsed. They must be administered and issue from the depths of a teacher's being and enlightened state of being.

VIOLENT DISCOURSE

Whatever method or combination of methods is preferred by a master, it occurs within the context of violent Buddhist discourse, which strikes a student of Mahāyāna Buddhism as remarkably strange because the *bodhisattva*, or ideal paradigm, is not conceived or defined as a religious figure who engages in violence. Rather the *bodhisattva* attempts to perfect virtues such as compassion, altruism, nonviolence, and wisdom. Instead of non-harmful and passive language, the Chan tradition uses aggressive and violent discourse. The master Zhaozhou compares

---

44. Yampolsky, *Hakuin*, 164.

his violent teaching methods to a diamond sword that can cut off the head of someone who hesitates to respond to a question or can snatch away your eyes.[45] Referring to the story of the Buddha's birth when he announced that his present birth would be his last and that he was the world honored one, Yunmen reacted aggressively by saying, "Had I seen him then, I would have struck him dead with one blow and fed him to the dogs, so that there might be peace in the world."[46] Another example of this iconoclastic spirit is evident when Linji advised that when you meet a Buddha or a Patriarch you should kill them in order to be free of any form of attachment.[47] A reader does not have to grasp these injunctions to commit violent actions literally, but one should recognize that they fall into a pattern of discourse that is associated with violence and justified by a philosophy of emptiness. This type of philosophy is a non-dual position, rendering both violent and compassionate actions ultimately empty and indistinguishable.

This violent discourse is sometimes rather innocent and playful sounding. The path to enlightenment is associated metaphorically with the courage of an aspirant to enter a tiger's cave to retrieve the tiger cub. Or the danger is associated with grabbing the tiger's whiskers. A Chan teacher must be willing to let his student grab the tiger's whiskers. The purpose of this type of teaching style is explained in the following way: "In reality there is no other purpose but to dissolve fixations and untie bonds, to get rid of what blinds and burdens people."[48]

If freedom of the student is at issue, how can a method such as a shout be considered dangerous and violent? Linji compares a shout to a sword or a golden-haired lion crouching on the ground.[49] The master Touzi, a discerning, truthful, and plain teacher, is described as cutting off the tongue of a questioner.[50] The raising of a finger appears to be a nonviolent method of teaching, but it has the potential to become violent, as when Judi cut off the finger of an attendant as noted previously along with other examples. The shout also gives the appearance of being nonviolent, but there are exceptions, as evident when Baizhang tells the

---

45. Cleary, *Blue Cliff Record*, 62.
46. Cleary, *Blue Cliff Record*, 97.
47. Sasaki, *Record of Linji*, 236.
48. Cleary, *Blue Cliff Record*, 93.
49. Cleary, *Recorded Sayings of Linji*, 52.
50. Cleary, *Blue Cliff Record*, 349.

story of how Mazu left him deaf for three days after shouting at him.[51] Even when there is no overt violence in the Chan discourse, there is the constant threat of violence. After a physical altercation between Linji and Huangbo, the duty-distributor responded to Huangbo's call for assistance by helping the monk to his feet, who responded to his act of kindness by hitting him. Then, Linji said the following: "Everywhere else they cremate with fire. Here we bury them alive for a time."[52] Therefore, the physical violence, shouting, and finger raising are teaching methods that are not only violent in themselves, but they also occur within a wider cultural context of the threat of violence.

If one subtracts the violent encounters recounted in the ancient Chan literature, there remains a pervasive discourse that is violent in this literature. A monk training in this way is described as a warrior wearing battle armor and ready to kill or die.[53] Baizhang is described by a commentator as someone who is unconcerned about danger or death and brave enough to enter a tiger's lair to capture a tiger cub. Not avoiding life or death, he dares to grab the tiger's whiskers. In a similar vein, Zhaozhou is described by using violent discourse. Zhaozhou encounters situations in life, according to the commentator, like a diamond sword. For those that hesitate to answer his question, he cuts their head off, or steals their eyes. He dares to grab he tiger's whiskers.[54] The same text with these descriptions of two famous masters instructs a reader that to be a monk and to become a Buddha means that one must be willing to kill someone: "Whoever would uphold the teaching of Chan must be a brave spirit; only with the ability to kill a man without blinking an eye can one become a Buddha on the spot."[55] It is not unusual to encounter a nonviolent dialogue but to then read a commentary containing violent imagery. For example, Baizhang asked Wufeng, "How will you speak with your mouth shut?" Wufeng responded, "You should shut up too." Baizhang said, "I gaze out toward you where there is no one."[56] The commentator of this narrative says, "Baizhang's question is like a hawk; Wufeng's answer is like an arrow."[57] Later in the same text, the commentator explains what hap-

51. Cleary, *Blue Cliff Record*, 70.
52. Cleary, *Recorded Sayings of Linji*, 57.
53. Broughton and Watanabe, *Chan Whip Anthology*, 161.
54. Cleary, *Blue Cliff Record*, 148.
55. Cleary, *Blue Cliff Record*, 36.
56. Cleary, *Blue Cliff Record*, 320.
57. Cleary, *Blue Cliff Record*, 321.

pens when a novice asks a question by saying that the master responds by cutting off his tongue.[58]

In addition to describing masters and their methods as violent, classical Chan texts also portray spiritual dilemmas in terms of violent situations. In *Wumen's Gate*, master Xiangyan said, "It is like being a man up in a tree [supporting himself by] holding a branch between his teeth, with his hands and feet not touching the tree branches. Beneath the tree there is someone who asks about the meaning of the coming from the West... If he does not reply, he spurns the questioner's question. If he does reply, he perishes [by falling]. At such a moment, how should he answer?"[59] The imminent threat of death forms the discursive context for this dilemma. In another case, the threat of violent death helps one to concentrate. The master Jinglon stopped lecturing to concentrate on meditation, but continually was overcome by sleep as he tried to meditate. To focus his mind on meditation and to warn off sleepiness, he sat cross-legged on a thousand-foot-high cliff and spied a tree jutting out from the side of the cliff. He made a straw cushion, placed it on the tree, and sat on it in a meditative posture where he sat day and night with his life in the balance. He had an absolute fear of death that helped to focus his mental concentration until he attained awakening.[60] This episode elucidates the fact that the potential for a violent death can help one focus on a single thing. Another monk uses an awl to jab himself to keep awake during all-night meditation.[61] These two episodes clarify that violence can be put to pragmatic use to help one to concentrate. Even if one does not achieve enlightenment, these types of practice can protect a meditator from the influence of unmerciful karma and negative rebirth prospects. Nonetheless, violent methods and an emphasis on a context of pervasive violence created an environment of actual and potential conflict and harm.

The apparent willingness of Chan to accept violence and the acknowledged success of these aggressive methods did not guarantee that everyone accepted them. The *Blue Cliff Record* testifies to the fact that some individuals did not embrace the physical violence. The master Wujiu asked a monk how the teaching method of Dingzhou, a master of another region, was different from his. The anonymous monk replied that it

58. Cleary, *Blue Cliff Record*, 349.
59. Cleary, *Wumen's Gate*, 75.
60. Broughton and Watanabe, *Chan Whip Anthology*, 134–35.
61. Broughton and Watanabe, *Chan Whip Anthology*, 136.

was not different. Wujiu, replied, "If it is not different, then you should go back there," and hit him. After a flippant reply about Wujiu's staff having eyes, the master hit the insouciant monk again three times, causing him to protest of an unjust beating. Wujiu volunteered to turn the staff over for the unjustly violated monk. After Wujiu handed the monk his staff, he proceeded to hit the master three times. In response to this violence, Wujiu berated the monk for an unjust beating, which suggests that the encounter came full circle.[62] From one perspective, this scenario suggests that two unjust beatings cancel each other out in an encounter that is indicative of something comical and farcical.

A WESTERN PERSPECTIVE ON ZEN TEACHING METHODS

Lifting a single finger, shouting a meaningless sound, or administering a blow to someone can all be understood as a form of language. Although beatings and raising a finger are physical acts, they are still forms of language. The phenomenologist Merleau-Ponty writes, "It is the body which points out, and which speaks . . ."[63] This comment suggests that the body is a form of expression and language. The Zen phenomena under consideration are more particularly all forms of language called performative utterances, as developed by J. L. Austin. At first glance, these Zen methods do not adhere strictly to Austin's criteria for a performative utterance. However, it will be demonstrated that they do function as such.

Like a performative utterance, these Zen phenomena do not describe or report anything; they are neither true nor false. For language to be classified as a performative utterance, the uttering of a sentence must be part of the doing of an action.[64] For example, in a typical wedding ceremony, the bride and groom reach a moment in the ceremony when they say, "I do," which means that they accept each other in marriage. Thus, the saying and doing are intimately related. If either party does not respond, there is not a successful conclusion of the marriage ceremony. In other words, the marriage contract is void.

Austin enumerates certain conditions that are necessary for a performative utterance to be successful. He writes, "There must exist an

---

62. Cleary, *Blue Cliff Record*, 332–33.
63 Merleau-Ponty, *Phenomenology of Perception*, 197.
64 Austin, *How to Do Things*, 5.

accepted conventional procedure having a certain conventional effect, the procedure to include the uttering of certain words by certain persons in certain circumstances."[65] Within the Zen context, the master is the appropriate person by his enlightened state of mind; he possesses the authority, like a mayor or governor declaring a bridge open, to utter the correct words or make the appropriate gesture to make something happen. The conventional procedure in the Zen case is the unorthodox teaching methods. And for a method to affect the desired results, the circumstances must be appropriate. It can misfire because the procedure invoked is not accepted or understood by the student. For example, a steward informed Linji that he had gone to the provincial capital and sold his supply of millet. Linji drew a line in front of the steward with his staff and said, "But can you sell this?" The steward responded with a shout. Thereupon, the master hit him.[66] In other words, the steward made the wrong response.

Austin asserts another condition: "The particular persons and circumstances in each case must be appropriate for the invocation of the particular procedure invoked."[67] When Mazu twists Baizhang's nose after seeing wild ducks fly overhead, the latter is enlightened.[68] In this case, the persons and circumstances are appropriate to the action and the desired result is attained. According to the commentator, Mazu's intention is to reveal everything spontaneously for Baizhang, but he did not understand and says, "Flown away." Thereby, he missed twice to give the right response.[69] Neither time did Baizhang come prepared to the moment to understand, and thus he did not come ready to grasp the point of his nose being twisted by Mazu. He experienced and endured the pain of his nose being twisted for nothing. In short, it represents a wasted opportunity for an awakening breakthrough.

The final criterion for a successful performative utterance, according to Austin, is that the procedure must be executed by all participants correctly and completely.[70] It is common in Zen literature to find examples of a master beating someone without sparking off an enlightenment experience. In such cases, there is a misinvocation, misexecution, or

65. Austin, *How to Do Things*, 26.
66. Sasaki, *Record of Linji*, 44.
67. Austin, *How to Do Things*, 34.
68. Cleary, *Blue Cliff Record*, 255.
69. Cleary, *Blue Cliff Record*, 259.
70. Austin, *How to Do Things*, 35–36.

misapplication. The novice, for instance, may not have been sufficiently ready for the master's raising a finger for this gesture to trigger an enlightenment experience. This point is humorously illustrated on the impending death of Linji; he was concerned that his correct understanding of Zen be transmitted after his death. Therefore, he inquired of those assembled how they would respond to someone wanting to know what the master taught. In response to Linji, Sansheng uttered a "Ho!" The dying master then said, "Who would have known that my eye for the true Dharma would perish with this blind donkey." As his words concluded, he died sitting upright.[71]

Although beating someone with a stick or raising a lone finger are physical gestures, they are forms of self-expression; they are forms of communication. They attempt to express something that ordinary modes of expression cannot capture in words and sentences. In a similar fashion, a meaningless shout is intended to cut off words. The objective is to see the truth outside of any pattern.

The shout, the beating, and the single finger held aloft are all performative utterances, occurring within an encounter dialogue in which a usually anonymous monk and a known teacher exchange words. They are not always successful because the uninitiated is not spiritually ripe or prepared to understand. When they are successful something happens. If the circumstances are appropriate, they can trigger an enlightenment experience. As in a performative utterance, there is an intimate relationship between the expression and making something happen.

Agreeing with the observation that these encounter dialogues are performative, McRae calls attention to three features of these encounter dialogues: they are presented as written transcriptions of real oral dialogues between historically identifiable people; the dialogues use vernacular speech to achieve their effects, giving the impression of real exchanges between identifiable historical speakers; there is no evident exchange of ideas, although there is logical disjunction, inexplicable and iconoclastic pronouncements, strange gestures, and physical assaults.[72] The Chan encounter dialogues are different from the Pāli and Sanskrit texts that usually provide a social context for a reader. These social, historical, or cultural contexts are just not as important to Chan because it is not concerned with explaining the *dharma* in a comprehensible and

---

71. Cleary, *Recorded Sayings of Linji*, 63.
72. McRae, *Seeing through Zen*, 77–78.

expository language; it is rather focused on shocking students in a totally new direction. There is no evidence for encounter dialogues during the Tang dynasty. There is, however, evidence for them around 952, which convinces some scholars that they originated in the Song dynasty.[73] Their primary goal is to indicate to students how they can extricate themselves from the bottom of a deep well without a rope.[74] In short, the master wants to make something happen. These performative utterances and physical gestures are intended to act as a catalyst for an awakening breakthrough by an aspirant.

VIOLENCE AND PLAY

The various methods of Zen masters reviewed in this chapter often involve some degree of violence. The provoking of violence does not mean that the master is a mentally ill figure who enjoys inflicting pain on others. Instead of this type of misconception, we should view violence in the context of student-master encounters as part of a situational and pedagogical process that is dynamic in nature.[75] Violence shares its contextual characteristic with play.

Another way to look at violent beatings, shouts, and finger raising is as a ludic encounter between the master and student. To grasp the play element involved in these encounters, it is necessary to review the nature of play. The activity of play involves risk, insecurity, and ambiguity. With respect to violence, play can result in injury or worse. If a situation in which the student asking a question often precipitates violence by the master, the student knowing this operates from a position of insecurity as she quests ironically for certainty. When a person enters play, there is always the risk of winning or losing and the insecurity of not knowing how it will eventuate in the end. The participant also plays with ambiguity personified by violence.

To play involves a decision to be in the world, a decision that sets the *bodhisattva* (master) apart from others: "Play is being in the world, through objects, towards others."[76] This implies that to play means to be human. By entering into play, a person comes to understand the world,

73. Schlütter, *How Zen Became Zen*, 16.
74. Cleary, *Blue Cliff Record*, 106.
75. Collins, *Violence*, 10.
76. Sicart, *Play Matters*, 18.

grasp one's existential and social surroundings, and engage with others. By means of their recorded encounters with aspirants, Zen masters demonstrate the personal nature of play that stresses the individual effects of play and its creative aspect by bringing novices to awakening.

Play is an activity that possesses the potential to challenge traditional values by subverting established hierarchies. It can also invert accepted meaning, and it can become a form of perversion that is subversive. With these types of potential, it is possible to understand its appeal to the iconoclastic spirit of Zen Buddhism. The spirit of play is illustrated by a story about the master Mazu and a student who asked him why Bodhidharma come from the West. Asking the monk to be quiet and move closer, the master boxed the student on the ear, and he said: "Among six ears one does not scheme plots." When Mazu was asked the same question by another monk, Mazu asked him to bow down to him. While the monk was bowing, Mazu gave him a kick that caused the monk to have a great awakening and to respond with laughter and profuse joy.[77] If we review these two separate episodes, it is possible to learn some lessons about the nature of play. In the first episode, Mazu's blow to the ear of the monk was intended to sever his attachment to words. This is also true of the kick in the second scenario. Unlike the victim of the playful violence in the first episode, the monk in the second narrative enters the spirit of play due to his awakening experience. This is made possible by the realization of emptiness that renders the possibilities for play limitless.

Play embodies what can be called a to-and-fro spirit. A dialogue between two monks exemplifies this back and forth movement. The first monk said: "The master normally tells us to follow the bird path. I wonder what the bird path is?" The master Dongshan replied, "You don't meet anyone." After the first monk inquired how it is possible to follow such a path, the master replied that "one should go without hemp sandals on one's feet." The monks insightfully asked, "If one follows the bird path, isn't that seeing one's original face?" The master inquired, "Why do you turn things upside down so?" Then, the monk asked to be shown how he had accomplished upsetting everything. The master said, "Let there be no self in your footsteps" The monk responded with another question: "If I travel the bird's path, is this not the original face?" Responding to this question, the master replied, "It does not follow the bird path."[78]

77. Poceski, *Record of Mazu*, 55.
78. Cleary, *Blue Cliff Record*, 439.

Since the bird path is strictly speaking a no-path, there is no need to wear sandals when traveling on this non-path. The advantage of traveling on this no-path is that it is possible to discover one's true face—the no-face. Moreover, the master is indicating that there is no path and nothing to find. Then, what is the point of the ludic dialogue? The master wants to point to the fact that path and face are right here in the present moment. It is not a matter of looking for the path and your original face; it is simply a matter to see that here it is in the present moment.

The playfulness of the teaching methods examined in this chapter is evident in the spontaneous and often meaningless responses of the masters. And yet these responses embody the wisdom of the master. For instance, a monk asked Zhimen, "What is the body of wisdom?" And he responded, "An oyster swallows the bright moon."[79] The spontaneous nature of the response is evident in the response of the master, although the wisdom might not be as apparent. The unity of playfulness, spontaneity, and meaninglessness is evident in an episode involving Yaoshan. A monk asked Yaoshan, "On a level field, in the shallow grass, the elk and deer form a herd: how can one shoot the elk of elks?" Yaoshan said, "Look—an arrow!" The monk fell down. Yaoshan responded, "Attendant, drag this dead fellow out." Then, the monk ran out. Yaoshan responded by saying, "When will this guy playing with a mud ball ever be done?"[80]

The relationship between the Zen master and student is a good illustration of the game as an encounter, a dialogical exchange between people. Since one does not know the true intentions of the other, the master's play exhibits freshness or novelty, a presumption that what is to happen has not occurred prior to this encounter, even though there is a repetitive aspect to the game between the master and the novice being beaten, which are social episodes that construct a new world, an enlightened one. When participants in the encounter maintain their sense of connection and separation there is created a successful encounter.[81] The Zen encounter episodes enable interaction between actors during which subjects act and react, which is a process that occurs within the world. The Zen master plays at being violent and with a novice.

---

79. Cleary, *Blue Cliff Record*, 397.
80. Cleary, *Blue Cliff Record*, 357.
81. Henricks, *Play Reconsidered*, 150.

CONCLUDING REMARKS

In retrospect, the overwhelming majority of those discussing the nature of violence fail to notice its close association with play. This failure by theorists is a bit difficult to understand because many games involve violence. A board game like chess originated within the symbolic context of Indian warfare. American-style football is non-symbolically violent and dangerous as evidenced by broken limbs, dislocated joints, ligament damage, paralysis, concussions, and even brain damage from repeated blows to the skull. A major advantage of the many examples cited in this chapter help a reader grasp the close association between violence and play within certain contexts.

Besides their connection to play, these violent encounters manifest a context that is combative. The Zen master plays with the aspirant seeking enlightenment by tricking the seeker, inflicting violence, or surprising the novice with a gesture. In short, the encounter is a hagiographical account of a contest between two or more participants. In a peculiar way, the master is only a winner when the aspirant attains enlightenment. But when the seeker remains in a condition of ignorance that person is a loser. Nonetheless, both participants win when the aspirant achieves enlightenment. But the attainment of enlightenment does not mean that the game is over. Because once a person gains awakening he is then free to continuously play. At this point, all rules are suspended because one has transcended them. The purest form of play is the ability and freedom to play within emptiness. All is play. All is emptiness.

Although beatings and finger raising are non-verbal actions, they—like the shout—enable one to hear the truth that words cannot express. These actions enable the correctly prepared aspirant to hear the message of emptiness and to play in emptiness. The master Hakuin helps to illustrate this point, "When the [Sound of the] Single Hand enters the ear even to the slightest degree, in the mind with which all men are originally endowed, not one bit of ignorance exists, not one bit of birth and death remains. All is vast perfection; all is vast emptiness."[82] The sound of silence can only be heard when one ceases to speak. The aspirant must listen for the sound of his own Buddha-nature.

The lone finger perceived, the beating received, and the shout heard enable one to walk in the path of birds and play like them. They enable you to see your original face and hear the sound of one hand clapping.

---

82. Yampolsky, *Hakuin*, 166.

They allow you to get the goose out of the bottle without breaking the bottle or killing the goose. In short, they make something happen. Therefore, it is fair to say that no Zen master can inflict enough violent beatings on a sufficient number of aspirants for enlightenment, assuming that the goal of human existence is liberation from suffering.

5

A PAINTING OF A RICE CAKE CAN SATISFY HUNGER

THE TITLE OF THIS chapter is derived from a saying by Chan Master Xsingyan: "A painting of a rice cake cannot satisfy hunger." It is possible to imagine many different meanings for this statement. We can, for instance, acknowledge that rice cake is not eatable, whereas a real rice cake can satisfy your hunger. The Japanese Master Dōgen Kigen, the founder of the Sōtō school in the thirteenth century, offers a non-dual interpretation of the statement by denying the ordinary view that the painting is unreal while assuming a rice cake is real. From his non-dual perspective, Dōgen states that the painting represents a totality of all things including Buddhas, sentient beings, illusion, and enlightenment, which suggests that the painting is not any different from any other form of existence.[1] This aspect means that there is no actual difference between an actual rice cake and a painting of one. Dōgen's position seems to contradict our common sense. Dōgen consistently makes statements that offend our common-sense view of life and the world, but he is consistent concerning his position. If a reader grasps his position, his radical statements are much less outrageous and begin to make perfect sense. What Dōgen enjoys doing in his writings is playing with his reader. In other words, Dōgen plays with his reader's rational mind. It is as if he is playing soccer with his reader's mind that functions as the ball that is kicked every which way.

---

1. Dōgen, "Genjō Kōan," in *Shōbōgenzō*, 1:87.

Writing about the painting of the rice cake, Dōgen uses this painting to draw some lessons about illusion, which is symbolized by unsatisfied hunger. In short, the point that he makes is that a person loses her hunger by becoming detached from the opposites of enlightenment and illusion. From his non-dualistic position, when you become hungry, the entire world becomes hungry just as there is no real difference between a rice cake and a painting of this object.[2] However, why is this the case? The so-called eatable rice cake and the painting of such a cake, along with personal hunger and world hunger, are both empty. Thus, either can satisfy one's hunger. For the insightful eye, it is possible to see the entire universe in the painting, the truth of the Buddha's teachings, one's authentic self, both movement and inertia. Since this is true, the painting of a rice cake can potentially point a person in the direction of liberation. The experience of awakening functions to actualize the painting for Dōgen, making it possible to satisfy one's hunger. To comprehend Dōgen's non-dual philosophy, it is necessary to review his notions of perception, *zazen* only, Buddha-nature, being-time, non-thinking, and self and other.

THE BUDDHA-EYE

To truly see correctly and insightfully, a person needs to see via a combination of the seer and the seen, or subject and object. We are hindered in achieving this non-dualistic type of perception because we ordinarily see things through our preconceptions about the nature of things and events, our prejudices, or our prejudgments that combine to influence the way that we usually perceive things. From Dōgen's philosophical perspective, we need to stop assuming that objects are external to our mind because they are instead the mind itself.[3] Thus, a perceiver and an object perceived are non-dual, although our preconceptions and prejudices give us the impression that there is a dichotomy between the subject (perceiver) and object (the seen). Dōgen's non-dual position has implications for the eye, physical instrument of perception, and the human body because the organ of perception is both primordial and directly connected to the body: "'Right vision' is within the enlightened vision of our entire body. That is why we must possess the eye which existed before our body was born. This vision sees all things as they are in their true form—the

---

2. Dōgen, *Shōbōgenzō*, 1:87.
3. Dōgen, *Shōbōgenzō*, 1:11.

actualization of enlightenment. We share that vision with the Buddhas and Patriarchs."[4] This means that the primordial eye and its insightful vision form a unity with the body. Thus, when Dōgen refers to the perception, he is not talking about ordinary seeing, which is something exercised by a subject on an object. What he is discussing concerns what he calls the Buddha-eye.

What Dōgen means by the Buddha-eye can be illustrated by an often-repeated apocryphal narrative about the origin of Zen Buddhism in which the historical Buddha is portrayed as preaching before a large gathering on Vulture Peak without saying a word. Instead of speaking, the Buddha held up a single flower and winked to a monk named Mahākāśyapa. The monk responded to the Buddha's gesture with a smile, indicating that he understood the Buddha's message, even though others in the crowd were confounded and left pondering the significance of the gesture.[5] This apocryphal story portrays the Buddha directly transmitting his teachings to a disciple, a motif that has been embraced and promoted by Chan/Zen masters for centuries as a unique aspect of the religion.

If we focus on Dōgen's comments about the eye, we learn that holding up the flower for everyone assembled to see this gesture is intended to suggest that the Buddha both conceals and reveals himself in the flower. This act involves more than using one's hand and fingers because it includes the vision and mind of the Buddha. By vision, it is possible to grasp that "mountains, rivers, heaven, and earth; the sun, moon, and earth; rain and wind; human beings and animals; trees and grasses—all these are nothing but the holding up of an adumbara flower."[6] Moreover, when the Buddha winks in the narrative all human beings lose their ordinary vision, and their Buddha-eye opens. Moreover, when the Buddha raises the flower for all to see it, everyone is performing the same action unceasingly from a primordial past with his or her entire body. Moreover, the Buddha-eye is concealed within the flower.

Dōgen continues to point out that when we open our Buddha-eye, it represents reflecting the eye of the Buddha in our eye because we now have the "Buddha's vision and original face."[7] We can now see the Buddha

---

4. Dōgen, *Shōbōgenzō*, 2:79.
5. Cleary, *Wumen's Gate*, 76.
6. Dōgen, *Shōbōgenzō*, 2:117.
7. Dōgen, *Shōbōgenzō*, 4:75.

face to face, which enables us to see the universal nature of the Buddha and to observe the "sun-faced and moon-faced Buddha."[8]

Once this occurs the entire world and all its inhabitants and all moments of time are nothing but the practice of seeing Buddha. In other words, to truly see the Buddha we must open our own Buddha-eye, suggesting that we see the Buddha by means of the eye of the Buddha, and to attempt to conceal this actualization is impossible because it will eventually emerge by itself.[9] Even more precisely, the type of perception associated with the eye of the Buddha is not-seeing, which involves seeing without subject and without an object that is seen. This experience is thus non-dual seeing because it is both subjectless and objectless.

Non-dualistic perception is a not-seeing that is not limited to perception because Dōgen argues that we can also hear sounds through our eyes. Consequently, it is possible to hear the teachings of the Buddha through one's eyes. Even though this assertion might sound absurd, Dōgen pushes his point to the limit: "Further, we can hear the sound throughout our body in every part of our body." To conclude that Dōgen is writing nonsense or that he is confused about different sense faculties would be incorrect and an application of one's assumptions, expectations, and prejudices. From Dōgen's perspective, sense faculties do not have fixed and predetermined functions because they can be modified or interchanged. What Dōgen gives his reader is the development of an entirely new sensory circuit based on the harmonization of the five sense faculties.[10] It is this harmonized understanding of the five sense faculties that forms the basis for his view that the painting of a rice cake can satisfy one's hunger.

ZAZEN ONLY

As previously mentioned, *zazen* means unmoved sitting in meditation. For Dōgen, *zazen* is indubitably the best practice because, in part, it represents the primordial form of Buddhist life and the support for everything else associated with the Buddhist quest for liberation. It takes precedence over *kōan* practice, although Dōgen does not entirely reject using *kōans*. The rationale for this preference and emphasis will become

---

8. Dōgen, *Shōbōgenzō*, 4:75.
9. Nagatomo, "Analysis of Dōgen's 'Casting Off Body,'" 229, 232.
10. Nagatomo, "Analysis of Dōgen's 'Casting Off Body,'" 229, 232.

evident as we progress. A significant advantage of *zazen* is that it is not explicitly associated with any single school. From Dōgen's perspective, all schools of Buddhism are derived from it, a position that tends to stress its foundational character.

Zazen is not a technique by which a person comes to realization, according to Dōgen. In other words, it is not the cause of *satori* (enlightenment). On the surface of it, this seems like an odd position to assume. What Dōgen wants to affirm is that *zazen* is already realized, even if you sit in meditation for the very first time. This claim is related to Dōgen's vision of the unity between practice and enlightenment that we will review shortly. It is important to recognize that *zazen* does not represent the obliteration of a person's conscious experiences with absorption into some undifferentiated realm. It is preferable to grasp *zazen* as the non-thinking mode of consciousness, which will be discussed more fully later in this chapter. *Zazen* enables a meditator to realize "thinking of the unthinkable."

It is possible to comprehend Dōgen's position more fully by noting that there is a unity between practice and enlightenment. Therefore, *zazen* is referred to as practice based on enlightenment and not an activity before enlightenment. Dōgen steals an emphasis from the Rinzai school by calling *zazen* the *kōan* realized during life. This position does not mean that one seeks a unique state of consciousness or strives to become a Buddha through seated meditation, but it rather implies that one follows the way that is equally the same at the beginning, middle, and end. What Dōgen wants to stress is that the way is an active undertaking, that enlightenment is also something dynamic, and that it is not a static state of attainment. This dynamic notion of practice and enlightenment is related not only to their unity, but it also possesses implications for the authentication of *zazen*. What Dōgen means is that proper sitting authenticates the enlightenment that is already present in a person sitting even for the first time. A significant implication of this position is that a person does not practice *zazen* to become enlightened, because to practice *zazen* is to be enlightened. The unity between practice and enlightenment is analogous to a medical doctor because we do not say about a heart doctor, for instance, that he practices medicine to become a heart doctor, but we instead assert that to perform angioplasty is to be a heart doctor. Moreover, to practice *zazen* is to accept Buddha-nature as it is. From a slightly different perspective, to authenticate the presence of Buddha-nature is enlightenment.

Although the point seems rather obvious, it is essential to acknowledge that when a person sits in meditation that person does so with their body-mind (*shinjin*). Dōgen departs from the earlier Pāli Buddhist tradition and its emphasis on controlling the body and becoming detached from it. For Dōgen, the human body is not a hindrance to enlightenment; it is instead a vehicle through which enlightenment is realized. Dōgen wants to stress that human beings' quest for liberation with their bodies, practice with their bodies, understand with their bodies, and attain enlightenment with their bodies, which gives the body a metaphysical and religious significance that is not shared by the Pāli tradition.

This significance and Dōgen's overall conception of the body-mind becomes evident when it is examined in relationship to the world. Dōgen views the body and mind as interwoven. Therefore, it is incorrect and even illusory to conceptualize the mind as a permanent entity and the body as something impermanent and perishable. The body and the world are also inseparably interconnected. Dōgen illustrates what he means by the analogy of riding in a boat in which the sailor uses the sails of the boat and its tiller to steer the vehicle to its intended destination. The sailor performs various actions to navigate the way successfully, but it is the boat that carries the sailor to his destination. If it is agreed that the boat functions as a mode of transportation, it is still the sailor that makes it a boat and a world for the sailor instead of a series of wooden planks nailed and glued together flowing aimlessly on a body of water. When the sailor boards the boat, the sailor's body, mind, and the world are all representative of the dynamic working of it. In other words, the dynamic working of the boat includes the body of the sailor that works the tiller, the mind that navigates the boat, and the earth and all space in which it travels.[11] What Dōgen wants to make clear with his analogy is that the body, mind, and world are not only dynamic, but they are also non-dual.

Consequently, he can state that the body and mind are the entire universe since everything represents a single and total body. Thus, it is not possible to claim that human beings are separated from the world by their bodies. We cannot be certain where the human body ends and where the external world commences or vice versa for that matter. The human body is not an entity that participates in the external world because it also participates in one's inner world, and both worlds participate in each other through the human body. Since the mind, body, and

11. Dōgen, *Shōbōgenzō*, 1:81–82.

world interpenetrate each other, it is impossible to demarcate them and to affirm unequivocally to which sphere each belongs. Dōgen's position possesses ecological implications because when a person takes a shower and washes with soap, that person is cleansing her mind as well as the world. It could be asserted that a clean environment begins with a person's body-mind.

Dōgen's thoughts about the body-mind possess important implications for the act of understanding. If we assume Dōgen's position concerning the body-mind, it is only possible to understand as a participant in the totality of mind, body, and world. Thus, it is possible to understand the world with one's mind and/or the body. Since understanding is indispensably associated with one's whole being, it is incorrect to affirm that we act first, and then we attempt to understand as if action represents a special mode of understanding. When a person treats, for instance, another person who is ill, or if an adult reads a book to a young child, there is only that act of treatment or reading being done in the entire world. In other words, attending to a sick person or reading to a child represent actions that are not actions among other actions. Dōgen makes it clear that such actions are the action, since now of action—treatment or reading—there is no other action taking place. In fact, the entire world is created in and through that action. This understanding of action only makes sense from a non-dualistic position. Moreover, from Dōgen's non-dualistic position, all modes of understanding are actions and expressions because being and knowing are one. Thus, it can be asserted that a person is what that person understands since Dōgen unites being, knowing, and liberation. If a person understands garbage, one is, for instance, garbage. If one understands Buddha-nature, one is, likewise, Buddha-nature. However, since garbage and Buddha-nature are empty, garbage is Buddha-nature, which will become more lucid when we discuss the latter.

In addition to practice with the body-mind, the other part of the unity along with practice related to *zazen* is enlightenment, which is a conscious and luminous experience. It is also an experience of being. If one recalls the image of taking a step beyond the top of a hundred-foot pole, Dōgen makes use of the same image to elucidate how ordinary consciousness is released and transcended and the importance of casting off body and mind. The latter activity is not construed as a negative activity; it rather means that the meditator does not remain attached to any personal viewpoints or preconceptions. If you do remain attached to such mental phenomena, it is equivalent to holding onto the top of the pole and not letting go. What Dōgen thinks we must do is to rid ourselves of all relativistic things and world opinions no matter how wise they seem to us. By casting off body and mind, we experience verification that there is no distinction between cultivation (i.e., practice) and authentication (i.e., enlightenment). Since practice and realization are identical, *zazen* is not the cause of enlightenment.

The casting away of body and mind also represents the revealing of one's original face and the shining forth of the Buddha-nature. Intuitively seeing the Buddha-nature or one's original face with the enlightenment experience does not mean that this is the end of the path. Dōgen insists that seated meditation must continue for two reasons: (1) it represents practice in enlightenment and (2) enlightenment must continually be confirmed in *zazen*. Moreover, awakening does not occur once. It is something that must be ever-continuing and ever-renewed.

BUDDHA-NATURE

Dōgen discusses Buddha-nature as paradoxically something that is openly manifest and simultaneously concealed. This situation concerning the Buddha-nature is explained as being analogous to attempting to see your eyes with your own eyes. Although you cannot see your eyes with your own eyes, you are convinced that you have eyes because you can see the ducks swimming in the lake. Thus, your eyes are concealed from your view, but they are also a manifest aspect of your face. It is like the Buddha-nature that eludes our grip of knowledge because it is so manifest. It is as if Dōgen is saying that it is so apparent that it evades our grasping it. It is like losing your eye-glasses and looking all over for them before you realize that they were on your face all the time.

There is a passage in a Mahāyāna Buddhist text called the *Mahāparinirvāna Sūtra* that states, "All sentient being possess the Buddha-nature without exception." Within the historical context of Mahāyāna Buddhism, this statement confines Buddha-nature to just sentient beings, which are defined as thinking, perceiving, feeling beings, and living beings that transmigrate in the six realms of life (e.g., worlds of hell, hungry spirits, animals, demons, humans, and divine beings of traditional Buddhist cosmology) and it affirms that.

They innately possess Buddha-nature. In a sense, Dōgen takes this statement and makes it more radical by stating that Buddha-nature is all existence; moreover, all existence is equated with sentient beings. Unlike the earlier limits on sentient beings, this means that sentient beings include plant and animal life, as well as the inanimate world. Therefore, a carrot and a flower, a zebra and a monkey, a tree and a rock all possess the Buddha-nature. In comparison to the earlier limited notion of Buddha-nature, Dōgen transforms its meaning and makes it inclusive of previously characterized insentient beings.

Buddha-nature is further defined as beings and being itself. If Buddha-nature is all existences (e.g., sentient and insentient beings), it is possible for it to be the possession of these beings. Moreover, the all-inclusiveness of Buddha-nature suggests that all existence is immanent within it and not that it is immanent in all existence. By this abstract sounding notion that is ultimately concrete when one grasps its meaning, what Dōgen intends to state is that Buddha-nature and all existence are not identical, although they are not different. If we consider an apple, an orange, and a banana, we can agree that these three items are all fruits and yet they are all different kinds of fruits. This example offers us an approximation of what Dōgen is attempting to convey about the characteristics of Buddha-nature. What Dōgen wants to avoid is creating a wall or circumference around his notion of Buddha-nature. Although he does want to affirm that all existence and Buddha-nature are neither identical nor different. This position leads him to equate a particle of dust with all the infinite Buddhas of the Mahāyāna pantheon. Likewise, a person's body and mind are neither identical nor different than a blade of grass.[12]

If Buddha-nature is both beings and being itself, what does he say about non-being? Dōgen examines the traditional use of the term *mubusshō* (no Buddha-nature), and he indicates that it previously signified the absence of the Buddha-nature, which is analogous to the notion of non-being standing antithetically against being. Again, this is a traditional type of position that Dōgen alters to fit his redefinition of Buddha-nature. From Dōgen's perspective, non-being is an integral aspect of the Buddha-nature in the sense that it negates and transcends concrete realities. It also refers to the liberating and transcending powers inherent in the Buddha-nature. A significant philosophical advantage to Dōgen for including non-being within Buddha-nature is its liberating us from focusing on just the particularities of existence. If the inner structure of Buddha-nature embodies non-being, it is possible to ask Dōgen, as

---

12. Dōgen, *Shōbōgenzō*, 2:125.

someone did during his life, a famous *kōan*: Does a dog have the Buddha-nature? Dōgen's answer is yes and no—being and non-being. By adopting this philosophical path, Dōgen intends to stress both the emptiness of Buddha-nature and the Buddha-nature of emptiness and to emphasize that the ground of non-being is emptiness. In the final analysis, Buddha-nature both subsumes and transcends being and non-being.

By stressing the emptiness of Buddha-nature, Dōgen wants to call attention to its dynamic and creative aspect. This aspect is illustrated by a Zen narrative that draws the attention of Dōgen: One day Shigong asked Xitang: "Can you grasp emptiness?" Xitang replied: "Yes, I think I can." So, Shigong continued: "How would you grasp emptiness?" Xitang then demonstrated by grasping his hand in the space. Shigong stated: "You don't understand how to hold emptiness." Xitang responded: "How do you grasp it, then?" Shigong seized Xitang's nose and pulled it. Xitang exclaimed: "Ouch! Ouch! You are going to pull out my nose!" Shigong said: "You can grasp emptiness only this way."[13] Dōgen comments on this story by basically saying that that which grasps and that which is grasped are one and the same emptiness, that is, emptiness grasping emptiness. This position is confirmed even further when Dōgen defines the essence of emptiness: "the emptiness of emptiness is emptiness."[14] This definition is an acknowledgment that emptiness cannot be captured in language because it cannot be represented as you can create a tax form or a driver's license. Dōgen's definition also suggests that the realization of emptiness represents nothing but emptiness.

The dynamic and creative aspects of Buddha-nature are tied to its impermanence. For someone uninitiated into Dōgen's philosophical worldview, this assertion seems especially strange. However, he is being perfectly consistent. By the impermanent nature of Buddha-nature, Dōgen means that aspect that eternally comes into being and passes out of being. Within its eternal process, being and becoming are not separate because they are identically part of the same process of impermanence. Dōgen illustrates what he means with statements that upset and violate our common-sense view of the world:

"The blue mountain always walks." "The eastern mountain floats on the water." Common sense tells us that mountains are not blue except in a poetic sense, that mountains do not possess locomotion, and they do not

13. Kim, *Dōgen Kigen*, 170–73.
14. Dōgen, *Shōbōgenzō*, 4:125.

float on water. So, what is Dōgen trying to convey to us? Or is he merely playing games with our minds? What Dōgen wants to teach us is that the universe is not fixed and immovable like one ordinarily associated with the nature of mountains. The universe is a being in time. Moreover, parts of the universe like mountains are also beings in time. Again, this points to the dynamic nature of Buddha-nature.

EXISTENCE AND TIME

Like everything associated with Buddha-nature, existence and time form a unity that is called *uji* (being-time) in Japanese. Of course, this is not the ordinary view of being and time. Dōgen paints an image of a conventional understanding of time. Imagine a person who lives in a valley. She travels from the valley, crosses a river, and climbs a mountain to reach the summit. After reaching the top of the mountain, she relegates the valley, river, and mountainside to the things of the past that have no relationship to the present moment at the summit of the mountain. Dōgen claims that we usually measure time by discrete now moments that we connect in a linear series. Instead of this linked series of now moments, what Dōgen wants to substitute, or to have us realize more precisely, is primordial time, a being-time.

Dōgen describes primordial time as non-substantial, which means that it is not objective. Therefore, it cannot be measured like you would by using a clock or another type of mechanical device. It is also non-reductive, which suggests that time forms a unity. Being-time is non-anthropocentric because it includes the human sphere and the natural realm. Thus, it is not confined to human experience. Primordial time is non-differentiated in the sense that there is a unity of time and existence and truth and time. Being-time does not possess status as an independent mode of existence or beyond it.

Dōgen identifies explicitly two essential perspectives on time that are grounded in an authentic reflection of the temporal mode of human experience, with neither being more primary, that are: *nikon* (right-now) and *kyōryaku* (totalistic passage). The former means the now-moment that represents a complete spontaneous presencing of being-time, which extends simultaneously throughout the past, present, and future. Totalistic passage denotes an experiential continuity that refers specifically to the non-directional, continuing and connected aspects of time. It unites all aspects and dimensions of the three moments—past, present, and future—in the here and now, but it also allows for their diversity, variety, and differentiation. Since neither *nikon* nor *kyōryaku* possesses priority over the other, their difference is more a matter of perspective, reflecting a surface viewpoint for *nikon* and a cross-section perspective for totalistic passage. For instance, if we consider the metaphor of ascending a mountain, *nikon* refers to the activity of ascent, whereas totalistic passage suggests the entire context of a person climbing a mountain within the universe. By taking these two aspects of time together, it is possible to account for the completeness of each moment with each including a complete range of multiple perspectives and situations. Where does this position leave Dōgen?

His notion of being-time (*uji*) implies that things and events within the universe are time. Thus, he says things that initially confound us like mountains and oceans are time. Does this line of thinking apply to Buddha-nature? Indeed, the being of Buddha-nature is time. Both enlightenment and illusion are Buddha-nature, and each contains all of reality. Moreover, time is both temporal and spatial, which suggests that they inseparably interpenetrate each other. However, each now-moment constitutes a unique whole of actuality. This point means that the Buddha-nature is an actuality in the present moment and not some potentiality to be actualized in the future. The Buddha-nature is realized simultaneously with activity because it is identical to time.

Dōgen proceeds to explore the possibility of experiencing time, and he concludes that we experience neither time nor being in themselves because what we experience is temporal existence. This experience implies that we overcome grasping time as three consecutive moments. We also experience a stream of ever-changing phenomena with our pre-reflective consciousness that also embodies change. Dōgen does not, however, confine change to either the self or the object. We experience continual flux when we accept the experience of change as it is, and we fail to make projections beyond what is manifested. From Dōgen's sagacious perspective, by projecting something else on, for instance, the self, we create a false self that we might think is unchanging.

In contrast to such false projections, Dōgen wants us to merely accept phenomena as they are in the flux of change or time. Why does he want to do this? He wants us to see that all things and beings are impermanent, which is precisely what is shared by being and time. For Dōgen, the impermanence of everything is exactly what the Buddha taught centuries before Dōgen's historical period. In summary, it can be asserted that Buddha-nature is the experience of the presence of impermanence, which is identical with it. To grasp Dōgen's perspective, a reader must recall that he is writing from the position of an enlightenment master with a non-dualistic position.

PATH OF THINKING

In the previous chapter, the significance of what a person does from the top of a hundred-foot pole was used to illustrate the necessity of letting go of one's body and mind. Dōgen also uses this *kōan* to emphasize that the thinking characteristic of enlightenment entails a leap. Is this a leap into an abyss? Dōgen agrees with the spirit of the Rinzai position discussed in the previous chapter that to think in the way that he understands it involves taking a step from the top of a hundred-foot pole, which means to cast away both body and mind. It also means to think the unthinkable. To understand what Dōgen means, it is necessary to grasp his thoughts on the path of thinking leading to the leap of thinking.

For Dōgen, thinking is a way of living one's life, although it is impossible to reach one's goal by continuing to think within the confines of thinking patterns with which a person becomes accustomed over a long time. By reflecting upon your lifelong process of learning that took you through primary and secondary schools, maybe even college, and the lifelong learning outside the context of formal schooling, you have been accumulating much knowledge. Some of it will prove useful, and some of it you will never use. However, during this period of learning, you tended to assume that you were making progress by accumulating knowledge. From Dōgen's perspective, this would be a false assumption.

If a person spends her lifetime accumulating knowledge, this is not the type of path envisioned by Dōgen because ordinary modes of thinking cannot reach the goal of enlightenment, and the proper path is not forward. It involves a radical backward movement instead. Dōgen gives this advice: "You should, therefore, cease from practice based on intellectual understanding, pursuing words and following after speech, and learn the backward step that turns your light inwardly to illuminate yourself."[15] This way involves questioning all previous knowledge and being willing to cast off completely all previous thoughts and concepts. What Dōgen

---

15. Dōgen, *Shōbōgenzō*, 4:122.

is proposing is a way of unlearning rather than learning. His rationale is that we must unlearn what we previously accumulated because our preconceptions interfere with the new way of thinking that he is proposing. It is as if we have spent our entire lives acquiring incorrect thoughts by erroneous modes of thinking that merely take us in the wrong direction away from the goal of enlightenment. Therefore, we need to radically unlearn what thinking has been traditionally and our complicity in this wayward process.

If our old mode of thinking represents a dead end and we must unburden ourselves of all our prior useless modes of thinking, we cannot simply discover a new way of thinking by constructing a definition of it. Dōgen raises a rhetorical question: Can you learn the art of swimming by reading a treatise on it? Answering his question, Dōgen states that "only the leap into the river tells us what is called swimming."[16] Dōgen intends to affirm that one must engage in thinking to discover what genuine, liberating thinking can be. This intention does not mean that we should think about what thinking is because this course of action would be engaging in logic. It is also important not to waste your time due to the brevity of life: "Think only of this very moment and waste no time in turning your minds to the study of the Way."[17]

The path of unlearning that Dōgen alludes to begins in *zazen* (seated meditation). Without repeating our prior discussion, it is possible to ask the following question: What is it that one learns by sitting in meditation? The meditator discovers the ground of one's self. This discovery is part of Dōgen's path of unlearning: "To learn one's self is to forget one's self. To forget one's self is to be confirmed by all dharmas. To be confirmed by all dharmas is to affect the casting off one's own body and mind and the bodies and minds of others as well."[18] The result of the unlearning process is that there is no trace of mind and body along with no trace of enlightenment. We will turn to a complete discussion of the self below.

The path of thinking that Dōgen wants to bring to our attention does not involve our active seeking or waiting for it. The seeking and waiting that he thinks is best is no-seeking and no-waiting. If you strive for your goal, you will either lose it or become further removed from it with the result being the same. The path envisioned by Dōgen involves no seeking and no-waiting. There is also no duality of someone seeking

16. Dōgen, *Shōbōgenzō*, 4:128.
17. Dōgen, *Primer of Sōtō Zen*, 40.
18. Dōgen, *Shōbōgenzō*, 4:123.

or waiting. There is only arrival. By affirming that it might arrive is the same as claiming that it is already here. What Dōgen means is that it is unnecessary and impossible for the Buddha-nature to come out of the past and arrive at the now moment because there is no time that does not arrive. Moreover, there is no Buddha-nature that is not Buddha-nature manifested at the now moment. Since the present is already here, its arrival implies the immediate manifestation of the Buddha-nature. To understand how Dōgen philosophically reaches this point, it is instructive (in his sense of the term) to review his distinction between three types of thinking: thinking (*shiryō*), not-thinking (*fushiryō*), and non-thinking (*hishiryō*).

Thinking (*shiryō*) represents the weighting of ideas by considering one idea against another competing idea. This ordinary type of activity possesses the tendency to objectify that which it is considering. This type of thinking is negated by not-thinking (*fushiryō*). With its focus on thinking itself, not-thinking represents the negation or denial of thinking. In comparison to the initial two modes of consciousness, non-thinking is more fundamental than these modes of thinking. Unlike the initial two modes of thinking, non-thinking does not assume any intentional attitude. This kind of thinking means, for instance, that it neither affirms nor denies the existence of objects. It does not accept or reject the results of consciousness. Moreover, it does not believe or disbelieve some fact or statement. If this is the case, how does it function?

It functions by going beyond thinking and not-thinking in the sense that it involves accepting the presence of ideas and objects without affirming them or denying them. It also functions by uniting and sublating thinking and not-thinking. Non-thinking represents the pure presence of things as they are. If it becomes aware of a large grey mass with four legs, a trunk, and a tail, it does not call it an elephant, a zebra, a lion, Jane, or Fred. It does not name its color, identify any of its parts, or give it a name. It merely lets it be present. In other words, non-thinking represents the pure presence of things as they are. Since it represents the pure presence of things as they are and is more fundamental than the initial two modes of thinking, non-thinking supplies the primary material from which thinking develops.

Non-thinking is additionally thinking of the unthinkable. What is the unthinkable?

Dōgen equates the unthinkable with emptiness. Therefore, non-thinking is emptiness, which suggests that it is objectless, goalless, formless, and purposeless. It is possible to illustrate what Dōgen means by looking at the fifth case of the *kōan* collection entitled the *Mumonkan*:

> It is like a man up a tree who hangs from a branch by his mouth; his hands cannot grasp a bough, his feet cannot touch the tree. Another man comes under the tree and asks him the meaning of Bodhidharma's coming from the West. If he does not answer, he does not meet the questioner's need. If he answers, he will lose his life. At such a time, how should he answer?[19]

Dōgen offers an analysis of this *kōan* by stating that the man hanging from the tree is not merely suspended in space. It is more accurate to affirm that he is hanging in emptiness, which is also true of the questioner, the tree, and the question itself. It is imperative for the man hanging from the tree to answer the standing man's question because it is a matter of life and death, and it is not simply some silly question about some character coming from a particular direction. Of course, it is only by responding to the question that the suspended man can assist the man standing on the ground. Although non-thinking is without intention and purpose, it can give some insight into the complicated situation of the *kōan* and assist with discerning a pragmatic solution. Since the question and any possible answer are equally empty, any response that is natural and spontaneous will meet the needs of the questioner. As we witnessed in chapter 4, a shout, raising a finger, or an obscene response would do fine. In the analogous case of being at the top of the hundred-foot pole, the man suspended in emptiness must let go and respond. Whatever the form of the response taken by the suspended man when he lets go it signifies thinking the unthinkable. This aspect means that non-thinking is an intuitive realizational type of seeing. It is also a non-dualistic mode of thinking (an inadequate term under the circumstances). When the man suspended in emptiness responds to the questioner he is also responding to the never-ending call of his Buddha-nature to realize it. This feature is a call that makes no noise, a primordial and undifferentiated sound that is the source of all that is. About the sound that is before the time of creation, Dōgen states, "The sound that issues from the striking of emptiness is an endless and wondrous voice that resounds before and after the fall of the hammer."[20] What is the message of the Buddha-nature? What can a person say in response? Since it is equivalent to emptiness,

---

19. Dōgen, *Shōbōgenzō*, 1:116.
20. Dōgen,"

Buddha-nature is the power of articulating no. If emptiness is expressing no, can a person respond with an affirmative answer? Dōgen answers: "One does not say emptiness, because it is emptiness. One does not say no, because it is no. One says no because it is Buddha-nature emptiness."[21] What Dōgen intends to make clear is no one can adequately express that emptiness. Moreover, since the call is never-ending, it does not terminate with enlightenment and the realization of one's Buddha-nature. A person continues to answer the call and authenticate realization by practicing *zazen* (seated meditation).

INAUTHENTIC AND AUTHENTIC SELF

The historical Buddha's teaching about the five aggregates (*skandhas*) is used to illustrate in part how people obtain a false sense of an enduring self, whereas the self is forever changing. Thus, there is nothing permanent that we can genuinely call a self. Dōgen agrees with this position that the self possesses no permanence or enduring presence because it is continually changing. Dōgen makes his agreement with the Buddha clear when he states: "That is when our 'self' is the true Self then our self is not ours and not others—it is the four elements and the five skandhas."[22] What Dōgen means is that the self is not something that we can possess like an automobile or a pair of shoes; it is also not something that another person can possess. Dōgen also intimates that the genuine self is something concrete because it represents the immediacy of experience, assuming we can retrieve the genuine self lost in the split between subject and object due to unenlightened consciousness. This loss of original selfhood prompts Dōgen to distinguish his understanding of selfhood into the inauthentic self and the authentic self.

Dōgen traces inauthentic selfhood to a tendency of human beings to superimpose what he identifies as patterns of thinking, categories, and concepts onto human experience to manipulate that experience. When encountering experiences from the outside world, the self projects itself outward toward the empirical world and attempts to impose meaning on it. This type of process distorts the authentic self because it is not actively and directly involved in the process of experiencing. There is also a lack of conveying the genuine self to experience or conveying the experience

21. Dōgen, *Shōbōgenzō*, 1:47.
22. Dōgen, *Shōbōgenzō*, 1:47.

to itself because things or events advance in themselves. In other words, Dōgen is suggesting that the inauthentic self is a victim of things or events happening to it rather than being the master of its destiny, although Dōgen would not use this type of terminology.

If the inauthentic self is the result of a process of the self conveying itself toward things, the authentic self represents the exact opposite type of experience. Dōgen makes this process clear: "Conveying the self to the myriad things to authentic them is delusion; the myriad things advancing to authenticate the self is enlightenment."[23] Besides, the inauthentic self is abstract because it originates from memory based on past concrete experiences, whereas the authentic self is concrete. The point that Dōgen is attempting to make clear is that the inauthentic self is a product of the mind's self image of itself. This point implies that the mind is bifurcated, and it tends to think of itself as a self. This bifurcation leads to an apprehensive obsession by the inauthentic self for its security and endurance, whereas the authentic self is liberated from such fear, and it does not cling to life or fear death. The root problem for the inauthentic self is ignorance with its inability of the self to realize its impermanent nature and to insist on believing that one is an enduring entity.

To overcome this ignorance, Dōgen proposed a process of authentication of the self grounded in *zazen* (seated meditation) and completed by enlightenment. Now, this process is not a single, one-time event because he insists that it needs to be continued forever. It begins by "dropping off mind and body" discussed previously in this chapter, which results in the restoration of original unity. This restoration represents a unity of subject and object in concrete, immediate experience. The meditator becomes aware that the self continually changes because its experience is continually changing. The recognition that the self is not permanent and unchanging is not to be lamented because it shares its impermanent nature with its Buddha-nature. Therefore, when Dōgen refers to the authentic self, he means the Buddha-nature, which implies the dynamic and active nature of the authentic self. Thus, the authentic self is profoundly immersed in the world of experience, and it is also transcendent in the sense of being self-transcendent and not transcendent of the world.

This lived experience of authentic selfhood and its immersion in the world necessarily suggest that the self lives in the world with others and is essentially related to them, a radically existential and social way

---

23. Cook, *Sounds of Valley Streams*, 66.

of being in the world. Within the context of discussing the nature of a *bodhisattva* (enlightened being) and this figure's identification with the suffering of those human beings to be helped, Dōgen also discusses the term *dōji*, which he defines as a foundational virtue of being able not to differentiate oneself from others.[24] This virtue is based on an intuitive insight by Dōgen that all things are interrelated: "Each particle of the phenomenal world is interrelated, but still each particle exists of itself."[25] This insight contains epistemological implications for Dōgen that recall the philosophies of the Huayen and Tiantai schools of Chinese Mahāyāna Buddhism: "If we can understand a speck of dust we can know the entire world; one who truly knows one dharma can understand all dharmas."[26] Besides this epistemological implication for Dōgen, the important point for relational implications of this term is that each self is necessarily interrelated with every other self within a mutual web of responsibility for the welfare of everyone. Therefore, to be an authentic self from Dōgen's perspective involves being a self for others.

The relationship between the authentic self and other is grounded in his understanding of the Buddha-nature. Dōgen illustrates his grasp of this relationship with an anecdote about a master, a layperson, and a worm. After the master cuts the worm in half, he asks the layperson which of the two moving sides of the worm possesses the Buddha-nature. Dōgen offers two reasons for not drawing distinctions between the two halves: (1) the two moving halves of the worm represent the simultaneous action of meditative concentration (*samādhi*) and wisdom (*prajñā*); (2) Buddha-nature, and non-Buddha-nature co-exist in both life and death. Grounded in these examples of unity, the authentic self is by nature relational. It represents the other in a real way and not as an embodied entity that is divorced from the world. Not only does the self encompass the other, but it also embraces the totality of events that constitute experience. Therefore, the authentic self is both related to others and involved in the world.

When the authentic self looks at the other, it does not see the face of Harry or Sally. Instead, it sees the face of the historical Buddha because of the face of the other and the Buddha is non-dual. Dōgen elaborates what he means, "In each generation, every face has been the face of Buddha,

---

24. Dōgen, *Shōbōgenzō*, 3:137.
25. Cook, *Sounds of Valley Streams*, 66.
26. Dōgen, *Shōbōgenzō*, 1:12.

and this original face is direct, face to face transmission."[27] If you consider this position carefully, this direct face to face contact makes it possible for the transmission of teachings from the Buddha to the teacher and a student. Thus, there is a single tradition of giving and receiving face. Dōgen intimates that this transmission is personal, immediate, and direct. Since the face of the Buddha and the faces of the student and teacher are all empty, this means that there is simply no-face.

GOOD AND EVIL

Suppose you eat the painting of the rice cake and get very sick. Assuming satisfying your hunger is good and getting ill is evil, or contrary to what is right, does this mean that such an action can be good or evil? Are there ethical implications associated with the act of eating a painting? What would Dōgen say to these types of naive or inane questions? For Dōgen, good and evil have no self-nature because they are both empty. This aspect implies that they have no metaphysical or theological ground or source like divine laws in the major monotheistic faiths. Moreover, to commit an evil deed is incompatible with enlightenment that embodies an amoral or trans-moral sensibility that is intrinsic to it. Dōgen refers to the example of the old narrative about Nanquan killing a cat because two monks were attached to it and arguing about who was the rightful owner of the cat. Dōgen maintains that the killing of the cat was both a sinful act and a Buddha-act because both types of acts co-exist in the same act. This case shows that an enlightened person can use evil freely for the ultimate good.

From Dōgen's non-dualistic perspective, good and evil are *dharma* (teaching, doctrine), which is neither good nor evil. *Dharma* is non-dual just as is good and evil. Dōgen clarifies further that authentic morality arises spontaneously from enlightenment. This implies that their relationship is not like that of cause and effect or means and ends. Both good and evil are intrinsic to the structure of *dharma*. According to Dōgen, morality is non-dual when it becomes effortless, purposeless, and playful. The highest morality occurs when ought become "is" in the transparency of thusness (emptiness).

27. Dōgen, *Shōbōgenzō*, 2:138.

CONCLUDING REMARKS

This chapter gives a reader a glimpse into the non-dual position of a remarkable figure in world religion and philosophy. Dōgen shocks a modern reader out of their complacency about the nature of the world and their self. To claim that he gives us a different perspective on human existence is a gross understatement. Dōgen is an edifying thinker who broadens our vistas and suggests another way of grasping reality. He graciously invites us to join him by sitting in meditation. It is from this foundational stance that the real adventure starts and play begins. Moreover, within the Buddha-nature, a person is both released and free to play. Concerning play, there are no limitations on it in the Buddha-nature.

Dōgen suggests that play is built into the Buddha-nature. It is possible to find evidence for this position in his illustration about the earthworm that is cut in two. Since both ends of the severed worm move, this makes it possible to ask which part contains the Buddha-nature. Dōgen urges a layperson to think about the original condition of the worm in its wholeness and the post-cut worm. Dōgen says the two halves are without distinction, representing simultaneously concentration (*samādhi*) and wisdom (*prajñā*).[28] Within the realm of emptiness (Buddha-nature), seriousness and play dance together. It is fair to say then that Dōgen does philosophy in the spirit of play. A significant implication of this way of doing philosophy is that the philosopher is in harmony with the world and his readers.

---

28. Dōgen, *Shōbōgenzō*, 4:39.

6

MADNESS, THE EROTIC, HUMOR, AND PLAY

WITH LANTERN IN HAND, the madman ran to the marketplace in the early morning crying out that he sought God. The populace laughed at his antics, and they paid no heed to his announcement that God was dead. The people simply stood silent and looked at the madman in astonishment. Throwing his lantern on the ground, it broke, and its light was symbolically extinguished. The madman of Nietzsche's work *The Gay Science* acknowledged that he had come too soon. The truth of his prophetic proclamation was still on the way. Four hundred years before Nietzsche wrote his first book, another literary madman made his appearance in Japan. Just as Nietzsche had criticized a decadent Christianity of his time, a Japanese madman named Ikkyū Sōjun (1394–1481) was trying to call attention to a degenerate Zen Buddhism. Ikkyū stands in a long line of mad holy figures that stretches back to Chinese history.[1] And he conceives of his own antics as exemplifying the spirit of that tradition.

Ikkyū, a colorful exponent and practitioner of madness in Japanese religious history, lived during some painful and turbulent times in the history of his country. During his lifetime, there were disorders in the eastern provinces, the assassination of the shōgun Yoshinori, various agrarian and other uprisings, the natural disasters of 1459–62 and subsequent starvation, and the destructive Ōnin War. This tumultuous historical period left some monasteries and temples in ruins and dislocated numerous monks and nuns. Not only had the Rinzai sect, of which Ikkyū

---

1. See Strickmann, "Saintly Fools and Chinese Masters," 35–57.

was a member, grown powerful and wealthy, they also engaged in questionable and illegal practices like selling seals of enlightenment, secret answers to *kōans*, and certificates of appointment. As Ikkyū protested in some of his poems, leaders of the Rinzai sect were motivated by greed and lust for power. If the times were a bit brutal, turbulent, and uncertain, and if Zen Buddhism was in a state of general decay, the period called for a creative genius, even a madman, to cope with the multitude of problems.

As a point of clarification, to be declared a madman does not necessarily mean that one is clinically insane, although this could be the case. The use of the term *madness* in this chapter is intended in more of a humanistic sense rather than in a clinical way. To be mad means to act abnormally; to act contrary to accepted norms of behavior or what people expect, in this instance, of a Buddhist monk. To deviate from the decorum of a Buddhist monk, a person runs the risk of being labeled crazy. And this is the way Japanese laypeople classified Ikkyū, and how in fact he understood himself, or at least wanted to be viewed by others. This chapter will demonstrate that his madness is the cutting edge of his creative genius. To accomplish the task of this chapter, it will be necessary to investigate not only what Ikkyū tells us about himself in his poetry, but also how others understood his personality and behavior. This procedure will involve using stories from popular literature composed after his death—the *Tokugawa Tales*—which may not be precisely historically accurate, but they embody the spirit of the man in the popular imagination and probably reflect to some extent some historical truth. These tales are examples of Zen Buddhist hagiography.

To call these narratives hagiography does not imply that they are false or fabricated to fool readers. The contents of these narratives to people outside of a religious tradition often sound fanciful and untrue, although believers within a tradition often find inspiration from the deeds of the holy figures. Hagiography is not true in a factual sense and not something verified by eyewitnesses. It is what Paul Ricoeur calls "truth of manifestation."[2] Ricoeur implies that the narrative simply shows itself without the possibility of being empirically proven. Although the narratives cannot be verified in any scientific way, or falsified for that matter, they are legitimate forms of historical writing that could be called sacred history. The hagiographical writer provides readers of these stories with knowledge, a gift that is meaningful to readers. Like any historian, the

---

2. Ricoeur, *Figuring the Sacred*, 36.

hagiographical writer interprets data, but does not do so in an unbiased and objective historical account.[3] There is a problematic bifurcation between hagiography and history, however, because the former pertains to faith, while history occurs in space that is devoid of the sacred. There is a richness and openness to these texts that reflect a particular time and place, but they are not static because texts change as they are redacted and rewritten.[4] There are instances when hagiography, a bridge between the past and the present, is composed during periods of historical transformation that reflect socio-political, institutional, or theological/doctrinal changes. These narratives function as teaching tools, inspirational motifs, and edifying tales. It can also be affirmed that the narratives about Ikkyū embody a strong element of play, a topic that will be addressed later in this chapter.

MADNESS AND ENLIGHTENMENT

After his enlightenment experience in 1420, Ikkyū's erratic behavior began to exhibit itself. Having accompanied his master Kasō Sōdon to a ceremony at Daitokuji at which all present were properly dressed according to the pomp and splendor of the occasion, Ikkyū wore his usual black habit and worn-out straw sandals. His master turned to him and said, "Why aren't you more dignified?" Ikkyū replied, "I am the only one who makes the crowd colorful."[5] As this example illustrates, Ikkyū refused to conform to the norm for a Zen Buddhist monk. He rejected the regimentation and discipline of monastic life. It was during the period between 1426–32 that he probably left religious life, became a layman, married, and fathered a son.[6] Although it is not unusual for a monk to leave the Zen order, Ikkyū returned to the Zen fold in the 1430s to become famous for his wild style of Zen.

Since Zen Buddhism had deviated from the true spirit and practice of its predecessors, Ikkyū assumed an unusual and critical posture toward his own enlightenment. After Kasō confirmed his enlightenment experience and wrote a document attesting to its authenticity, Ikkyū refused to accept it and threw it on the ground. Kasō entrusted it to a woman who

---

3. Monge, "Saints, Truth," 7–22.
4. Smith, "Devotion, Critique," 30–31.
5. Arntzen, *Ikkyū Sōjun*, 17.
6. Sanford, *Zen-Man Ikkyū*, 32.

gave it to a minister of the imperial court for safekeeping, which was to be given to Ikkyū when he had become humbler. While staying with the minister entrusted with his seal of enlightenment, Ikkyū acknowledged to him the reasons for his dismay and distress concerning the Buddhism of his time. Asking the minister for the document, Ikkyū tore it to pieces and burned it.[7] Ikkyū was not only indignantly upset about the degenerate condition of the Rinzai sect of this time, but he also wanted to divorce himself from such a religious body and its corrupt practice of selling such documents.

In addition to being critical of giving seals of enlightenment, Ikkyū was also disparaging of fellow monks. As mentioned in an earlier chapter, in his prose-poem work *Skeletons*, he has a dream after falling asleep at a remote temple that elicits an awareness of death and life. The liminal nature of dreams enables one to see both the real and the unreal. Ikkyū dreams that he sees many skeletons at the back of the temple. A skeleton tells Ikkyū that it is his destiny to become like them—a skeleton. It is no accident that Ikkyū encounters skeletons at the rear of the temple because they are alive monks, who are spiritually dead from his perspective.[8] Ikkyū is making his case that Buddhism and its monks are dead and/or corrupt. Ikkyū elucidates further those monks are devoid of wisdom and find *zazen* (seated meditation) boring, their practice of meditation is superficial, they suffer from pride, and they are nothing more than ordinary people in priestly garments. Religious practices such as funerals are in vain because a cremated body turns into a cloud that is blown by the wind, creating an image of the temporary and transient nature of life.[9]

In his poems, Ikkyū revealed to his readers that he comprehended his enlightenment and poetic creativity within an ancient tradition. He viewed himself as the sole, living transmitter of an ancient, wild, bizarre type of Zen. A poem on a *chinso* (portrait painting) of Ikkyū in his hand in Shuonan confirms that he thought that he was the lone transmitter of an authentic Zen tradition: "For thirty years the weight on my shoulders has been heavy; Alone I have borne the burden of Sung-yuan's Zen."[10] His other poems are also informative in this respect when one views the predecessors that he praises. In some poems, he praises Xutang, a monk despised by others of his time and detached from his status as a monk.

7. Arntzen, *Ikkyū Sōjun*, 6.
8. Blyth, "Ikkyū's 'Skeletons,'" 122.
9. Arntzen, *Ikkyū Sōjun*, 6.
10. Blyth, "Ikkyū's 'Skeletons,'" 122.

Xutang, who served Ikkyū as an image for himself, was solely concerned with the correct transmission of Zen.

Ikkyū's poems praising Puke (Japanese: Chinshu Fuke) are especially interesting and instructive. Puke, a famous Tang dynasty eccentric, was noted for his madness and frequent use of a bell that he would wave in the air or ring violently in someone's ear after having surreptitiously slipped on a victim. In the forty-seventh chapter of the *Linji lu*, a story about the death of Puke is given that relates that he climbed into a casket and had it nailed shut over him. The crowd that had gathered opened it and found it empty, although they could, however, hear the faint sound of a bell. It is possible to grasp these poems of praise for former Zen masters by Ikkyū as composed from a sense of obligation and written without very strong convictions.[11] If one takes into consideration Ikkyū's critical stance toward the decadent Zen of his time and the personal characteristics of his subjects, it is more likely that Ikkyū intended to exalt previous monks who exhibited the same characteristics that he thought he possessed.

In his poems of praise for former monks, Ikkyū was accomplishing two things: he was exalting those personal characteristics that he thought should be preserved; and he viewed himself, for instance, as carrying on Puke's tradition of madness. Ikkyū writes about Puke:

> Arguing first the Bright Head, then the Dark,
> That Zen-fellow's tricks fooled them all.
> Now, blowing up again, the same old madman,
>   A sensual youth, howling at the door.[12]

The initial two lines of this poem are about Puke, whereas the next two lines are autobiographical in nature.

Moreover, Ikkyū understood himself as a madman. He called himself "Crazycloud," and he viewed himself as Linji's blind donkey. The latter was a reference to the great Chinese master Linji's reference about the transmission of his teachings to a dull monk at the end of his life. By assuming the role of the madman, Ikkyū was assuming the burden of preserving authentic Zen. Since he alone was keeping the genuine Zen tradition alive, Ikkyū was a "wanton madman stirring up a storm."[13] He alone had the courage and fortitude to preserve the Zen tradition and fight the corruption of the current leaders and their followers. By praising

11. Sanford, *Zen-Man Ikkyū*, 139.
12. Sanford, *Zen-Man Ikkyū*, 148.
13. Sanford, *Zen-Man Ikkyū*, 130.

Zen masters who exhibited odd behavior, by referring to himself as crazy, and by engaging in bizarre behavior, Ikkyū wanted to call attention to himself and his message. It appeared that he was successful because others certainly thought that he was mad. In fact, Ikkyū's master was aware that others thought that he was crazy. When he was asked who would maintain and transmit his teachings, Kasō said, "Although you say he's crazy, it will be Ikkyū."[14]

The composers of the *Tokugawa Tales* certainly thought that Ikkyū was crazy, which is evident when people in the tales identify him as mad. There is a story that relates that Ikkyū happened to spy a woman with her skirt up, while he was crossing a river. Ikkyū stopped, making three reverential bows toward her sexual parts. Meanwhile, some men saw this odd behavior and concluded that the monk must be mad.[15] If Ikkyū were an ordinary person, his action would have been considered a bit odd. But since he was a monk, his behavior was mad and out of character for someone of his position in life. From Ikkyū's point of view, his action was entirely consistent. He wrote in an autobiographical vein, "Among fools and idiots, a free spirit."[16] Thus Ikkyū understood himself as totally free from all constraints, a free, flowing breeze among the fools and idiots of ordinary existence.

MADNESS AND THE WORLD

While residing for a few days in the province of Kai, Ikkyū decided to investigate a mountain and its ruins located within an area called "Hell." Apparently, Ikkyū's reputation as a witty speaker preceded him, and a local lord wanted to encounter the monk on the path to the mountain. Not letting Ikkyū know that he was aware of the monk's identity, the lord asked the monk to tell him about heaven and hell. To the outraged lord, Ikkyū replied, "Oh, shit!" Thereupon, the lord instructed his attendants to tie up the foul-mouthed priest so that he learned to keep his mouth shut. After Ikkyū was pummeled to the ground and had his arms tied behind his back, he turned to the lord and said, "Now see what is meant by 'Hell.'" The lord descended from his horse and unbound the monk. Then, he insisted that Ikkyū mount the horse and accompany him to his

---

14. Arntzen, *Ikkyū Sōjun*, 17.
15. Sanford, *Zen-Man Ikkyū*, 238.
16. Sanford, *Zen-Man Ikkyū*, 145.

manor for a day of feasting. After eating all sorts of delicacies, Ikkyū told the lord, "And this is what I call heaven."[17] This story from the *Tokugawa Tales* illustrates that the world is a combination of heaven and hell, pleasure and suffering, joy and sorrow. But neither opposite is permanent nor possesses any self-nature (*svabhāva*). Thus, the world—heaven and hell—and its contents are all empty (*śūnyata*).

From the perspective of enlightenment, there is no heaven or hell because each is empty. Therefore, hell is paradise: "For the wise, who know this, there is no sin in any action."[18] Ikkyū indulged himself fully in the sensuous pleasures of the world and committed acts that were contrary to monastic regulations. He was, for instance, a frequent visitor at brothels where he exercised his passions. Since the world has "become a kingdom of beasts" and the Japanese nation was "lost to lechery," the *bodhisattva* must venture where the people were to be found enjoying themselves. If the *bodhisattva* turned his back to the world or remained aloof from lechery, he was far removed from Buddhahood. A line from one of his poems summarizes Ikkyū's attitude: "one trip to a brothel brings Great Wisdom."[19] For Ikkyū to know the nature of the world's delusions, he was convinced that a person needed to enter direct contact with them and experience them firsthand. In other words, for a monk to remain in solitude within the walls of his monastery involved residing in a state of ignorance.

Besides his patronage of brothels, Ikkyū was also known as a frequent patron of the local wine shops. In an autobiographical poem, he admitted, "Racing back and forth from brothel to wine shop."[20] Although Ikkyū rewarded his taste buds with sake, he remained in control of his wit. According to a *Tokugawa Tale*, having heard what a quick-witted fellow Ikkyū was, a monk decided to put him to a test. When this monk arrived at Daitokuji Ikkyū was not present because he had gone to a local wine shop and had gotten very drunk. A temple acolyte went to tell Ikkyū about his visitor, but he found the master too inebriated to stand. On a second attempt to retrieve Ikkyū, the acolyte witnessed the master snore and fall over backward with his bodily appendages sprawling every which way. The acolyte related his dilemma to the waiting monk back at the temple, who decided to visit Ikkyū at the wine shop. Slipping quietly up to where

17. Sanford, *Zen-Man Ikkyū*, 259.
18. Sanford, *Zen-Man Ikkyū*, 241.
19. Sanford, *Zen-Man Ikkyū*, 156.
20. Sanford, *Zen-Man Ikkyū*, 131.

Ikkyū was lying in a drunken stupor, the monk dragged Ikkyū into a sitting position and screamed a question into his ear, essentially asking Ikkyū to tell him in ordinary language why Bodhidharma came from the West. Without hesitation and quite loudly, Ikkyū replied, "You're what's common and ordinary." Thereupon, Ikkyū flopped over on his back, leaving the monk speechless, full of wonder, full of admiration, and acknowledging that the drunken Ikkyū must indeed be a living Buddha.[21]

Ikkyū's bizarre antics were a form of *upāya* (skillful means), a form of instructive pedagogy. When exercising *upāya* the teacher must take into consideration the level of awareness of his audience, their spiritual progress, and their cultural environment to fit his message to their level of comprehension. Thus, one notices Ikkyū playing the role of a madman in the streets of Sakai, by brandishing a long, genuine-looking sword with an elegant hilt and scabbard. The local folk would stop the crazy monk to point out to him that a sword was the proper possession of a warrior and not of a monk. When accosted in this manner Ikkyū would withdraw his sword from its scabbard and show that the blade was merely wooden, much like fake jewelry used to enhance someone's appearance. Ikkyū equates his false sword with false wisdom, neither of which has any value to give or to take life.[22]

Besides the false wisdom and delusory appearances of the world, Ikkyū's madness was also directed to common religious practices. The most outrageous, humorous, and shocking example of Ikkyū's madness directed toward an ordinary religious ceremony can be found in a tale from the Tokugawa writers about a Buddhist eye-opening ceremony. Having built a statue of the *bodhisattva* Jizo at Seki, the people discussed who they should invite to perform the eye-opening ceremony (a ritual means of giving life to a statue by painting in its eyes as the final part of the ceremony). Since Ikkyū was the most famous monk in the area, they agreed to invite him to perform the ceremony. Ikkyū accepted their invitation; since he planned to make a pilgrimage to the Kanto region, he would be able to stop at the town and perform the ceremony. The people of Seki were overjoyed at having such an eminent monk perform the religious ceremony, and they made meticulous preparations for the big event. When Ikkyū arrived the townsfolk excitedly ran to meet him, but he approached dispassionately the happy throng. The monk was

21. Sanford, *Zen-Man Ikkyū*, 260–62.
22. Sanford, *Zen-Man Ikkyū*, 38.

shown the beautifully decorated statue, and everyone edged toward the front and stood on tiptoe to see this important religious event. Climbing up the ladder to the statue, Ikkyū stood in front of the image, and to everyone's utter astonishment he proceeded to urinate on Jizo's head. With all the offerings and statue thoroughly soaked with urine, Ikkyū announced the end of the ceremony and walked off rapidly toward the east. The townsfolk were literally outraged. They proclaimed, "What kind of filthy outrage is this? That skinny priest is out of his mind. The gall of him, taking a leak on our important *bodhisattva*; it makes me boil. After him! Don't let him get away." While some people angrily gave chase, some lay nuns cursed Ikkyū for his sacrilege, began to wash the statue, replaced the offerings, and asked Jizo to forgive them. As they worked to clean the venue, the women, however, began to have second thoughts about washing the monk's urine off the statue. They began to think that there must be some profound, mysterious reason for Ikkyū's actions. Forgetting their earlier outrage and disgust and having rethought the significance of Ikkyū's action, they decided to catch the monk and ask him to return to repeat the ceremony. While Ikkyū was boarding a ferry, the women caught up with him and related their request. Ikkyū pleaded inconvenience, but he gave the women his own loincloth, which he told them was very old and could cure ills instantly if tied around the head of the statue. The women carried out Ikkyū's instructions, even though they feared committing a sacrilege; they did not want to miss the opportunity of seeing a miracle.[23] Ikkyū's sacrilegious act was certainly outrageous behavior, but it is consistent with his wild style of Zen and within the tradition of Zen iconoclasm in which the Buddha, idols, scriptures, and ego must be destroyed.

What is especially interesting is the reaction of the people, which moves from outrage to wonder to reflection. Since the action was so disgusting, especially for a religious leader, it must have some deeper significance. But what could this be? The townsfolk never discovered the deeper significance of Ikkyū's action because they were too attached to their fine statue and sunk in their own superstitious ignorance. Ikkyū succeeded in outraging, astonishing, and getting the people to reflect on his behavior, but they were not prepared to understand that the statue was a meaningless object.

---

23. Sanford, *Zen-Man Ikkyū*, 291–95.

Ikkyū continued his humorous ruse and the folly of his ways by giving the credulous women his allegedly illness curing, miracle making, and ancient loincloth. Ikkyū not only gets the first laugh, but he also gets the final one. He uses the seriousness of the situation to project his joke, but the simple townsfolk never catch the punch line of his humor. The occasion was too serious for Ikkyū. His madness cut through the façade of seriousness in which people were attached to their object. Furthermore, the statue of Jizo symbolizes order and the urine of the madman represents disorder and impurity. After he has broken down order, the lay nuns are uncertain as to what is impure and pure. By his outrageous antics, Ikkyū has upset the boundaries between pure and impure, order and disorder. Thus, the old categories have been called into question.

MADNESS AND THE EROTIC

Ikkyū's relationship to the leaders of the Rinzai order was very critical. He attacked, for instance, Yōsō Sōi (1376–1459), who inherited the leadership of Daitokuji on the death of Kasō, for being a false and deceitful monk who sold the Zen *dharma* (teachings) for profit and fame. In a series of vitriolic poems, Ikkyū called the older monk a leper, a pervert, and a betrayer of his spiritual predecessors. Ikkyū was also critical of the decadent Zen of his time. Ikkyū referred to the "ornamented chairs, wooden floors," which were metaphors for a Zen of fame and profit, or a false Zen.[24] And beneath the false exterior of Zen lies corruption: "Under the saffron robe, a spirit soaked with the stink of leprosy."[25] It appears that later in his life, Ikkyū had qualms concerning the possible devastating effect of his vitriolic poems. In "Confession of a Malicious Tongue," he pondered, "With spears of words how many men have I murdered."[26] Although he had reservations later in life, Ikkyū's vitriolic poems of Buddhism and its leaders were reformist in spirit, since Zen Buddhism had deviated from the true spirit and practice of its eminent predecessors.

Ikkyū's unusual behavior for a Buddhist monk, which began after his full enlightenment, continued into his old age. While leader of his religious community of monks, Ikkyū had a love affair with Mori, a blind

---

24. Arntzen, *Ikkyū Sōjun*, 31.
25. Sanford, *Zen-Man Ikkyū*, 136.
26. Keene, *Appreciations of Japanese Culture*, 62.

singer, having initially met her when he was seventy-seven years old. She was the subject of many of Ikkyū's most emotionally moving poems:

> With Mori, I am lost in a garden of dreams,
> Pillowed on drifts of white plum blossom—the essence of faith
> Drinking my fill of a pure, sweet, but shallow stream.
>
> What new song can I sing to the moon at dawn?[27]

Although Ikkyū expressed his profuse love for Mori in this poem and numerous other pieces, there was a pervasive melancholic tone to the above poem. The plum blossom was not a symbol of spring because it better expressed the lingering of winter with its blossoms that bloomed so early as to be out of season.[28] Due to his advanced years, Ikkyū's love affair was, like the plum blossoms, out of season, and he could only drink from a shallow stream of love and not a deep one because his life was ending. Sometimes his poems about Mori were erotic, which manifested the madness of his love.

The erotic is a type of play that is associated with anticipation and tension, because the erotic builds up like a never-ending sexual tease that is never fully satisfied as evident by its repetitive character. What is operating in the human mind is its capability for imaginative fantasy, a form of play that arouses an individual to heights without limit, enhancing one's experience in the present moment to something more wonderful, rich, and creative. Fantasy is associated with anticipation that in turn relates to the promise of culminating in sensual pleasure. Being aroused by fantasy and anticipation, the erotic manifests features such as emotion, mutual arousal, touching and being touched, and sharing flesh. Eroticism is excessive because it pushes beyond social and moral limits, which is certainly the case for a Zen monk who has vowed to adhere to a prescribed set of rules. In the case of Ikkyū, eroticism is doubly radical and antisocial because it breaks down normal patterns of social and monastic behavior that is manifested by nakedness, a dispossession of the self, and revealing of one's flesh.

Ikkyū's eroticism is not only repetitive but is also marginal because it marks a being on the periphery of society and monastic life. The erotic marks the limits of human experience, and yet it is potentially subversive because it is associated with transgression, insatiability, and ceaseless

27. Sanford, *Zen-Man Ikkyū*, 167.
28. Sanford, *Zen-Man Ikkyū*, 186.

desire. The marginality of Ikkyū's eroticism also suggests liminality, a neither here nor there, a something in between being a monk or not. This liminal nature invites inversion, experimentation, and a new mode of thinking. By playing the roles of madman and the erotic figure, Ikkyū creates a counter-world, an upside-down world.

Besides his loving relationship to the blind Mori, Ikkyū was concerned throughout his life with the plight of others, his relationship to other people, and his relationship to his Buddhist predecessors and current leaders. He composed poems, for instance, about starvation in 1461 and about the plight of men being hung for crimes committed against the state. He was prepared to risk, by means of his actions and words, everything to assist others. Ikkyū confessed that "poetry paves the road to hell."[29] Unless the *bodhisattva* was prepared to descend to hell and to forsake all, he could never save others, an attitude that justified his patronage of brothels and consumption of rice wine.

A *Tokugawa Tale* humorously illustrated Ikkyū's compassion for a young couple. The young, prosperous, successful, married proprietors of a wine shop lived happily together. Their lone misfortune was that they were unable to have children. They visited many religious shrines and temples to ask for the blessings of the Buddha but without any success. Finally, resigned to their fate to be childless, they obtained a cat and showered their feline with all their affection. After a brief illness, the cat died to the consternation and despair of the young, loving couple. In their profuse distress, the couple approached Ikkyū to ask him if he would perform funeral rites for their departed animal in the hope that it would become a Buddha in its next life. Ikkyū was captivated by their tearful story, the strangeness of their request, and the oddity of the deceased being a cat. Ikkyū assured the bereaved couple that he would perform a fine service and see that the animal received the seed of Buddhahood. Instructing the couple to stand and listen, Ikkyū began to chant:

> While you were alive,
> You caught many mice
> And reaped human kindness as a reward
> And lived a contented life.
> Now, whatever you're born as, be sure to catch a Buddha.
> Amen.[30]

---

29. Sanford, *Zen-Man Ikkyū*, 179.
30. Sanford, *Zen-Man Ikkyū*, 268–71.

Before Ikkyū could leave, the couple told him that his words had led them to enlightenment.[31] The message of this narrative is that Ikkyū used the dead cat as a vehicle to spiritually awaken the young couple. This incident was a manifestation of his compassion for their spiritual hollowness and misplaced love. It was also performed in the spirit of play.[32] Thus, Ikkyū plays with the grieving couple to bring them to an awareness of the truth.

In a world in which social position, fame, and wealth were important to people, Ikkyū literally sought to cut through the delusory appearance to the truth. According to the hagiographic *Chronicle of Ikkyū* by Bokusai, Ikkyū paraded through the streets of Kyoto waving a human skull that was attached to the end of a long bamboo pole. This bizarre gesture and hideous sight were his way of wishing others best wishes for the coming year. Ikkyū's creative skill as a teacher of Zen Buddhism can be noted in the linguistic coincidence between the terms *medetō* (best wishes) and *me-detō* (with eyes popped out), the latter obviously referring to the eyeless and open sockets of the skull.[33] Expressing the truth of pain, suffering, impermanence, and death, skulls and skeletons are important motifs in Ikkyū's writings. "The Skeleton," a title of one of his prose works, is a valid symbol of the living who are more spiritually dead than alive. In his work entitled *Skeletons*, Ikkyū raises the question "Who among us is more than a skeleton?" Since the world is populated by skeletons and since the *bodhisattva* must enter relationships with them to instruct them, one must become a madman to communicate with those who are already spiritually dead.

MADNESS AND MEANING

Ikkyū's actions appear to be the random behavior of an insane, often obscene person without apparent meaning. He is considered mad by others because his actions do not manifest to them any apparent intention. Taking into consideration his enlightened state, his understanding of his role in the Zen tradition, and the personal acknowledgment of his madness, Ikkyū's madness is not without meaning.

---

31. Sanford, *Zen-Man Ikkyū*, 93–94.
32. Sanford, *Zen-Man Ikkyū*, 39–40.
33. Sanford, *Zen-Man Ikkyū*, 203; Blyth, "Ikkyū's 'Skeletons,'" 116.

Madness is a mark of Ikkyū's freedom and transcendence. A symbol of Ikkyū's freedom is the wind. In *Skeletons*, he writes, "Cast aside the idea of self-existence, simply entrust yourself to the world's vagrant winds and go where they take you."[34] Like the wind, the mad monk is free to act in unpredictable and tumultuous ways. He is free to wander alone or to seek the company of others in the city streets, wine shops, or brothels. He is free to fall in love with a blind singer or study Buddhist scriptures in solitude. He can express his emotions or hide them in his poetry. Not ensnared by the world, not encumbered by society, and unbound by monastic decorum, he can act mad and practice his wild Zen in total freedom.

Ikkyū's freedom and madness place him outside the confining structure of the world and the social patterns of society. I have given numerous examples where Ikkyū acts contrary to social and Zen monastic norms, even taking into consideration the odd behavior of previous Zen masters, which means that he does not follow the conventions of established order. His radical freedom, which is based on his madness, breaks down all order. Thus, Crazycloud is a social misfit and demonstrates contempt for social and monastic status. On the one hand, he plays the impostor by carrying a wooden sword and arrogates the dignity of the warrior. On the other hand, Ikkyū gives up the dignity of his monastic position to help others. Finally, his insane actions indicate the absurdities of conventional social life and corrupt monastic life.

Ikkyū's madness is ontological because the distinction between opposites is transcended. He can compose poems about heaven and hell, enlightenment and delusion, beautiful blossoms and his own penis, lust and compassion, humans and fleas, and life and death. His transcendence of phenomenal dichotomies enables him to write about and lament that humans are fornicating like animals in broad daylight and still indulge his sense pleasures in wine and sex.

The antics of the mad monk are often not without humor, even though the victims of his humor often fail to laugh or appreciate it. Why would they fail to laugh? Conrad Hyers makes an informative assertion: "In humor there is transcendence and freedom. The free man is the one who is free to laugh and to see things in the light of laughter."[35] The ordinary folk unable to laugh are the ones who are benighted and bound by their lack of true insight. Ikkyū's humor that is grounded in his madness

---

34. Sanford, *Zen-Man Ikkyū*, 204; Blyth, "Ikkyū's 'Skeletons,'" 119.
35. Hyers, *Zen and the Comic Spirit*, 126.

gives his Zen a dynamic quality rather than the static type of Zen he criticized in many poems.

MADNESS AND PLAY

The madness of Ikkyū is playful. He plays with lay women in the eye-opening episode by giving them his ancient, illness curing loincloth. He playfully counteracts the magical flames created by a *yamabushi* (a member of a magico-religious fraternity of mountain ascetics) by urinating all over the flames;[36] and he plays with the monk who puts him to the test, even though Ikkyū was totally drunk. He plays with townsfolk while carrying his wooden sword and the skull attached to a long bamboo pole. D. T. Suzuki elucidates the nature of play in Zen, as he writes, "For playfulness comes out of empty nothingness, and where there is something, this cannot take place. Zen comes out of absolute nothingness and knows how to be playful."[37] To be able to play is to be free, whereas to work is to be limited and confined. The free and voluntary nature of play is a source of joy and amusement.[38]

The play of Ikkyū is neither foolish nor disinterested. He enters play voluntarily. His play manifests meaning, even though it is the play of a madman and possesses an irrational character. The play of Ikkyū manifests his transcendence of earthly dichotomies and absolute freedom. Huizinga writes, "Play lies outside the antithesis of wisdom and folly, and equally outside those of truth and falsehood, good and evil."[39]

The play that Ikkyū practices, however, is different from ordinary play explained by Huizinga in his work. Ikkyū's play is unique because of its mad quality. His play differs from that identified and explained by Huizinga for the following reasons: It is not an interlude in his life and does not have the character of disinterestedness; it is not limited and played out within certain limits of time and space; and it does not create order. The mad play of Ikkyū is grounded in his compassion for human beings; it is beyond the confines of time and place because it can take place in the streets, brothels, monastery, in poetry, and at any time. It seeks to create disorder rather than order associated with ordinary play.

---

36. Sanford, *Zen-Man Ikkyū*, 280–83.
37. Suzuki, *Sengai*, 7.
38. Caillois, *Man, Play, and Games*, 6.
39. Huizinga, *Homo Ludens*, 6.

By madly playing with others, Ikkyū's actions express his understanding of human existence and the world. Ikkyū's mad antics are a strong indication that Buddhist practice can represent an attempt to realize enlightenment through ludism.[40]

PLAY AND LAUGHTER

Joining the monastery where Mazu was the master, the monk Shuilao asked the master, "What is the purpose of the coming from the West?" Mazu commanded the monk to bow down. As Shuilao was bowing, Mazu gave him a kick. Thereupon, Shuilao suddenly had a great awakening. Standing up and clapping his hands together, he laughed aloud, expressing how exhilarating the experience was by stating, "How wonderful! A hundred thousand samādhis and an infinite number of mysterious truths all have their origin on the tip of a hair!" Bowing respectfully, he withdrew from the presence of the master. He later said to others: "From the time when I received Master Ma's kick until now, I cannot stop laughing."[41] As this story suggests, to become awakened means that one is free to laugh. Moreover, to find something humorous in a situation expresses insight and liberation. This episode is indicative of the close connection between laughter, humor, the comic, play, and Zen Buddhism, which serves as the theme of this chapter and another example of the role of play in the Zen tradition.

Previous chapters have made it clear that truth in Zen Buddhism is not something that a person can teach to another person no matter how much talent a person possesses. Since truth is not a matter of conveying information, a learner cannot strictly learn the truth like a person can assemble a table or a car engine because the truth is something that a person already possesses and knows. It is more a matter of re-recognizing and re-realizing the truth in a person's possession. Even when a person realizes the truth that is previously present, it cannot be communicated to others. The Chinese Chan master Yunmen warned:

> There are those who, upon seeing an old monk opening his mouth to speak, put his special words into their own mouths to chew them. They are like flies struggling to gobble up manure.[42]

---

40. LeFleur, *Kama of Words*, 54–58.
41. Poceksi, *Record of Mazu*, 55.
42. Luk, *Ch'an and Zen Teachings*, 2:189–90.

Those who are like flies think that the truth can be abstractly realized or accumulated like books. In fact, the truth can only be realized existentially, implying that knowing cannot be separated from being. When truth dawns, a person does not see and experience any specific thing differently; it is rather that a person sees and experiences everything differently.

A major obstacle to realizing the truth is seriousness. By taking oneself or one's situation too seriously, a person increases craving and anxiety. Being overly serious is also a manifestation of clinging to self and grasping after pleasures that one mistakenly assumes will alleviate one's anxiety or satisfy one's cravings. If seriousness results in attachment and bondage, the Zen message is the following: be serious but not too serious. It is important to learn to laugh at the folly of the craving self. The Chan master Xuefeng said, "The whole earth is one eye of a monk; where will you defecate?"[43] If a person cannot laugh at the human condition, this overly serious person remains in a state of bondage. In fact, Zen means never to stop laughing.[44]

THE COMIC AND HUMOR

The comic is something that teaches us nothing, but it does function to call attention to the ambiguity in all things. It recalls for us the finiteness and fallibility of everything. The Zen Buddhist monk and poet Ryōkan (1758–1831) captures these aspects of the comic in a poem: "I've forgotten my begging bowl, but no one would steal it no one would steal it—how sad for my begging bowl."[45] From the Zen perspective, the comic represents an example of *upāya* (skillful means), serving as a device to bring Buddha-nature into conscious awareness and existential realization even when encountering the absurd. Yunmen, for instance, said, "Your body is the size of a coconut, yet you can open such a big mouth."[46] The juxtaposition of a person's body and mouth is both absurd and comic.

There is an intimate connection between the comic and the absurd. Rather than representing despair, alienation, or anxiety, absurdity manifests the inadequacy of reason, an important theme in Zen with its

43. Cleary, *Blue Cliff Record*, 38.
44. Blyth, *Zen and Zen Classics*, 2:95.
45. Watson, *Ryōkan*, 29.
46. Cleary, *Blue Cliff Record*, 80.

emphasis on intuitive insight. The inadequacy of reason and the comic is brought to life with an odd exchange between two Zen characters. Zhaozhou asked, for instance, Master Huanzhong, "What is the essence of wisdom?" The master repeated the question, as if an echo. Zhaozhou burst into laughter and walked out. The next day finding Zhaozhou sweeping the yard, the master demanded, "What is the essence of wisdom?" Zhaozhou dropped his broom, burst out laughing, and clapped his hands in delight.[47]

There are times when the perception of absurdity precipitates laughter. While a *roshi* lay dying, a senior monk asked him if he, for instance, had any final words of advice or instruction for his monks. The master slowly opened his eyes and in a weak voice whispered, "Tell them truth is like a river." The senior monk passed these words to others, but a young monk did not understand the words. The senior monk returned to the master and asked what he meant by saying "Truth is like a river." Slowly the master opened his eyes and in a weak voice whispered, "Ok, truth is not like a river."[48] This type of anecdote suggests that absurdity is a matter of taking things as they are. To embrace absurdity is akin to accepting life and celebrating it.

The comic plays with absurdity, and it revels in its irrationality. For instance, master Baoche was asked about the nature of Zen. He stood up, pivoted around his stick, raised up a leg, and then asked in return, "Do you understand the message?" When a monk did not understand, he struck him with his stick.[49] The comic uses absurdity for its own ends, which is illustrated in the narrative of Puhua, who received a premonition that his end was near. He announced to the people that he would go the next day to the eastern gate of the town and die there. The entire community went in a procession behind him and assembled outside the city wall to pay their final respects. Puhua then announced, "A funeral today would not be in accord with the blue crow [a mythological bird], I will pass away tomorrow at the southern gate." People followed him again the next day, but he announced, "It would be more auspicious to leave by the western gate tomorrow."[50] On the third day fewer people came; he then decided on the north gate instead of on the following day. On the fourth day, he picked up his own coffin and carried it out of the north gate.

47. Ogata, *Transmission of the Lamp*, 2:9.170.
48. Hyers, *Zen and the Comic Spirit*, 103.
49. Sasaki, *Record of Linji*, 54.
50. Cleary, *Blue Cliff Record*, 310.

Shaking his bell, he entered the coffin and died.[51] This tale illustrates that out of absurdity can come an unexpectedly different way of perceiving and responding to life in a humorous way.

Humor functions in a variety of ways. It functions as a technique for precipitating understanding, and it works as an expression of new levels of insight and freedom. An encounter between two monks illustrates a way that humor can operate to improve understanding. Yangshan asked Sanshang, "What is your name?" Sansheng said "Hug." Yangshan said, "Hug? That's me." Sansheng said, "My name is Huiran." Yangshan laughed.[52] The commentator calls attention to the fact that Sansheng's meaning was beyond Yangshan's words because the words do not fall within the realm of common sense; this makes them difficult to comprehend. Then, the commentator concentrates his remarks on the laugh when he says, "Yangshan laughed; there was both provisional and true, both illumination and function. Because he was crystal clear in every respect, he functioned with complete freedom. This laugh was not the same as Yantou's; in Yantou's laugh there was poison, but in this laugh the pure wind blows chill for all eternity."[53] This encounter sheds light on laughter itself and suggests different motivations prompting laughter.

Humor also functions to reveal the ego as a mask that one wears to hide one's identity. A modern Zen master named Sogaku (1871–1961) instructed his students to be great fools because a small fool is an ordinary person, but a great fool is a Buddha.[54] Moreover, humor enables one to break down identities and distinctions. This function is illustrated nicely by an anecdote about Ikkyū when he was invited to a banquet given by a wealthy patron. Ikkyū arrived at the banquet dressed in beggar's garb, and he was sent away by his host, who did not recognize him. Ikkyū returned later wearing his purple ceremonial robe and was welcomed by his host. Upon entering, he took off his purple robe, revealing the beggar's robe underneath. He said, "Apparently, you did not invite me, but the purple robe!"[55] By means of his sense of humor, Ikkyū can leap into play, demonstrating a freedom to play and to laugh that is embodied in humor.

51. Cleary, *Blue Cliff Record*, 311–12.
52. Cleary, *Blue Cliff Record*, 311–12.
53. Cleary, *Blue Cliff Record*, 311–12.
54. Stryk and Ikemoto, *Zen Poems, Prayers*, 98.
55. Sanford, *Zen-Man Ikkyū*, 28.

The iconoclastic spirit of Zen monks like Ikkyū implies that anything can become a legitimate object of laughter. This type of attitude presupposes that to take things too seriously is to be dependent on them and to be caught up in a cycle of attachment. This is certainly not true of Qilin when he enters the Buddha Hall in the monastery and scolds the image of the two *bodhisattvas* Mañjuśrī and Samantabhadra, saying, "You are both devils." Then he would brandish a wooden sword, pretending to spar with them, and shout, "Surrender."[56] The comic iconoclasm is grounded in a perception about the uncommon nature of ordinary things. Yunmen is asked, for instance, to expound about enlightenment. He responds by saying, "Pulling a plough in the morning and carrying a rake home in the evening."[57] These types of everyday activities possess a mysterious quality that is called *yūgen* (deep reserve) in Zen aesthetics. Even acknowledging the existence of this mysterious depth to the ordinary, there is a spirit of humorous acceptance and joyfulness about the mundane. Once when all the monks associated with Master Daizhu were tilling in the fields, for instance, there was one monk, upon hearing the dinner drum, at once raised his spade and gave out a hearty laugh and went off. Daizhu remarked: "What an intelligent fellow! This is the way to enter the Guanyin gate of truth." When he returned to the monastery, he sent for the monk and inquired, "What was the truth you saw a while ago when you heard the drum?" Answered the monk, "Nothing much, master. As I heard the dinner drum sound, I went back and had my meal." This time the master gave out a hearty laugh.[58] On the surface of this anecdote, there does not appear to be anything humorous here. However, the laughter evoked is that of appreciation for the little things of life, wonder at the ordinary, and acceptance for whatever is. There is no attempt here to superimpose one's own perspective or views about the way things should be.

The laughter of the monk provoked by hearing the dinner drum represents a participation in the immediacy and spontaneity of the present moment. This is manifested by the antics of Wangxia (eighth century), who was nicknamed Ink Wang because of his unconventional approach to art and his creative use of wine. When drunk, he would splatter ink on the surface, while laughing and singing. Then, he might kick it on or rub it on with his hands. Or he would dip his head in a container

---

56. Ogata, *Transmission of the Lamp*, 7:3.35.
57. Luk, *Ch'an and Zen Teachings*, 2:188.
58. Luk, *Ch'an and Zen Teachings*, 2:33.

of ink, and he would paint with his hair serving as a brush.[59] Laughter can also suddenly call an abrupt halt to following the wrong path. When Wen Zhenjing was asked, for instance, "Who is the Buddha?" he just laughed. The questioner was confounded: "I do not see why my question makes you laugh so." Wen replied, "I laugh at your attempt to get into the meaning by merely following the letter."[60] By grasping the point of the laughter, a person enters the genuine path to liberation. This suggests that there is a direct connection between laughter and enlightenment. Hsing-yen studied books, for instance, to no avail. He burned his books and became a wandering monk. While collecting grass one day at the ruins of a monastery, he picked up a broken tile and tossed it away. It struck a stalk of bamboo, making a ping sound. On hearing this, he was instantly awakened and began laughing heartily.[61]

From the perspective of Zen, laughter is a useful tool because it functions to debunk pride. For example, Zhaozhou was asked what he thought was the most important principle of Zen. He abruptly excused himself, saying, "I must now go pee. Just think, such a trifling thing that I have to do in person."[62] Laughter also functions to deflate the ego. This is expressed nicely by a poem by Issa: "He who appears / Before you now are the toad / Of this thicket."[63] Laughter mocks the tendency to grasp and to cling to things. It also upsets hierarchies, and it then collapses them. A poem by Demaru illustrates this:

> Sitting like a Buddha,
> But bitten by mosquitoes
> In my Nirvana.[64]

Besides overcoming preexisting hierarchies, laughter conquers dualities. For instance, the Zen artist named Sengai made a sketch of a frog with the following inscription: "If by sitting in meditation one becomes a Buddha, then all frogs are Buddhas!"[65] In summary, laughter helps one to overcome egoism, helps to sever grasping at things within the world,

---

59. Hyers, *Zen and the Comic Spirit*, 49–50.
60. Suzuki, *Essays in Zen Buddhism Third Series*, 105.
61. Luk, *Ch'an and Zen Teachings*, 1:129.
62. Wu, *Golden Age of Zen*, 146.
63. Henderson, *Introduction to Haiku*, 142.
64. Blyth, *Haiku*, 4:49.
65. Suzuki, *Sengai*, 96.

controls one's desires, conquers ignorance, subverts social hierarchies, transcends dualities, and enables one to achieve insight into reality.

HUMOR AND PLAY

In his book on the element of play in culture, Huizinga remarks that humor can be placed in the category of non-seriousness.[66] The opposite is also true because seriousness is the ground of the comic. Without the precondition of seriousness, humor would be reduced to cynical contempt, which potentially leads to despair.[67]

To be in a condition of despair or to be unable to laugh is to be in a state of bondage. With a keen sense of humor, the Zen artist Sengai painted a puppy tied to a stake.[68] The puppy, a metaphor for humans, is yelping because it does not like being tied to the stake and wants to be free. On the other hand, Ikkyū uses somewhat different images to depict the bound condition of humans. In a poem entitled "Puppets" Ikkyū writes:

> Whole men appear on the stage.
> Some as kings, others as common peasants.
> We forget the strings, right in front of us.
> Dummies; talking about "the original man."[69]

Not only are humans ignorant, foolish, and morally imperfect, but they are also puppets, victims of social mores and manners who have lost their freedom. Humans are also like frogs: "They are pitiable, those at the bottom of wells, calling themselves great."[70] Ikkyū burlesques the folly and finitude of beings caught in their own limitations and captive to the mercy of unremitting, unseen, impersonal forces of karma. Moreover, beings are products of their own delusions: "so deep we cannot fathom their delusiveness."[71] To assist others toward liberation, Ikkyū's comic behavior functions as a visual *kōan* for others to discern or solve. Like a *kōan*, Ikkyū's behavior is paradoxical and absurd, which tends to destroy

---

66. In Miller, "Clown in Contemporary Art," 324.

67. See Hyers, *Zen and the Comic Spirit*; and his "Comic Profanation of the Sacred" and "Dialectic of the Sacred and the Comic," in *Holy Laughter*.

68. Blyth points to the vital connection between Zen and humor in *Oriental Humour*, 87–97.

69. Sanford, *Zen-Man Ikkyū*, 32.

70. Sanford, *Zen-Man Ikkyū*, 132.

71. Holmer, "Something about What Makes," 170.

our common-sense understanding of the world. The humor evoked by the antics of the Zen clown is radically anti-essentialist and seeks to subvert the sense of ego that holds one captive to this world. Ikkyū's antics also point toward freedom, but one must concentrate on the clown's *kōan* with all one's energy and finally resolve it by an intuitive insight. When pondering his antics it is permissible for a reader to laugh at the cavorting, gaiety, and insouciance of Ikkyū, which is true both before and after enlightenment.

Humor, like play, is an interlude within our lives, representing a pause that enables us to see the incongruities of life. Human existence is full of realized hopes and disappointments, of triumphs and frustrations, or rationality and irrationality, of periods of peace and violence, of certainties and contingencies. The individual who can respond with laughter to the incongruities of human existence demonstrates her wisdom and insight into the true nature of the way things are in truth. This is not to imply that humor is something objective, merely an emotion, or something stupid. Holmer accurately states that "one has to be in the game of life: then laughter is not stupid. It is stupidity within the game at which one can smile."[72] This statement can be applied to Ikkyū, who was immersed in the game of life, although the laughter of the Zen poet both is within existence and transcends it.

If Blyth is correct when he asserts that the great defect of humanity is precisely a deficiency of humor,[73] the comedian, then, helps us recover our humanity.[74] Ikkyū's bizarre antics remind us that we are deeply rooted in the world. Humans are contingent, imperfect, benighted beings tied to the tangible things of the world. Thus, the purpose of Ikkyū's clowning is to awaken us to our humanity and to recognition of our true status, which can function as a lever to shift our center of gravity and enable us to recognize our innate Buddha-nature. Although often beaten and defeated, the comic arises victorious and triumphs over the world's obstacles.[75] By assuming the role of a clown, Ikkyū vividly demonstrates his commitment to his fellow beings and brings them a visual message of hope.

The actions of Ikkyū, like those of a comedian, are excessive. The Zen comedian overdoes it, neglecting any rule of moderation. Ikkyū's New

72. Blyth, *Oriental Humour*, 201.
73. Blyth, *Oriental Humour*, 201.
74. Miller, "Clown in Contemporary Art," 327.
75. Vos, *Drama of Comedy*, 23.

Year's skull is a bizarre type of feast of fools where excessiveness reigns supreme. In his prose work entitled *Skeletons*, Ikkyū writes, "Beneath the skin of the person we fondle today, there, too, is a skeleton propping the flesh up."[76] If one could see beneath the flesh, one would recognize that one is an empty skeleton living among other skeletons playing behind the temple. Thus, Ikkyū's clowning actions are not superficial, because he recognizes the tragedy of life.

The excessive behavior of the Zen comedian and the laughter that it evokes are dangerous to the established order. Laughter breaks down boundaries and helps us put the events of our lives into a different and often more lucid perspective. In the hagiographic *Chronicle of Ikkyū* by Bokusai,[77] the biographer of Ikkyū, there is a story about the master's visit to the home of a parishioner where he found an old cow and composed a poem as a joke which he hung on the tip of the bovine's horn. The poem was a ruse about the cow's identity as a monk in its previous life. The cow died that evening. The following day its owner teased Ikkyū that he had eulogized the animal to death. Ikkyū responded with just a smile. Since Ikkyū's body and mind had fallen away with his enlightenment, it is not difficult to imagine a smile like that of the Cheshire Cat of Alice's wonderland. To be able to laugh at life and death demonstrates one's freedom and potential danger to a static society. To be able to laugh is to be able to play and vice versa.

As suggested by previous remarks, comedians are not mere entertainers who perform to provide comic relief to the solemnity and formality of religious ritual, interpersonal relationships, human-divine relations, or the quest for liberation. Should the success of the comedian's performance be measured by the extent of the laughter that he provokes? Rather than using the amount of laughter provoked, it would be wiser to evaluate the comedian according to the successfulness of his teaching methods. Does the comedian successfully teach us about the foolishness of ourselves and our society? The clown presents us an upside-down picture of ourselves and our society, and to be able to comprehend the comedian we must stand on our heads to view the portrait. When our folly is exposed publicly and properly comprehended by us, we can hopefully get back on the right track.

---

76. Sanford, *Zen-Man Ikkyū*, 204.
77. Sanford, *Zen-Man Ikkyū*, 90–91.

THE COMIC AND PLAY

It is obvious that play is intimately connected to the comic. The comic is a subsidiary of play that is beyond foolishness. Play is not antithetical to wisdom and folly because play subsumes and transcends both opposites. The spirit of this type of play is evident in a poem by Ryōkan:

> The wild geese and ducks have flown off and left me—
> I'm glad my bean curd doesn't have wings![78]

Humor is a form of play that is fundamentally a useless activity because it is not for the sake of something else. Humor is only useful for itself.

Humor is an entertaining type of play that suggests the lightness of play, which implies that play is an effortless activity. In other words, there is an ease of play that suggests the absence of strain. We can get absorbed in play and humor and lose ourselves, a feature that is parallel with meditation. When one is absorbed, one becomes oblivious to what is occurring around one in the world. The comic as a form of play can become a mode of escape from personal problems and the stress of everyday life. Ryōkan writes playfully and comically about being drunk:

> On three cups five cups of this fine wine, I' drunk and once drunk
> I can pour for myself.[79]

The comic can also be an escape from the world of work, a confining mode of life, unlike the freedom afforded by play and its promise of relaxation.

Not only is humor an expression of insight and liberation, but it also suggests that to be awakened involves the freedom to laugh. Humor and laughter are forms of play, akin to playing for its own sake. While engaged in the play of humor and laughter, a person is purposeless for the sake of being purposeless and is nonsensical for the sake of being nonsensical. And yet, humor and laughter accept others despite their differences. The freedom afforded by humor and laughter is grounded in the freedom of enlightenment, implying that humor transcends all categories yet arises from an inner harmony and assurance associated with enlightenment.

We have noted that the comic calls attention to what is finite and fallible, and functions to intuitively elicit an awareness of our Buddha-nature. The comic is associated with the absurd that exposes the inadequate

---

78. Watson, *Ryōkan*, 55.
79. Watson, *Ryōkan*, 54.

nature of reason and precipitates laughter. Absurdity accepts things and events as they are and celebrates life. For all the talk about suffering, ignorance, and rebirth, Zen is a celebration of life. As the figure of the comedian makes clear with his decorum and antics, we can embrace life because everything is empty and possibilities are endless.

By enabling a person to transcend their social situation, comic play facilitates the achievement of a state in which categories, tools of order, and rationality do not exist because the comic moves within the freedom of irrationality, of suspended order and nonsense. The comic represents a chaos of infinite potentiality and creative possibility. The comic can thus collapse cultural categories and confuse or blur social distinctions. In its playful mode, the comic perspective helps humans understand their basic awkwardness with the world, which suggests that to be truly human one must be able to laugh at oneself and one's situation in the world.

Zen stresses the importance of the now and its realization by an individual. And it is laughter that can help a person participate in the immediacy and spontaneity of the present moment. Laughter can be a means to enter the path to liberation just as much as it can signal enlightenment itself. Laughter can even function to help a person meet their goal by debunking pride.

CONCLUDING REMARKS

Ikkyū's madness, eroticism, and humor are forms of play. His play is immersed in a game of impersonation. He plays, for example, the enlightened master and monk; he makes believe that he is a samurai warrior carrying a sword; he plays at being a drunk and a lecherous monk; he pokes fun at peasants attached to an icon of a *bodhisattva*; he assumes the demeanor of a foul-mouthed monk, performs a funeral for a cat, and waves a human skull from the end of a long bamboo pole in public. His life pattern conforms to the to-and-fro movement of the nature of play when he leaves the priesthood, returns to lay life, gets married, fathers a son, and then returns to monastic life; and while the abbot of a temple he has a love affair.

Throughout these various adventures in his life, Ikkyū acts like a mime, occupying a position on the edges of Japanese society. The "mime's" actions allude to something but refer to nothing. He mimes the role of husband and father, monk, and warrior with his fake sword. As a mime, Ikkyū plays various social roles during his life as he swings from one role to the next. By playing the role of a mime, Ikkyū reflects no reality, but does produce reality effects such as madness and eroticism.

Ikkyū manifests a liminal nature by virtue of his participation in play. Between their sanity and insanity, normalcy and abnormality, these holy figures represent liminal players. The liminal nature of play invites inversion, experimentation, and a new mode of thinking and being. The liminality of play generates an inner dialogue in the mind of the outsider as viewpoints are compared. This is an internal dialogue that allows the outsider to simultaneously embrace opposites as exemplified by the mad figures. The evidence of this chapter suggests that play is not antithetical to wisdom and folly because play subsumes and transcends both opposites.

In summary, the Zen of Crazycloud is obscene, frightening, astonishing, unusual, contemptuous, and wild. It breaks down boundaries and allows us to see the truth in the empty eye-sockets of a skull. It surprises us, makes us laugh, and provides an opportunity for us to reflect on the folly of human existence. It embodies an iconoclastic and irrational spirit. Ikkyū's style of Zen embodies a comic spirit and points toward freedom without forgetting or neglecting the mundane. It points to our essence and enables us to see into our own being. To see into our true nature, we must look beyond the bizarre, obscene, outrageous, and wild antics of a crazy monk, just as we must look beyond the façade of this insane world and our striving for fame and fortune. In summary, the hagiographical tales about Ikkyū include many elements of play that both entertain and edify a reader.

7

ZEN AND JAPANESE FINE ARTS

PREVIOUS CHAPTERS HAVE CALLED attention to the fact that Zen Buddhism is an experience, awareness, or intuitive flash of insight called *satori* (enlightenment), although this observation is not intended in a reductionistic spirit. Nonetheless, this profound experience represents a transformation of one's consciousness and level of awareness. We have seen that this crucial experience is an awakening to the immediacy of experienced reality before all description, before naming, and preceding reflection; it is also before subject/object consciousness. We have also witnessed that ultimate reality and meaning are discovered right here in the present moment within the living emptiness of things.

These points also pertain to the Zen-influenced artist who wants to express reality immediately, which suggests that Zen-inspired art points to itself and not beyond itself. Zen art shares with the Zen ethos several important aspects. These shared aspects reflect an art that is formless and trackless and expresses immediate emptiness. Zen-influenced art is spontaneous, which suggests that it is not thought out before the artist applies, for instance, a brush to rice paper or composes poetry. Ideally, Zen art is performed without any conscious intention. The spontaneous nature of this art implies that it flows immediately and formlessly from a mind associated with emptiness. This type of art does not intend anything; it does not intend, for instance, to capture beauty, truth, courage, or some socio-political message. It only points to the right here and now; it does not point beyond itself to some transcendent realm.

Zen-inspired art is transformative in the sense that it serves as a vehicle, process, or technique for moving forward religiously in the sense of enabling one to realize one's Buddha-nature. This type of art is performed rather than merely appreciated. This performative feature of Zen-inspired art is connected to religious transformation. Besides its transformative aspect, Zen art represents a way of life in which the artistic master lives his art in his everyday life. In Japanese, this way is termed *dō* or *michi*, and there are several of these ways: the way of tea (*chadō*), the way of painting (*gadō*), the way of poetry (*kadō*), the way of flowers (*kadō*), and the way of calligraphy (*shodō*). Borrowing a term from western art that does not do violence or distort these Japanese ways of art, we can call these the fine arts, whereas the way of swordsmanship (*kendō*) and the way of archery (*kyudō*) can be distinguished from these fine arts as the martial arts. These various ways suggest that there is no art apart from life and no life apart from art. Thus, it is possible for a genuine artist to live, for instance, her life on the model of the tea ceremony or the way of archery.

The way of Zen art involves a progression from the mastery of rules and techniques associated with each artistic way to no-mind. When the artist reaches the point of no-mind she possesses free artistic creativity in her art and life. Since there is a parallel between the various ways of art and the religious way, art can serve as a way of creating enlightenment (*satori*) experience within the midst of phenomenal existence. This chapter explores the Zen-influenced fine arts of Japanese culture, while the next chapter turns its attention to the martial arts. The various ways of Zen art are also intertwined with play, a feature that will become evident in this chapter. Before turning to examples of these fine arts, it is useful to examine some Japanese aesthetic features.

BASIC AESTHETIC CATEGORIES

The emotion evoked by hearing the melancholy calls of birds and beasts is represented by *aware*, a term that became tinged with sadness. Within this aesthetic category, an artist like a poet becomes aware of a combination of beauty and the perishability of a sight or sound. As the sight or sound fades, the artist realizes it is passing away. If an artist or any sensitive person, for instance, is viewing an especially brilliant sunset, *aware* gives birth to possibly the thought that beauty must die, which represents its interior aspect or internal response by the artist to what is perceived.

By contemplating the beauty of a flower, for instance, it is possible to have a poignant experience evoked by the object and to reflect on the transience of it. Besides this internal response to some stimuli, *aware* is also related to the properties of the external phenomenon. In summary, *aware* includes the external nature of what is perceived and the internal response or reaction to that perception by the artist.

With the original connotation of being desolate, the aesthetic category of *sabi* later becomes associated with growing old. By the thirteenth century, it suggests not merely being old but the pleasure in what is old, faded, or lonely. Phenomena like a withered branch or the moon obscured by rain clouds would be examples. Instead of the gentle melancholy of aware, *sabi* does not suggest lamenting, for instance, for a fallen flower, but a person instead merely loves it, although this aesthetic category does include melancholy overtones of loneliness. The essence of beauty for *sabi* is the old, worn object that possesses a quiet, peaceful air that exudes tranquility, dignity, and character. In short, it can be characterized as the dignity of old age.

Closely related to the category of *sabi* is that of *wabi*, a term associated etymologically with being wretched. *Wabi* originally referred to a miserable feeling that comes from material deprivation, although it does not mean to be completely bereft of material possessions. It instead suggests a lack of things or having things run contrary to our desires. When this occurs, of course, we feel frustrated with our wishes. The formative meaning of *wabi* includes notions like disappointment, frustration, and poverty. *Wabi* also means to penetrate to a thing's true essence and therein to discern beauty, although it is important to indicate that this is a beauty of restraint.

Along these aesthetic lines, *wabi* glorifies artificial poverty with its element of forced restraint, because in genuine poverty there is nothing to restrain. For example, during the tea ceremony, there is absolutely no hint of wealth or worldly status, which must be left outside of the tearoom. In this way, *wabi* is indicative of the self-transforming beauty of the impoverished. This aesthetic category deplores nonfunctional decorative objects, polished surfaces, or artificiality in shapes or colors as it deliberately turns away from the ostentatious. *Wabi* can be viewed as an impetus toward a state of mind that embraces a simple, unpretentious beauty. With a mind sensitized to *wabi*, a person discovers in poverty a world of spiritual freedom unbounded by material things and un-trappable by worldly values. Instead, a person finds a transcendental serenity apart from the world. *Wabi* represents the beauty of great depth that is expressed in unpretentious and straightforward ways. The deep beauty associated with *wabi* is imperfect and irregular. Wabi is an aesthetic category that embraces the notion that the imperfect and incomplete, like cracks in tea bowls and tears in calligraphy, are not flaws with which to find fault, but they represent a deeper kind of beauty than an unblemished piece of art. The notion of beauty associated with *wabi* is an austere, stark loveliness of original non-being, which is latent with unlimited energy, change, and potential.

The fourth important aesthetic category is *yūgen*, which suggests something profound, remote, and mysterious. It refers to an unknowable, invisible, and subconscious beauty. It is not something, however, that can be apprehended intellectually. Within the context of the Nō theater, an example of *yūgen* would be when the actor slowly raises his hand as if the actor is indicating something eternal rather than a mere representation of a gesture. *Yūgen* involves the recognition of something mysterious and strange in which one gets a glimpse of something eternal within the world of flux. From another perspective, *yūgen* is an extension of *aware* in the sense of a poignant foreboding. *Yūgen* relates, for instance, an awareness that not merely does beauty fade but life also does. The significance of *yūgen* extends beyond mere worldly phenomena to the realm of the eternal. Moreover, *yūgen* is profoundly suggestive because its mysterious nature forces an observer to feel truths through suggestion. Moreover, yet, in the final analysis, *yūgen* cannot be explained or even expressed in words; we can, however, intuitively sense it.

A final aesthetic category of significance is the notion of *ma*, which refers to an interval between two or more spatial or temporal things. Thus, it refers to a gap, an opening. It can refer to space between or time between something. A room is *ma*, for instance, in the sense that it refers to the space between the walls. If one considers music, rest during the playing of music represents *ma* because of the pause between the notes or sounds. The term can also mean "among" as in the example that "Jane stands among the monkeys." *Ma* is also the ground of all existence in the sense that it stands between non-being and being. Within the context of this between-world, it renders possible the coexistence of opposites like, for instance, reality and non-reality. The major actor suggests *ma* in a Nō drama by doing just enough to create a gap, a blank space-time moment, where nothing is done. The greatest playwright of the Nō theater, Zeami, put it this way: "What the actor does not do is of interest."[1] Therefore, *ma* is where the true interest lies for the audience. This interest is equally true of the ink landscape paintings of an artist like Sesshū (1421–1506) because the unpainted part of the work is what commands the greatest interest.

ZEN AND GARDENS

Before we examine landscape and rock gardens in any detail, it is wise to look at the role of nature in Japanese culture and Zen. The Japanese attitude toward nature has been historically shaped originally by the Shinto religion that views nature as both awesome power and beauty. Without getting into elaborate detail, the Shinto creation myth recounts the creation of the Japanese islands by heavenly *kami* (spirits). They dipped their long spears into the depths of the primal waters, bringing up mud from the depths of these waters that dripped off their spears and formed the islands of Japan. Since this creative act is a mirror image of the heavenly abode, Japan is an earthly paradise and manifestation of divine power. This myth implies that nature is a hierophany or manifestation of the divine, that is sacred, beautiful, and pure. Many parts of nature in the Shinto religion are intimately associated with *kami* (spirits) like springs, rivers, mountains, hills, and trees.

Within the context of Zen, when you recognize nature as nature, it becomes a part of you to such an extent that you exist in nature, and it exists in you. This point necessarily implies that nature is not something over against you, which means that you and nature are not in competition, and thus it is unnecessary for you to seek to conquer it. Strictly speaking, nature is already you before any recognition on your part; otherwise, you could not emerge from it. This point is illustrated very nicely by a Zen anecdote. The master Ungan once asked a monk where he had been, and he was told that the monk was talking with a friend on a rock. Then, the master asked, "Did the rock nod, or not?" The puzzled monk did not reply, after which the master remarked, "The rock has been nodding indeed even before you began to talk."[2]

A genuine Zen master is, of course, identified with nature. And there are Zen narratives that support this assertion. A master took, for

---

1. Rimer and Yamazaki, *On the Art*, 96.
2. Suzuki, *Zen Buddhism*, 247–48.

instance, a monk who was eager to know the secrets of Zen teaching into the bamboo grove and told the monk: "You see some of these bamboos are somewhat crooked while others are growing up straight."[3] In a similar tale, a monk was anxious to learn Zen and said: "I have been newly initiated into the brotherhood and will you be gracious enough to show me the way to Zen?" The master said: "Do you hear the murmuring sound of the mountain stream?" The monk acknowledged that he did. The master said: "Here is the entrance."[4] These two anecdotes suggest two fundamental points. Nature can be a place from which to begin one's journey to enlightenment, and nature teaches some of the lessons of Zen for those who will take the time to look and listen. These Shinto and Zen Buddhist attitudes toward nature were incorporated into views about landscape gardens and rock gardens in Japan, although it is also important to grasp the influence of Chinese culture in Japan.

The term for a garden in China was *shima*, which means island. The development of gardens and their popularity was tied to Daoist influence that related stories about fantastic islands in distant places. In one such narrative, a young fisherman thrown from his boat is saved by a sea turtle and is taken to a magical island where he marries a beautiful princess, while time stands still. The young man becomes homesick, and he decides to return to his native village where he immediately becomes old and dies. Like the situation of the fisherman on the magical island where time stands still, stones give the appearance of defying time. In Chinese culture, there is a close connection between stones and mountains, which in the popular imagination are places impregnated by supernatural forces and represent the most majestic expressions of natural forces. In the Chinese imagination, mountains are connected to the numinous. The Five Sacred Peaks of ancient Chinese cosmology stood, for instance, at the center of the world. The Chinese drew a correspondence between rocks and mountains in the sense that rocks are microcosmic mountains, suggesting that rocks inherit the powers associated with mountains. Daoists, ascetics, and Buddhists located themselves in mountain retreats, monasteries, or caves to live a life of solitude and to meditate.

These types of notions about rocks and mountains formed the cultural context for landscape gardens (*shansui*), which means mountains and waters. The term *shansui* evokes the ancient Daoism ideas about

3. Suzuki, *Zen Buddhism*, 251.
4. Suzuki, *Zen Buddhism*, 153.

Islands of Immortality. It also refers to the alternating cosmic principles of *yin* (female) and *yang* (male).[5] For the phenomenon of *shansui*, there is a co-joining of the soft, feminine fluidity of feminine (*yin*) water with the rough hardness of masculine (*yang*) rock. The combination of water and rock produces aesthetic pleasure. In addition to aesthetic pleasure, rock gardens in China could thus be used for aesthetic contemplation and self-cultivation important for both Daoism and Confucianism.

While walking or sitting in the *shansui*, a person came into close association with various kinds of rocks. Besides the cosmic symbolism connected to these rocks in ancient China, rocks were not considered inanimate objects because they possessed cosmic energy (*qi*). The rocks were animated by this cosmic energy (*qi*). Rocks of especially unusual size or shape were believed to be special conduits of cosmic energy. By being in their presence, a person receives beneficial effects.

In Japan, some rocks were believed to be inhabited by *kami* (divine spirits), connoting that which is superior, extraordinary, and mysterious, although they are not considered omniscient or omnipotent. Because *kami* lack a specific shape, they can manifest themselves when evoked to assume some shape, a revelatory vehicle known as *yorishiro* that refers to *kami* assuming the form of natural objects such as trees, stones, pillars, springs, mirrors, or swords. *Kami* can also reveal themselves through human beings such as shamans (*miko*). Not only do the Japanese share Chinese attitudes toward rocks as embodying energy and spirituality, but they also believe that unusually impressive rocks were revered as something sacred. When the Japanese want to induce a shapeless *kami* to a specific place, they often built piles of rocks to attract *kami*. It is these types of notions and practices that helped to shape the ideology behind Zen rock gardens.

Besides these indigenous and foreign influences on Japanese landscape and rock gardens, another important line of influence came from Song dynasty ink paintings of China.[6] These paintings convinced Japanese artists that a garden should be a three-dimensional painting in the sense that the Zen garden is a landscape painting executed in natural materials. The Japanese artists discovered ingenious and creative ways to manipulate the visual perspective associated with viewing these gardens. The artist created, for instance, artificial depth through overt

---

5. Berthier, *Reading Zen in the Rocks*, 43.
6. Berthier, *Reading Zen in the Rocks*, 9–10.

foreshortening by making objects in the distance smaller, less detailed, and darker, which gave more depth to the scene. By using trees with large, light-colored leaves toward the front of the garden and putting small, leafed foliage farther to the rear, this also created an impression of depth. By creating meandering paths toward the rear of the garden that grow narrow with smaller and smaller stones, the artist created an impression of distance. Other techniques of creating the appearance of depth involved situating streams and waterfalls deceptively by having them vanish and reappear around and behind rocks and plantings, or the artist could have garden walls disappear by placing dark natural materials before a wall or camouflaging it by a bamboo thicket.

The landscape artists also used psychological tricks to great effect. If a pathway or stream disappears around the growth of a tree, for instance, a viewer assumes that it continues when it might not continue in fact. The strategic placement of foliage near the viewer causes a diminution of perception that the mind associates typically with distance, or large vacant areas can enhance the impression of size. The illusion of greater distance can also be created by dwarfing trees. The various devices used to create these tricks are made invisible by giving the garden an appearance of naturalness and age. A couple of ways that this can be accomplished is by applying moss to stones and burying rocks in the earth to give them an appearance of icebergs. Moreover, by making the garden appear unkempt, shaggy, and old, this gives the appearance of naturalness.

These landscape gardens are created in natural materials and are intended primarily for viewing. They are not intended for meandering through or for loitering. The garden is closed in upon itself like a form of curved space, producing the illusion of an infinite wilderness in a few acres. The style of the landscape garden tended to be angular and asymmetrical with a preference for naturalness in their stones, rejecting fantastic and grotesque contours. The garden is considered an extension of a person's dwelling that is constructed in such a way as to prevent someone inside from having to see outside the confines of the garden. The fundamental impression given by the garden is that of a symbolic world that is confined to a small space that simultaneously suggests the infinite.

Moreover, the viewer is given an opportunity to gain a deeper understanding of one's consciousness.

In contrast to the landscaped gardens, there are also rock gardens that are called dry landscapes (*kare sansui*) that are specifically intended for meditation. Many of these rock gardens are reduced in size to fit into a temple yard. Since these gardens are intended to be copies of paintings rather than nature, they are best grasped as abstract representations of nature. Creating a rock garden is a way to practice Zen. Thus, there is a close connection between the rock garden and the search for truth. Another aspect to consider when attempting to understand these phenomena is that nature is getting stripped of its essentials to reveal its substance, which in turn offers human beings an opportunity to discover by analogy their original nature.

There are strict limits on the kinds of material that can be used in a rock garden. It is mostly created by using rocks and sand and a little vegetation that might include slow growing evergreen bushes. This image gives the impression of a garden anchored in time. The rocks chosen for the garden tend to appear like mountains and crags in paintings; light-colored stones with striated sides and sharp edges are prized, and those with natural shapes like flat-topped and vertical-sided rocks are coveted because they look like volcanic islands. This appearance is enhanced by raking the sand in such a way as to appear to be waves hitting an island.

The arrangement of the rocks is extremely important. An oddly numbered configuration like 7/5/3 represents the male *yang* principle, whereas even-numbered rocks manifest the female *yin* factor. The odd is considered superior to even-numbered configuration just as *yang* is superior to *yin*. Another type of configuration is, for instance, the three-deity setting, which is composed of a large stone flanked by two comparatively insignificant diminutive stones, forming a vertical triangle with the peak of the largest stone representing the apex. Within the context of the odd-numbered stones, the number five is significant because it represents the central number within the initial nine numbers, and it is thus the symbol of the center. It also represents in Chinese cosmology the five primordial elements: wood (east), fire (south), earth (center), metal (west), and water (north).

Besides this cosmic symbolism grounded in ancient Chinese cosmology, rock gardens possess a profound subjective quality that is intended to evoke a sense of motion. Stones are placed, for instance, with their longer axis corresponding to that of the garden, and the sand is raked lengthwise, which makes observers' eyes sweep from left to right and vice versa. Empty areas suggest *ma*, a gap that reinforces an emphasis on the stones and invites the viewer's mind to expand into a cosmological infinity represented by the rocks. Therefore, rocks serve both a pedagogic function and a soteriological dimension by inviting the viewer to grasp them as embodiments of wisdom. Besides being able to use the rocks as companions to a more profound and insightful understanding and plays an important symbolic role in depicting emptiness. With its rich cosmological significance, Buddhist symbolism, and location in Zen monasteries, the rock garden functions as a visual *kōan* that is used for purposes of meditation by Zen monks.

Rock gardens embrace a sense of play in the way that the play of humans is a natural process suggesting that a player is a part of nature. The to-and-fro nature of play is embedded in the alternation of *yin* and *yang* in the gardens that reflect the nature of the movement of the cosmos. Play is predominant over the player's consciousness, which makes all play a being played. This point suggests that play is limited to representation itself and its mode of being is self-representation, making play a simple totality that connects it to emptiness.

ZEN AND PAINTING

Using very absorbent rice paper and black ink, the calligrapher or landscape painter seek to penetrate beyond the perceptions of the rational mind and senses. The landscape artists, for instance, do not attempt to depict the surface of nature, but they want to reflect its essence or to paint the moment of enlightenment. In other words, the artist wants to take a viewer beyond the mere surface painting into a third dimension.[7]

The materials used are very instructive. Because the rice paper absorbs the ink so quickly, the artist cannot alter the strokes once they are made on the paper. In other words, the artist cannot touch up or correct his work once it is painted. If the artist is dissatisfied with the product, he destroys the work and begins another piece. Instead of using colors, the Zen artist uses black ink because it is more expressive. It is also presupposed, on the one hand, that an artist cannot precisely capture the colors of nature, a realization that helps us to grasp a basic truth about nature. On the other hand, black ink is preferable because it can produce the illusion of color. Another way of understanding the use of black ink is to view it as a trick played by the artist upon the viewer to unwittingly supply one's colors. When a viewer supplies the colors that person is more apt to be in tune with nature. Embodied within this procedure is a

---

7. Carter, *Japanese Arts and Self-Cultivation*, 53.

fundamental Zen insight that informs us that the mind is a much richer source of inspiration than the brush.

Whether the artist is doing calligraphy or a landscape painting, the work produced must flow out of the Zen discipline grounded in no-mind. This feature suggests that the artist does not labor over each stroke and does not correct a stroke after it is executed. It is essential that the technique of the artist flows thoughtlessly and effortlessly. The objective of the artist is to capture the fleeting images of the inner sense that is beyond mind and ordinary thought. When the artist begins to work on a blank sheet of rice paper, it is perceived only as paper. By creating figures like trees, mountains, streams, waterfalls, and human beings, the artist transforms the blank sheet of rice paper into something empty. Thus, the use of empty space is always richly symbolic.

It is possible to view this richness in a landscape painting that is divided into three distinct tiers. In the typical near scene, there is often depicted individual leaves or trees, ripples on water, and a small figure of a human being that can often be missed or mistakenly viewed as something else. In the middle section of the painting, there may appear only the branches of trees with water often portrayed as a waterfall. In the far section, there are mountain peaks with fog or mist used to divide the painting into three planes. These ink landscape paintings do not yield all their secrets at first viewing. The *yūgen* element of these paintings and their depth mean that a viewer can always perceive something new with each subsequent viewing. In other words, the mystery and secrets of the landscape paintings are not yielded all at once. In retrospect, landscape painting aims to move beyond the surface to something three dimensional. This aim is an attempt to achieve wholeness and to see things holistically.

Besides calligraphy and landscape paintings, artists also created monochrome landscape works of art. The fundamental objective of these paintings is not a true representation of nature, but a depiction of an emotional response to nature. Another type of painting is the *zenkiga*, a didactic figure painting. These works often illustrate Zen parables, depict Bodhidharma, capture the critical moment of a *kōan*, or illustrate a Zen monk performing some form of labor as a form of self-discipline. And finally, *chinso* represents solemn portraits of well-known teachers and leaders.

The Zen artist—calligrapher or painter—wants to play with the mind and senses of the viewer of their works. They induce a viewer, for example, to supply the colors for a landscape, or encourage a viewer to return to a work of art to see something that they did not notice at a previous viewing. They introduce human figures so small that it is easy to miss them, although a clear message is that these figures blend into nature and are part of it. The artist's effortless actions flow with ease without a preset plan, a contrived concept, a thought-out paradigm, or a striving for perfection. In the spirit of play, the artist creates something empty by painting figures onto absorbent rice paper.

THE NŌ THEATER

Scholars have traced the origins of the Nō theater to Chinese circus forms of entertainment called *sarugaku*, which often displayed physical feats of daring, farcical playlets, and suggestive and even indecent dances. A common theme associated with these performances was the lampooning of the clergy within both the Buddhist and Shinto religions. From this type of entertainment, *sarugaku* evolved into a more structured drama (*sarugaku-nu-nō*), a Japanese equivalent of the European morality play that included singing and dancing performers. A chorus was added later to supply the verses during certain segments of the dance. By 1374, it had evolved from a village drama to theater. At one such show, the shōgun Ashikaga Yoshimitsu attended, and he became excited by witnessing a work of Kanrami (1331–1384), father of the Nō theater. Yoshimitsu became Kanrami's patron and supported the art form, which was to become an aristocratic art. Due to the Zen aesthetics surrounding the shōgun, this form of entertainment began to be shaped by religion. As this art form evolved, the most celebrated playwright became Zeami, a son of Kanrami.

The Nō dramas are a combination of text, music, and drama performed in a kind of ritual slow motion. The drama contains minimal realism, and instead stresses symbolism.[8] The drama uses a chorus, but it never participates in the action, confining itself to recitations for the principal dancer when he is performing his dance. The principal actor often wears rich robes and masks for his roles. The supporting actor (*waki*) is usually the first to enter the stage. It is not unusual for him to represent an itinerant monk dressed in black robes, and he begins relating the narrative. The richly costumed and frequently masked *shite* is the protagonist, forming a sharp contrast between his costume and the austerity of the stage and other costumes. As the narrative unfolds, the

---

8. Varley, *Japanese Culture*, 102.

shite is transformed from a human being into a soul that expresses its tortured inner emotions as a representative of universal consciousness. At the climax of the drama, the *shite* performs a highly stylized dance that embodies a sequence of mannered postures and gestures.

The principal actor performs on a stage that is a platform of polished wood covered by a roof like that in a Buddhist temple. Zen aesthetics influences the architecture of the stage in its simplicity, naturalness, austere sublimity, and tranquility. The actual theaters are small, in which the audience sits on three, or sometimes only two, sides of the stage. There is a raised passageway leading from the actors' dressing-room through the audience to the stage. Frequently, actors make their entrances through the audience, pronouncing their first words before reaching the stage. The stage and entrance ramp are symbolically separated from the audience by an encircling expanse of white sand. These types of features attempt to break away from a representational mode of performance, and are instead "meant to be outward, beautiful forms suggestive of remoter truths or experiences, the nature of which will differ from person to person."[9]

There are five primary categories of plays. These include god plays in which the principal actor (*shite*) is a supernatural being. In warrior plays, the main actor represents a military figure who may speak in universal terms about his tragedy. Thirdly, woman plays are often lyric evocations of a beautiful woman, who is frequently a courtesan, who has been unsuccessful in love. Madness plays often focus their attention on a historical episode that has driven the main actor to desperation or driven him to madness by guilt. Finally, there are demon plays in which the primary actor is a vengeful ogre. It should be noted that all these parts are played by males, even the so-called woman plays. Within the play, the plot is deliberately suppressed. However, the play explores an emotional experience or a state of mind like hatred, guilt, love, longing, fear, grief, or happiness instead. Dramatic components like confrontation, conflict, self-realization, development, and resolution that one could find in the western theater are nearly absent. What the audience receives is a ritualized rendition of an emotional state that infrequently develops or is resolved during the play. The actor describes the emotional condition of the audience.

The masks, dances, and poetry reflect the Zen influence with their suggestiveness. The masks are carved, for instance, to play off the lighting.

---

9. Keene, *Appreciations of Japanese Culture*, 16.

When the actor tilts his head this creates a different expression that is very suggestive. The slow motion of the dance movements is subtle, reserved, and suggestive. The use of gaps or intervals (*ma*) is also very suggestive. There are moments when the dancer is still, representing a perfect balance of opposing forces. The slow hand gestures are, for instance, a symbol of an eternal region of perpetual silence. Zeami refers to a point in the performance that he calls the "eye-opening" that occurs when the *shite* opens the mind's eye of the audience to the wondrous (*myō*), an ineffable experience.[10] The wondrous (*myō*) is devoid of form or is something that is not physically manifested.

Zeami uses the term *flower* (*hana*) to refer to the attunement between actors and audience. The term *flower* is also used metaphorically to refer to the art of the actor, a combination of sensibility and technical versatility, enabling an actor to read his audience and to adjust his performance as necessary.[11] Zeami also calls attention to "two modes and three styles" (*nikyoku santai*). The two modes refer to the actions of dancing and chanting, which form the foundation of training before playing roles, whereas the three styles refer to the three types of representation: venerable style, feminine style, and material style. The venerable style is related to elderly characters, the feminine style for females, and material style for warriors.[12]

According to Zeami, there are three basic elements of a Nō performance: skin, flesh, and bone. The bone element represents the actor's natural artistic strength. Flesh is a visible element that originates from the skills of the actor by mastery of chant and dance, whereas skin denotes the ease and beauty of a performance when the skin and flesh elements are perfected.[13] In summary, bones represent the naturally inherited talent, flesh stands for the actor's acquired skills in chant and dance, and skin is the elegance of the actor's outward appearance. By mastering these three elements, Zeami stresses that an actor becomes what he is performing. By playing an old man, an actor, for instance, assumes the posture of someone who is bent, walks fraily, and uses small gestures when moving his hands. Zeami stresses that what he is describing is "an art beyond mere appearance."[14] However, the most crucial moment in a performance, after

---

10. Quinn, *Developing Zeami*, 258.
11. Quinn, *Developing Zeami*, 3.
12. Quinn, *Developing Zeami*, 5–6.
13. Rimer and Yamazaki, *On the Art*, 69.
14. Rimer and Yamazaki, *On the Art*, 80.

the feelings of the audience are grasped intuitively by the *shite*, "is the moment when the experienced actor can absorb the concentration of the audience into his performance."[15] This scenario suggests an event akin to the back-and-forth characteristic of play.

Within his aesthetic theory, Zeami emphasizes that *yūgen* represents the highest expression of an invisible and subconscious beauty attainable in the Nō drama.

The spirit of the Nō drama is expressed in Zeami's aesthetic theory by sight, hearing, and heart. The drama succeeds by stirring the heart. By the principal actor reducing his movements of dance and mimicry to a minimum, the audience is presented with an austere drama, a kind of Nō drama of no-mind. The principal actor connects the moments before and after that instant when nothing happens by rising to a selfless level of art. He accomplishes this by developing a concentration that transcends his consciousness, not unlike a Zen meditator. It is also possible to witness the Zen influence concerning the intrinsic detachment from self and object in the Nō drama. Moreover, the stages of Nō drama culminate with the sixth stage of emptiness.

The ideal mental state of the lead actor consists of non-dual wisdom that realizes that objective and subjective distinctions are merely egotistical illusions. The mental condition of non-duality is called wondrous (*myō*) acting that suggests something exquisite, which means an image without form. The wondrous is removed from being/substance and non-being/non-substance distinctions but embraces both being and non-being. As the lead actor trains, he reaches a state of no-mind (*mushin*), which is a non-discriminating consciousness in which the dichotomy between actor and audience is overcome. This state of consciousness is without intention and free of self-consciousness. After achieving the level of no-mind, the actor attains one-mindedness (*isshin*), which refers to a mental concentration that connects the intervals between actions to the extent that intention is not even evident to oneself.[16] The actor is now free of objective or subjective thinking, which enables an actor to react spontaneously with his surroundings. In the final analysis, the actor rises to a selfless level of art.

In his book on Japanese culture, D. T. Suzuki overstates the Zen influence on the development of the Nō theater and forgets to include the

---

15. Rimer and Yamazaki, *On the Art*, 82.
16. Rimer and Yamazaki, *On the Art*, 96–97.

role of Neo-Confucianism, Daoism, Shinto, and devotional Buddhism (Amidism). The influence of Buddhism was diverse and not that associated with a specific school.[17] The Nō play *Nomori* (*The Watchman of the Plain*) is, for instance, about a *yamabushi* (mountain ascetic figure) that concludes with his vision of the universe and perception of his face in all the worlds, suggesting a non-dualism typical of some types of Buddhism and Daoism. Like the wandering lifestyle of the *yamabushi*, the theme of journey and the importance of place are common to Nō dramas. This wandering occurs within nature and its elements such as the full moon, water, a pine tree, or mountain that is typically inhabited by ancestral spirits. Throughout numerous dramas, there is a play of opposites like hot and cold, male and female, red and white, heaven and earth that reflect each other.

The Nō drama shares some features with the notion of play. It is, for example, an interlude in the life of a viewer. It is located at a particular place, limited, and secluded.

In Zeami's theory, there is an interaction between the actor and the audience. The Nō drama is a good example of play as a distinct form of human expression.[18] As a member of an audience watches the play unfold, she can transcend time and place.

ZEN AND THE TEA CEREMONY

There are some similarities between the Nō drama and the tea ceremony, although they are very different types of activities. Both suggest the measured movements, simplicity, serene action, austere sublimity, and the *yūgen* element. Besides, naturalness, freedom from attachment, and tranquility are all features that they also share. The Chinese took these features and combined tea drinking with writing poetry and spirituality.[19]

From a well-known drink during the period of Confucius (ca. 500 BCE) to the green-powdered tea dating to the Song dynasty (960–1279), tea was finally introduced to Japan by Buddhist priests who had studied in China. During the Kamakura era of the twelfth century, the Buddhist monk Eisai was given credit for introducing *matcha*, a powdered, bitter, tea into Japan, which was believed to have beneficial results for the

17. Tyler, "'Path of My Mountain,'" 151.
18. Henricks, *Play Reconsidered*, 184.
19. Sōshitsu, *Japanese Way of Tea*, 35.

human heart and served as an elixir of human longevity. In addition to these types of health benefits, tea drinking, a favorite activity among the merchant class, also had economic benefits, the social prestige associated with fine art, leveling of class distinctions, a type of social entertainment, and an opportunity to gain self-discipline and self-refinement for tea masters.[20] From Buddhist temples in medieval Japan, tea drinking spread to other areas of society. Within Buddhist temples, the diffusion of tea was associated with a practice called *obukucha*, which refers to offering tea to the Buddha and to the tea itself. Around the middle of the thirteenth century, a tea gathering called *ochamori* began at a Buddhist temple called Saidaiji, which consisted of temple priests drinking tea offerings at a shrine, although this practice was expanded later to include the laity. Among the laity, tea tasting contests (*tocha*) became a fashionable Japanese cultural event. These contests consisted of competitions aimed at distinguishing between different teas grown in different regions of the country. A contest called "four kinds and ten cups," for instance, involved drinking three cups of each of three kinds of tea and one cup of a fourth kind, which was known as the guest tea.[21] These contests evolved into excessive and extravagant affairs that frequently included gambling among the samurai, and the government later prohibited them.

Within the context of Japanese history, there has been a close connection between tea and Zen. During the Kamakura era in Japan, there was an aphorism that affirmed: "Zen and tea are one."[22] This intimate relationship is even based on a legend that attributes the origin of the tea bush to Bodhidharma, the legendary founder of Zen. According to the legend, Bodhidharma discovered himself falling asleep while meditating. To overcome his drowsiness, he allegedly tore off his eyelids and flung them to the ground, and they grew to be tea plants. The legend does contain a kernel of veracity because tea was used by Buddhist meditators to prevent drowsiness during long periods of sitting in meditation. In China, tea drinking became ritualized in Chan monasteries with monks congregating before an image of Bodhidharma and taking a sacrament of tea from a single bowl in his memory, a manifestation of a pious celebration of their religion and way of life.

Rules associated with tea drinking slowly emerged from those within the context of Zen temples connected to rules called *shingi* that

20. Ludwig, "Chanoyu and Momoyama," 77.
21. Yasuhiko, "Development of Chanoyu," 11.
22. Sōshitsu, *Japanese Way of Tea*, 93.

formed the basis of communal life. An aesthetic developed that was related to the notion of discrimination connected to the relationship between people and things with the connotation of attachment to things (*mono-suki*). There also arose principles of behavior (*furumai*) that were historically connected to interpersonal relationships at tea gatherings. Associated with an ethical sentiment, the principles of behavior were related to entertaining people and providing them with a feast. Early tea gatherings consisted of presenting tea (*suki*) and the activity of serving food (*furumai*). The spirit of the behavior was embodied in the expression "one time, one meeting," which expressed an image of a group coming together once in a lifetime and giving themselves to this event with absolute sincerity.[23]

These basic rules would later be developed by the greatest tea master's in Japanese history called Sen no Rikyū, who was born in 1522 in the city of Sakai and later experienced Zen training. To grasp the context of his historical period, it is important to note that the tea ceremony (*chanōyu*) became popular among warlords of medieval Japan because it represented a symbol of new wealth and culture, and these lords competed to invite tea practitioners and to hold tea gatherings. Rikyū was hired to serve as tea master for Oda Nobunaga. Rikyū distinguished his tea ceremony from others by making it more individualistic, which made it appear heretical during its historical period. Although previous masters of tea influenced him, Rikyū was especially influenced by the so-called *Shuko soan* (hut) tradition of Murata Shuko, who cultivated the astringent nature of tea that leads to an aesthetic of the "cold and withered." In turn, this resulted in reshaping the art toward simple and frugal settings and common utensils that were associated with the honesty of the heart. In 1582, Rikyū's patron Nobunaga was assassinated, and he was succeeded by Toyotomi Hideyoshi, who hired the tea master to serve him. This new position established Rikyū as the foremost practitioner of tea in the country.

For Rikyū to be admitted to the royal palace, he needed rank and office, and he received these by adopting the designation of Koji (Buddhist layman) and the Buddhist name of Rikyū. Over time, a rift developed between Rikyū and Hideyoshi over the issue of authority that the former was reluctant to grant. Finally, a wooden statue of Rikyū wearing straw sandals was placed atop the gate of Daitokuji Temple, an event that upset

---

23. Sōshitsu, *Japanese Way of Tea*, 29.

Hideyoshi enough that he demanded the tea master's suicide. Shortly after that, Rikyū received word from a disciple that he should commit *seppuku* (ritual disembowelment). Rikyū prepared for his death and awaited the arrival of the court official assigned to serve as a witness. Rikyū and the official drank tea together before the master committed suicide. Nonetheless, Rikyū's transformation of the tea ceremony was to endure beyond his passing, enhanced by principles that included harmony, respect, purity, and tranquility.

TEA CEREMONY AND ZEN AESTHETICS

A poem composed by Rikyū summarizes the spirit of the tea ceremony:

> Know that chanoyu
> Is simply this:
> Boil water,
> Prepare tea,
> And drink—that is all.[24]

Although this poem captures his emphasis on a natural, serene, and purposeless human activity, this poem is rather deceptive because the ceremony involves the mastery of over 350 steps that can take years of training. The rules combined samurai warrior etiquette and Buddhist monastic discipline. However, it is wise to conceive of the tea ceremony as a meditation in action.

Without getting into all the steps, rules, and nuances of the actual ceremony, it is possible to review the highlights of the ceremony. The tea bowl, which is a *raku* ceramic, undecorated object, is rinsed with hot water from the kettle and wiped with a napkin. The *raku* tea bowl possesses an austere, unpretentious, weathered grace because they give the appearance of being imperfect, old, and functional. A bamboo scoop is used to transport the powdered green tea (*koicha*) from the tea caddy into the bowl. A bamboo dipper is used to add the boiling water, which has been heated in a kettle set into a hole in the floor of the tearoom. The tea master blends the tea with a bamboo whisk, and he gives it to the guest of honor, who takes the first taste. After the guest salutes the host, the guest takes a couple of more sips, wipes the lip of the bowl with a napkin, rotates it, and passes it to the next guest, who repeats the ritual. The last person to drink must empty the bowl with only the host denied a taste. Then, the

---

24. Varley, "Chanoyu," 168.

bowl is rinsed, and the second batch of tea is made of a thinner variety called *usucha*. The host also offers a meal called *kaiseki* that consists of the Japanese characters for "bosom" and "stone," alluding to the practice of Zen monks using warm stones in the bosoms of their robes to stave off hunger. This etymological background of the term suggests that it is a simple meal to ward off hunger pangs and not a sumptuous feast. The cuisine is chosen to reflect the season of the year, and it is connected to sensitivity for human feelings. Since there are no pronounced flavors to the food, it invites the diner to sharpen one's senses and attune oneself to the world. The tea master and guests should ideally reach an experience of "one time, one place" (*ichigo*). This moment is not an abstract experience of time or experience of time mediated through language; it is an experience of the now moment—something that is once in a lifetime.[25]

The tea ceremony does not take place in a master's kitchen or living room. It occurs in a special thatch-roofed hut that gives tea drinking an air of conspicuous poverty, an embodiment of the Zen spirit with its dislike of materialism. The hut was constructed with a square hole instead of a doorway that was intended to convey the message that all worldly status and dignity were to be left outside of the hut and only the humble may enter. Leading to the hut was a garden path (*roji*) that signaled the initial stage of meditation. The term *roji* means dewy ground, suggesting a place of cleansing before one enters the tea hut.[26] The garden path functioned to sever any connection with the outside world and to create a fresh sensation conducive to the enjoyment of the aesthetics of the tea-room.

The tea-room itself was modeled on a monk's room in a monastery or a hermit's cave, which was purposely intended to give tea drinking an environment of conspicuous poverty, while other parts of the simple structure suggested other important notions. The tearoom was a four-and-a-half mat room, which was analogous to the size of the room of a hermit. The tearoom thus implied a rejection of differences associated with social status.[27] The thatched roof suggested something transitory, the slender pillars indicated frailty, the bamboo supports implied lightness, and ordinary materials suggested carelessness. Moreover, the utensils for a tea ceremony must harmonize with each other.

Many tea rooms have an art alcove (*tokonoma*) that is modeled on the altar of a Zen chapel that often contains a single decoration like a

25. Carter, *Japanese Arts and Self-Cultivation*, 73.
26. Sōshitsu, *Japanese Way of Tea*, 170.
27. Yasuhiko, "Development of Chanoyu," 25.

single flower in a vase. Other alcoves contain a hanging scroll (*kakemono*) of a painting or calligraphy, and some alcoves combine the hanging scroll as a background for a flower in a vase. What significance does the flower have? The flower is a symbol of the abstract aspect of Buddhist philosophy; it also embodies in its momentary explosion of beauty and fragrance all the mysteries of the cycle of birth, life, and death. The plum and cherry blossoms are, for instance, symbols of life's transient nature. From this simple setting, there evolved the art of flower arrangement (*ikebama*), which literally means "making flowers live." Since a flower grows from roots buried in the earth, to cut a flower would rather seem to kill it. But this demise of a flower is contrary to the Zen perspective because to cut a flower enables it to reveal itself.[28] It is the rootless nature of a flower after it has been cut that embodies a fundamental Zen truth: all beings and things in the world are impermanent.

Rikyū introduced a style of flower arrangement called *nageire*, which consisted of one or two blossoms placed in a pot devoid of any hint of artificiality and was called tea flowers (*chabana*). This style was an anti-philosophical attempt to achieve immediate unity with the universe. Since the flowers are cut, they are dying, but this fact is not to be lamented because after being cut they are at their brightest and best.[29] This style reflected *wabi* aesthetics by being informal and spontaneous in appearance. The style represented something instinctive and natural that served as a direct link between a person and their natural surroundings.

The tea ceremony was designed to soothe one's senses with the purpose of creating feelings of harmony and tranquility. The soothing of the senses was combined with an attempt to evoke aesthetic sensations like *sabi* and *wabi*. The loneliness associated with *sabi* was expressed by the uneven, cracked tea bowl, an ancient rusty kettle for heating the water, a solitary flower in the art alcove, and a ten-foot-square room. The tranquil deportment of the tea master expressed *wabi*, which represents the negation of all luxury, extravagance, and power. There were produced forms of simplicity, frugality, poverty, and the ordinary instead. *Wabi* comes from the term *wabu* (to be wretched), referring to miserable feelings that are evoked by material deprivation that is the beauty of the ordinary or restraint, whereas *sabi* suggests loneliness.[30] In short, the *wabi*-dominated aesthetic style forged by Rikyū renders his type of tea service imperfect.

28. Parkes, "Role of Rock," 134.
29. Carter, *Japanese Arts and Self-Cultivation*, 104.
30. Yasuhiko, "Development of Chanoyu," 125.

The imperfect *raku* bowl itself used for the tea ceremony was related to soothing the senses, because the term *raku* means pleasure or comfort. Historically, it was Rikyū who gave their development impetus after he took a fancy to roof tiles being produced by a Korean workman named Chojiro, which the tea master thought would be perfect for his *wabi* style tea. Developed and produced at the Zen stronghold of the city of Kyoto, the *raku* ceramic bowls were a mixture of clays blended to gain the desired consistency, lightness, and plasticity. The clay was fired in an unconventional way by thrusting it directly into a very hot charcoal kiln for thermal shock, which gave the bowls an instant look of the ravaged face of *sabi*. These bowls were not decorated with designs or color. These simple bowls were *wabi* and *sabi* with unpretentious, weathered grace. The bowls were also light and porous, which allowed for minimal heat conduction and comfortable handling. Their low center of gravity meant that it was very difficult to tip them over and allowed for easy whisking of the powdered tea. The imperfection of the bowls was related to the high temperatures to which the clay was exposed, and this gave them an old and weathered appearance. Thus, the bowls were out of shape, cracked, and contained blobs and ashes in the glaze, which invited a viewer to resort to a process of creation through their asymmetry and imperfection. These perfectly functional tea bowls embodied no suggestion that they represented a consciously produced work of art, which enabled it to embody the spirit of *wabi* aesthetics with its rejection of non-functional decorative objects, polished surfaces, artificiality in shape or color, and any unnatural materials used in its creation. The art connoisseur finds an inner warmth and lack of superficiality in *wabi* inspired art, whereas the suggestion of long years of use reflected the *sabi* element. The Zen-influenced tea ceremony has become part of the fabric of Japanese culture. Any student of Japanese culture would be wise to arrive at an understanding of this ceremony to grasp this Far East Asian culture.

Although it might be difficult to recognize beneath all the restraint of the way of tea, there is a discernible element of play. The Japanese tea historian Sōshitsu points to the place of play: "Tea is a meeting of *yin* and *yang*, and chanoyu has a well-defined order based on shifting from *yin* to *yang* and *yang* to *yin*. When the right-hand takes the tea scoop, the left-hand takes the caddy . . . one moment flows steadily into another, and the host can draw the guests firmly into the event."[31] This alternation of *yin*

---

31. Sōshitsu, *Japanese Way of Tea*, 240.

(feminine) and *yang* (male) principles is analogous to the to-and-fro movement of play. This movement suggests that play is built into the way of tea and the tea master is the prime player with the guests assuming the roles of participants. It is also possible to recognize that the tea ceremony shares with play other features such as being an interlude in a participant's life, a way to separate oneself from the continuities and complexities of everyday existence, a particular type of human expression and encounter, a repetitive nature, a voluntary aspect, a performance, and a unique type of action.

ZEN AND *HAIKU* POETRY

Among the most renowned poets in world literature, Matsuo Bashō (1644–1694) gained fame for his *haiku* poetry and travel literature. He was born into a family with prior blood relations to the samurai class that had fallen socioeconomically during the founding of the Tokugawa shogunate led by Oda Nobunaga (1534–1582), having become farmers to survive. In 1672, Bashō moved to Edo with the intention of becoming a poetic master at the age of twenty-nine. In the fall of 1684, he began a series of journals detailing events of his travels for a period that would last almost five years. On November 28, 1694, he died prematurely at the age of fifty-one of a stomach ailment, leaving behind him numerous followers and a school of poetry. In his poems, he incorporated not only Zen but also Neo-Confucianism, Daoism, and a Shinto reverence for nature.

In his poetry, Bashō developed the notion of "awakening to the high, returning to the low." Embodied in this notion was spiritual cultivation and return to the everyday, material world of ordinary people.[32] He also referred to "following the Creative," "object and self as one," and "the unchanging and the changing." These poetic ideals sought to unite contradictory trajectories. In short, Bashō was attempting to create a poetry that was simultaneously orthodox and unorthodox and that was transgressive.[33] Bashō alluded to a process of seeing an object such as a cherry blossom and fusing it within himself, a process of joining the way of the cosmos (*zoka*) with that internal to the poet, which is equivalent to spiritual cultivation. By being able to enter objects, the poet was able to discover the high in the low that enables the poet to find beauty in the mundane.[34] When pushed to

---

32. Shirane, *Traces of Dreams*, 255.
33. Shirane, *Traces of Dreams*, 257.
34. Shirane, *Traces of Dreams*, 263.

its extreme Bashō's technique renders the external internal and the internal external, resulting in a juxtaposition of opposites.

A *haiku* poem consists of a mere seventeen syllables in Japanese. This poetry demonstrates a profound Zen influence with its characteristics of selflessness, loneliness, grateful acceptance, wordlessness, non-intellectuality, contradictoriness, humor, freedom, non-morality, simplicity, love, and courage. Many *haiku* poems are expressions of temporary enlightenment into the life of things. The poem captures that moment and freezes it in time. An excellent example of such awareness is the following poem by Bashō, who is generally considered the greatest poet of this genre:

> In scent of chrysanthemums,
> Climbing through the dark
> At festival time.[35]

This poem is dated 1694, which is the year that the poet died. In this poem, he is traveling along a path in the cool, early morning, while he is lost in the all-pervasive scent of chrysanthemums. Suddenly, he realizes the darkness and the time of the year as he continues his journey.

The length of a *haiku* verse—seventeen syllables—consists of the number of words that a person can utter during a single breath. From a related perspective, this is precisely the duration of the experience of "ah-ness," which is a state of mind during which one stands still, struck with awe. The viewer is seized by the object, is aware of it for a moment, and sees something previously unrecognized. The viewer does not have time to emotionally feel, reflect, or judge about what one sees, an instant when a viewer forgets the relationship between subject and object and unites with the object.[36] The *haiku* poet gives the reader an aesthetic moment that is full of meaning and significance that the poet renders immediate for the reader.

By following an itinerant lifestyle, Bashō slept where he found himself at the end of a day. Sometimes, he found a place to sleep in a barn. He writes of one such experience:

> Fleas, lice,
> A horse peeing
> By my pillow.[37]

---

35. Barnhill, *Bashō's Haiku*, 152.
36. Yasuda, *Japanese Haiku*, 38–39.
37. Yasuda, *Japanese Haiku*, 94.

A reader's natural reaction to this image is repulsion and a lack of empathy. To react in this way is perfectly understandable when it comes to creatures that are nasty and disgusting and the abhorrent impurity associated with horse urine. But such a natural human reaction would miss Bashō's intention with this poem. If one puts fleas, lice, and horse urine into a cosmic totality where each thing has its place, it is possible to agree with D. T. Suzuki, "But in and through all this, there is to be a feeling of the whole, in which urine and champagne, lice and butterflies take their appointed and necessary place."[38] Thus, the evoking of disgust by this poem can point to a greater insight into the world.

Haiku poetry is like a landscape painting in words in which its scenes tend to become static. Bashō painted this scene with words:

> On a withered branch
> A crow has settled—
> Autumn evening.[39]

This scene is a landscape that any intelligent person can imagine. Typical of these poems, the author gives the time of day and the season. In this poem, it is possible to witness three elements that are typical of many *haiku* poems: where, what, and when. Thus, the location of the poem is often given, the event perceived by the poet, and the time of the day or year. In other poems, it is possible to witness the mind of the poet uniting with the world around him. Bashō expresses this through an insect:

> Butterflies only
> Fluttering in this field
> Of sunlight.[40]

This insect is the only such butterfly in the world at this very moment, and the poet feels unity with it. Thus, nature is used by Bashō to teach a truth relevant to Zen that the transient is part of the eternal. Within *haiku* poems, the transient elements are expressed by such phenomena like the chirps of insects, songs of birds, or scents of blossoms, whereas the eternal elements are expressed by more enduring or repetitive elements like water, wind, sunshine, the seasons.

---

38. Suzuki, *Zen and Japanese Culture*, 237.
39. Suzuki, *Zen and Japanese Culture*, 25.
40. Suzuki, *Zen and Japanese Culture*, 50.

ZEN AND JAPANESE FINE ARTS 203

Haiku poetry does not give its reader much of a hint about the sensations or feelings of the poet, who tends to give us the name of things. The poet also does not describe a scene as much as he presents it. Moreover, he does so in a way that does not give meaning. The *haiku* poet presents objects that have meaning. A poem by Bashō illustrates these points:

> Grave to move!
> My wailing voice:
> Autumn wind.[41]

Bashō presents his reader with a new grave, a response to death, and the wind. This poem weaves together the transient nature of human life with the wind of nature. The grave, voice, and wind are three phenomena with meaning because the death is recent, the grief is a genuine response to the death, and the autumn wind is associated with a time of the year when nature also dies. The seasons of life are like the seasons of nature by ending in death. It is typical of *haiku* poetry to find a reference to the season of the year, which often functions as the background for the picture portrayed by the poet.

The seasons or weather are frequently a way for the poet to evoke the reader's emotions. Bashō's following poem illustrates this point:

> Morning-glories
> Even they, too, are not
> My friend.[42]

The sadness suggested by autumn winds in a previous poem is missing here, but in its place, the morning-glory evokes sad feelings of quickly fading beauty and is analogous to quickly fading human life.

Many of Bashō's poems express humor and the spirit of play that was discussed in chapter 6. Bashō makes fun of his ineptitude in the following poem:

> Striking the fly
> I hit also
> A flowering plant.[43]

Sometimes, Bashō sees humans and things that are humorously juxtaposed:

---

41. Barnhill, *Bashō's Journey*, 71.
42. Barnhill, *Bashō's Haiku*, 139.
43. Barnhill, *Bashō's Haiku*, 145.

> In the same house
> Prostitutes too were slept
> Bush clover and the moon.[44]

The clover and moon are widely disparate things. This difference can also be discovered with Bashō and his traveling companion sleeping in the same inn with two immoral women of the world.[45] The women kept the two companions awake with conversations in a nearby room about their impending separation the next day from their elder escort.

Believing themselves to be victims of bad karma, the women were on a pilgrimage to the Grand Shrine of Ise, a Shinto holy place, to earn good karma to improve their chances in the next world because they feared retribution as punishment for their lifestyle. Although the humanity of these women emotionally touched Bashō, he found it a bit amusing for two itinerate poets to be in their midst, which is a situation as odd as that with the clover and moon. Bashō's humor is not always apparent to a reader, as in this example:

> Bagworms
> Come hear their cry;
> A thatched hut.[46]

On the surface of this poem, there is nothing very humorous. However, this is a kind of inside joke because a bagworm does not make any sound. It sits in its bag, gestating and metamorphosing into a moth.

The spirit of play, however, is evident in the next poem:

> Hey kids!
> Let's run around
> In the hail![47]

Bashō acts uninhibitedly by assuming the character of a child. While indoors with some children, Bashō perceives the hail, and he invites the youngsters to join him outside in a spirit of enthusiasm with him to see it. Bashō invites his reader to become child-like in the sense of reacting spontaneously. At other times, Bashō enters the spirit of play in solitude, like the following poem:

---

44. Barnhill, *Bashō's Haiku*, 145.
45. Barnhill, *Bashō's Haiku*, 98.
46. Barnhill, *Bashō's Haiku*, 61.
47. Barnhill, *Bashō's Haiku*, 107.

> With my fan
> I mime drinking sake—
> Falling cherry blossoms.[48]

During the historical period in which Bashō lived, cherry blossom time was the occasion for *sake* parties under the trees. Bashō joins the party and world of play from his solitude by miming drinking with his fan. Being free of bottles, he is engaged in the pure act of drinking.

As evident in earlier chapters, humor and play are germane to the spirit of Zen. In other poems, we find Bashō capturing the more philosophical implications of Zen and the Zen stress upon the limits of language and wordless communication:

> They spoke no word
> The visitor, the host
> And the white chrysanthemum.[49]

Without the utterance of words, there is nothing to stand in the way of the relationship between the visitor, host, and flower. Too much language can interfere with the direct relationship with others and objects.

The Zen spirit of no-mind is expressed in an onomatopoeic piece by Bashō:

> The old pond
> A frog jumps in—
> Water's sound.[50]

Besides the overgrown lily pond and frog making a sound, Bashō presents to the reader his mind as a timeless, endless, serene, and potent, old pond. Other poems relate something profound about the poet's relationship to the universe:

> Lightning—
> Into the darkness
> A night-heron's cry.[51]

Lying suspended in the darkness, Bashō is suddenly awakened by a lightning flash and then the darkness returns. A heron responds with a scream. Darkness is a metaphor for the undifferentiated absolute,

---

48. Barnhill, *Bashō's Haiku*, 38.
49. Barnhill, *Bashō's Haiku*, 137.
50. Barnhill, *Bashō's Haiku*, 137.
51. Barnhill, *Bashō's Haiku*, 150.

whereas light expresses the experience of the next phenomenal world. As the darkness and light alternate, Bashō is absorbed in a timeless, boundless universe. Another poetic product of his creative mind expresses an important message about the world:

> Summer in the world;
> Floating on the lake
> Over the waves.[52]

The waves represent the cycle of rebirth as the poet floats in a boat. Just as summer will give way to another season in a transient cycle that is endless, the other features of the poem like the world, floating, and waves are tied together to express the transient nature of life. Finally, Bashō expresses emptiness in some of his poems, like the following example:

> White chrysanthemum.
> Gazing closely,
> Not a speck of dust.[53]

The white chrysanthemum is usually a symbol of purity in Japan. In this poem, there is no hint of dirt or impurity to obscure perception. However, the experience of emptiness is a realization that arises from an attitude that is devoid of any distinction between what is pure or stained.

Other poems reflect a Zen influence with a message about our relationship to the universe. This message is evident in the following poem:

> Squeaking in response
> To the young sparrows.
> Mice in their nest.[54]

This poem depicts an intimate connection between the baby mice and sparrows, which is also true for humans, animals, and things. Although we are all completely dissimilar, we live within a web of life that makes us dependent upon one another in a symbiotic universe. Another poem combines the interrelatedness of things within the universe with an emphasis on their transitory nature.

> The hawk's eyes, too
> Have darkened now:
> Calling quail.[55]

52. Barnhill, *Bashō's Haiku*, 77.
53. Barnhill, *Bashō's Haiku*, 154.
54. Barnhill, *Bashō's Haiku*, 34.
55. Barnhill, *Bashō's Haiku*, 121.

When evening comes, the hawk cannot see as well, and the quail becomes emboldened and begins to chirp after hiding during the day from the hawk. Showing his sensitivity to the interplay of life in nature, Bashō indicates in a suggestive way that the hawk preys on the quail, and the quail upon insects, and insects feed on smaller insects in the cycle of life. As day gives day to night, and as hawk gives way to the quail, this suggests that it is possible to find experience at the edge of transitions.

CONCLUDING REMARKS

Just as rocks have energy and awareness and are arranged according to the flow of *yin* and *yang*, the artist invites the viewer to enter the playful nature of the gardens and to feel the flow and energy being exuded by the gardens. The creator of the garden plays with the viewer's sense of perception by employing visual tricks on their eyes. The rock gardens at Zen temples have pedagogical and soteriological dimensions by pointing to basic Buddhist teachings about the impermanence of everything, dependent co-arising, and emptiness. In a metaphorical sense, Zen monks strip nature bare with their abstract rock gardens and invite viewers to discover their original nature freed of historical, social, and cultural accretions that function to obscure the truth. The ink landscape artist also plays with a viewer's perception by, for instance, using black ink and allowing the perceiver to supply the colors of nature, which can never be precisely recreated by an artist. The game begun by the landscape artist never really ends because there is always more to see with subsequent viewings.

The Nō theater and the way of tea share a subjunctive quality like that found in play. The leading actor pours out his soul as if the narrative is authentic and is attuned to the feelings of his audience to the extent that he can alter his performance. The tea master conducts a ceremony in a rustic hut that blocks out the external world, as if nothing significant is happening beyond the confines of the hut, giving the impression that everything is tranquil despite what might be happening in the outside world. Playing a game and becoming absorbed in it is also a way to block out the external noise coming from the world.

Bashō's *haiku* poetry uses many different players to convey its message. There are flowers, a mountain path, an arrow, a butterfly, a grave, a fly, a bagworm, a hut, a fan, a frog, lightning, and mice that make their appearance in his poetic creations. The confinement of the poem to seventeen syllables is a challenge for the artist and functions as the width and length of the playing field within which his poetic game is played. Haiku often includes the season of the year and/or time of day. The poems also express the way that the elements fit together. Some poems have an innocent and spontaneously playful sense about them. Within the poems, the mundane encounters the transcendent and the eternal interacts with the transient. Moreover, the wandering lifestyle of Bashō is a good example of living life as play.

In summary, the path of Japanese fine arts informs a reader about the importance of the interconnectedness of all things and the necessity for self-cultivation. The goal is to transform oneself and to become more aware. These fine arts also stress unity, simplicity, austerity, and tranquility. The *haiku* poems invite spontaneity and love of nature, which is conceived as being alive with energy even in its stones. Harmony is expressed in the tea ceremony, landscape painting, and rock gardens. Finally, the Japanese fine arts are pervaded by Buddhist notions such as impermanence, concentration, self-control, and emptiness.

8

ZEN, DEATH, AND THE MARTIAL ARTS

THE MARTIAL ARTS ARE intimately connected to the samurai way of life and the *Bushidō* code of warrior conduct. This code means the determined will to die. An eighteenth-century text captures the spirit of an earlier period by giving the following advice: "Every morning make up thy mind how to die. Every evening freshens thy mind in the thought of death. And let this be done without end."[1] When a person is determined to die death loses its sting. We have already noted that Zen possessed many features that appealed to the samurai warrior class. Warriors were attracted to Zen because it represented practice in meditation. Zen was also anti-institutional, which allowed for more freedom of action and practice. The non-political nature of Zen and its emphasis on individual action was appealing to the warrior class.[2] The Zen attitude toward death was also influential on the samurai.

From the perspective of the Zen Master Dōgen, death is not an external power that arrives from outside of a person to claim one's life. It is rather co-present with life. Dōgen asserts that life and death interpenetrate each other: "Life is the total experience of life; conversely, death is the total experience of death."[3] Dōgen indicates that life and death do not obstruct each other. In another context, he writes, "There is life in death, and there is death in life. There is death that is constantly in death;

---

1. Suzuki, *Zen and Japanese Culture*, 73.
2. Wu, *Butterfly as Companion*, 30–32.
3. Dōgen, *Shōbōgenzō*, 2:81.

there is life that is always in life."⁴ If life and death interpenetrate each other, this means that death is not the termination of life. It is wiser to grasp birth and death as two discrete positions of time. Birth and death are both in a position of total time that possesses a past and future. Birth is non-birth and extinction is non-extinction. When either birth or death arrive, a person should surrender oneself to them without hating or desiring them. By choosing death by abiding in it, death is not a death among other innumerable deaths. It is rather the death that is paradoxically non-death, and yet it is a death that nothing can replace. It is this type of philosophy of death that made sense to the warrior class.

For its initial hundred years, it was common for Japanese citizens to view Buddhism as a cult centered on the worship of images by monastic figures.⁵ But during the sixth and seventh centuries of Japanese history, Buddhism began to develop expertise in death and came to monopolize death in the everyday lives of its citizens.⁶ This commenced the cultural practices of a couple getting married by Shinto priests and being buried according to a Buddhist service. The typical Zen funeral for a monk was a formal affair that included notification of the death to the government, gaining permission to conduct a service, preparation of the body of the deceased, dressing the corpse in clean robes and placing it in a coffin in an upright, seated position. Once the deceased is transported to the cremation grounds, the abbot lights the pyre in a ceremony that includes offering incense, a brief sermon, chanting of the name of Amida, and further scripture recitations. In a typical funeral, sermons do not eulogize the deceased, but are rather directed to the living observers about how they should face death. Overall, the entire ceremony is marked with choreographed movements that are punctuated with the ringing of bells and gongs. The ceremony concludes with a ritual transference of merit to the deceased monk to assist him to attain salvation in the Pure Land. The next day the ashes are collected and deposited in a stone pagoda or thrown into a river.

In comparison to the death of an ordinary monk, the death of a master became even more specially ritualized. The death of a master involved a three-step sequence:⁷ prediction of death, final words, and meditative absorption. It was commonly believed that an enlightened master

4. Kim, *Dōgen Kigen*, 226.
5. Bowring, *Religious Traditions of Japan*, 21–22.
6. Bowring, *Religious Traditions of Japan*, 41.
7. Faure, *Rhetoric of Immediacy*, 186–87.

had the ability to foretell his own death. By examining the presence or absence of bubbles in one's saliva, a master can be forewarned of his impending death because the presence of bubbles in one's saliva represents life, whereas their absence signifies death.[8] The second aspect of the death of a master is the composition of death verses, which is usually preceded by the designation of a successor. The verses are intended to testify to the degree of the master's enlightenment. Finally, the meditation posture is the final death posture of the master, requiring him to die in a seated posture to demonstrate practice until death, transforming the master's death into a public event.[9]

A popular death rite performed by Buddhist priests for the laity is the posthumous ordination of the deceased person, which is done in the home of the deceased. A small chapel is created near the deceased, verses are chanted, and the deceased is asked three times if he or she intended to observe the Buddhist teachings. The silence of the deceased is considered an affirmative answer. The ceremony includes the presentation to the deceased of a bowl, robe, and lineage chart, on which a Buddhist name is substituted for the deceased person's secular name. This ordination service for a layperson transforms him or her into a monk or nun, and thus includes shaving of the head of the deceased.

WAY OF DEATH AMONG THE SAMURAI

The term *samurai* is derived from a Japanese verb (*saburau*) meaning to serve. The term was used to refer to personal attendants. During the period between the tenth and eleventh centuries in Japan, it was applied exclusively to members of the provincial warrior class, who were destined to become the ruling elite of the country. During the Heian period (794–1185), the imperial court was deprived of its tax income because land fell into private hands. Therefore, the court was obliged to curtail its administrative services, which were transferred to local militia that assumed responsibility for maintaining order in the provinces. It was this transfer of power that served as the chief impetus for the rise of the warrior class.

Because techniques of massive troop movements and coordinated maneuvers did not develop until between the period of the fourteenth

---

8. Faure, *Rhetoric of Immediacy*, 187.
9. Faure, *Rhetoric of Immediacy*, 189–90.

and fifteenth centuries, samurai warriors fought individually against one opponent at a time, which suited their personal preference to fight alone. This style of single combat could be used to impress their lord, and it made it easier to know who was victorious, which was important for the redistribution of confiscated holdings and land by defeated foes. Single combat developed its own ritualistic mode of individual combat. This began with a warrior announcing his name, family pedigree, and an expression of personal humility; admitting that he was unconcerned about his own life or death; and challenging an opponent to test his skill and strength. The aims of this procedure were to raise the fighting spirit of one's side and to intimidate the enemy. It was also an expression of pride in one's lineage and family heritage. After the conclusion of the conflict, a warrior gave a great victory shout. Then the process of counting severed heads took place to determine who accomplished certain deeds. If one acquired the head of an ally, the warrior was punished by the severance of a finger from his right hand. Much of this procedure was important because the samurai fought less for himself than for his family and the perpetuation of its reputation and glory. The worst fate that a warrior could endure was not death, but it was rather disgrace in combat because a warrior's lack of courage or honor reflected negatively on the reputation of his family.

The centrality of the family in a warrior's life carried over to his relationship with his lord. The relationship between a samurai warrior and his lord was like that within a family. For instance, the lord often referred to his vassals as housemen and children of the household. This family bond was evident in the phenomenon of the vendetta. A genuine samurai would never live content in the same world as the slayer of his father or lord. In other words, it was his responsibility to avenge the death of his lord. This attitude and commitment led, of course, to a never-ending cycle of violence.

The samurai were not, however, a group of cold-blooded killers, seeking combat for thrills, vengeance, or an excuse to kill another person. They lived according to a strict code of conduct that was shaped by Buddhist, Neo-Confucian, and Shinto ideas. The lifestyle of the warrior was like an ascetic way of life because the warrior was instructed to lead a sober, restrained, and frugal existence. Frugality was, for instance, an obligation to reduce his consumption to a minimum, which was like that of a Buddhist monk. Some may find this strange because of the warrior life that he led, but the samurai had a very high regard for learning, although not for its own sake. The purpose of learning was the cultivation of the self and control of others.

In general, the *Bushidō* code was not a body of fixed laws, because it was more akin to an ideal of behavior. The spirit of this ethical code embodied eight basic attitudes. The first was understandably loyalty, which was directed to the emperor and one's lord. In the samurai mind, loyalty was closely linked to filial piety, a central Confucian virtue denoting devotion to one's parents. Other virtues included gratitude, justice, truthfulness, politeness, and courage, which entailed willingness to give one's life in service to one's lord. There were two additional virtues that included reserve, which involved concealing one's true feelings, and honor, which meant for the samurai that death was preferable to disgrace. Due to the importance of honor in the code and lifestyle of the warrior, he always carried two swords: a long sword to fight his enemies and another shorter one to use on himself in case of blunder or defeat.

According to the *Bushido Shoshinsu* of Taira Shigesuke (1639–1730), a Confucian scholar and military figure, a warrior is defined as "one who is supposed to be a warrior considers it his foremost concern to keep death in mind at all times."[10] By keeping the thought of death always on one's mind, one will enjoy fulfilling virtues such as loyalty and familial duties, avoid evil, be physically sound and healthy, live a long life, and improve one's character and virtue. Since the way of life of a samurai warrior was also a way of death, the symbol of a short life and early death of a warrior was the cherry blossom. There was a Japanese adage that went: "Among flowers it is the cherry blossom; among men it is the samurai." However, the great death of the Zen monk like that referred to by Hakuin served as the paradigm for the warrior. An accepted form of atonement for failure or misjudgment was suicide. Suicide was not considered a cowardly act, but it was instead an action possessing the qualities of nobility, strength, and determination. In short, it was the honorable way to die, and it was far preferable than dying at someone else's hand, which was considered a disgraceful way to die.

The samurai form of suicide was called *seppuku* (disembowelment). A grosser Japanese term was *hara-kiri*, literally belly slitting. *Seppuku* was a ritualized form of suicide for males, whereas *jigai*, a cutting of one's jugular vein, was the accepted form for women. For males, the cutting of the abdomen was symbolically important because it represent a person's

---

10. Cleary, *Code of the Samurai*, 3.

vital center. If one recalls the discussion of Zen meditation in chapter 3, this point about the abdomen being the vital center will be apparent. By cutting his abdomen, a warrior publicly acknowledged that his vital center was undefiled. A person performed an act of suicide in a kneeling posture, inserted his dagger into his left side, drew the knife across his abdomen, and made a final thrust upwards on the right side of the abdomen. Frequently, the person performing *seppuku* had a companion that used his longer fighting sword to decapitate the suicide and dispatch him as soon as possible to end his suffering. After performing the cutting of his abdomen, the suicide leaned forward, exposing the back of his neck to give his companion an opportunity to decapitate him. Due to the suicide's kneeling position and blow to the back of his neck and the keen sharpness of the blade, it was not unusual for his companion to sever not only his neck but in addition his knee caps. Besides being an honorable way to die, *seppuku* was also used to punish a person guilty of a serious crime, sparing him the shame of being executed by an executioner. Thus, *seppuku* was an honorable and face-saving way to die. A person might decide to commit *seppuku* for several reasons, which include the following possible scenarios: having fallen alive into an enemy's hands; as a protest of an unjust decision; to protest unfair treatment by authorities; and being deficient in performing one's duties.

If swordsmanship was originally an aggressive and violent activity, it became a more defensive and non-injurious action as the Japanese medieval period unfolded. The bloody, decade-long struggle of the Ōnin War (1467–77) marked a turning point for the samurai and his sword. In a profound sense, the sword was eclipsed in fourteenth-century warfare by various types of projectiles and missiles that caused the bulk of the battlefield injuries.[11] Thus, the intimacy of a sword duel was overshadowed by long range weapons. The end of the destructive Ōnin War opened the cultural door for the ascent of the Shinkage school of swordsmanship that sought ways to make peace and avoid war. This school was centered in the village of Hotokuzen, and was associated with the family temple of the Yagyū clan, being more precisely founded by Takuan Sōhō (1573–1645), a Zen priest and abbot of Daitokuji temple in Kyoto, who brought swordsmanship under Zen influence. Takuan likened the art of swordsmanship to a *kōan* that is impossible to solve rationally. The crux of the problem was: How does one establish nonaggressive peace? He

---

11. Haskel, *Sword of Zen*, 21–22.

answered this *kōan* by means of the sword that was no-sword, a sword connected to no-mind.

In his theoretical texts, Takuan compared the mind to water that never stops, never stays in a single place for long, and is always flowing. What he is indicating is a mind that is unattached to anything. By being unattached or fixated on one thing, the mind of the swordsman cannot be caught off guard. By having an unattached mind, the swordsman's body can move freely, much like water. Conversely, a mind attached to the opponent's blade causes one to lose freedom and be slain.[12] Takuan illustrated his point by recalling the image of the *bodhisattva* Kannon with his thousand arms when he writes, "It's just because its mind doesn't become fixed at any one place that all its arms work."[13] What Takuan is discussing is evoked by the image of the *bodhisattva* Mañjuśrī that appears in many meditation halls (*endo*) of many Zen temples. Mañjuśrī is depicted holding a sword that symbolically represents *prajñā* (intuitive wisdom). Within the confines of the meditation hall, the meditation monitor walks up and down holding a warning stick (*keisaku*) used to awaken those meditators, personifying the figure of Mañjuśrī, who have fallen asleep or fallen into the incorrect posture.

Beyond these metaphorical figures, Takuan discusses the original mind, our basic endowment, and the deluded mind that is attached. The original mind or no-mind is equated with emptiness and inherent Buddha-nature. This no-mind is perpetually responsive because it is free and devoid of thought or intention. Takuan compares no-mind to a scarecrow that scares away birds and deer, even though it does not act.[14] For Takuan, swordsmanship is something immediate, direct, natural, and spontaneous. Takuan defines the master of the sword as someone who does not use his weapon to kill an opponent but rather to bring the other to life.[15]

ZEN AND THE ART OF ARCHERY

Besides the proper stance, the archer must learn to draw the bow properly because it symbolically encloses everything when it is drawn. When drawing the string one must not exert the full strength of one's body. A

12. Haskel, *Sword of Zen*, 33.
13. Haskel, *Sword of Zen*, 35.
14. Haskel, *Sword of Zen*, 36.
15. Haskel, *Sword of Zen*, 51.

student must learn to let only his hands do the work, while the arms and shoulder muscles remain relaxed. This might sound easy to execute, but these bows were very long and difficult to pull with ease. Central to learning the art of archery is the accompanying breath control. Each phase of the process begins with inhaling and ends with exhaling. Breath control is used with each sequence of grasping the bow, nocking the arrow, raising the bow, drawing it, and releasing the shot. Assuming a student has mastered the control of his breath, these various steps must be done without effort, purpose, or thinking. A person must simultaneously be relaxed during the various phases.

On a more theoretical level, the archer aims at himself and yet not at himself. His objective is to become the aimer and the aim, the hitter and the hit, which suggests a non-dualistic position. The archer must also withdraw from all attachments and become egoless, and this detachment includes one's weapon. It is assumed that if one's mind is not attached to any place, it is present everywhere. When practicing this art, the archer must forget about hitting the target, although paradoxically one concentrates entirely on the target. In fact, hitting the center of the target is irrelevant. It is thus possible to become a master without hitting the target. Therefore, one does not strain for accuracy, which simply comes because of intuitively applying perfect technique. Just as a Zen meditator forgets body and self and discards them at a certain point, the archer must also forget technique, bow, draw, and release. In other words, the steps culminating with the release of the arrow must occur without intention or deliberation. The archer reaches a point where he is totally unaware of his actions. The goal of the student is for the bow, arrow, goal, and ego to melt into each other to the extent that there is no longer a separation between them. In short, this is an artless art.

In 1953 in the West, a German professor of philosophy named Eugen Herrigel published the English version of his book *Zen in the Art of Archery*, a work based on his personal experience studying with a master in Japan after World War II, a work that captured the imagination of its readers. Japanese scholars have called his description of his experience into question because it does not fit the actual art of archery. What Herrigel does not tell his reader is that there have been numerous lineages teaching different methods. The two main categories of Japanese archery are ceremonial archery that is concerned with ritual and thaumaturgic aspects and military archery that is divided into foot, equestrian, and temple forms of archery. The initial military type refers to foot soldiers, the second to shooting from horseback, and the third type is indicative of a contest between archers.[16] If the third type of military archery is associated with sport, the initial two are directly related to the possibility of death. Herrigel's account does not mention any of these distinctions. The Zen connection of Herrigel's teacher has been called into question as has their ability to communicate lucidly. In short, the art of archery is not strictly a product of Zen, but also includes Neo-Confucian, Daoist, and Shinto elements that helped to shape it.

ZEN AND THE ART OF SWORDSMANSHIP

The symbolic significance of the sword was deeply embedded in Japanese culture. In addition to the mirror and jewels, the sword of the emperor was one of the three imperial treasures. The emperor's sword symbolized the sword of Susano, Shinto god of thunder, which he wrested from an eight-headed, eight-tailed monster during the primordial period. The sword of the emperor has become part of imperial regalia, which is housed in a sacred Shinto shrine at Atsuta.[17] If the sword helped in part to define the status of the emperor, the sword was equally significant to the warrior because it defined his identity and status.

The craft of sword making embodies a mythical and religious aura. It was believed, for instance, that the character of the smith entered the very nature of the blade.[18] The sword assumed a *yūgen* (mysterious) and nearly sacred character within Japanese culture. The maker tried to touch it with only clean tissues to prevent rust and to render it respect as a special object. The warrior carried two types of swords: a curved blade used for slashing and a short sword with a blade of sixteen to twenty inches used for close hand-to-hand combat. The samurai were so wedded to their swords to the extent of being a part of their identity that they rejected using guns, which represented a challenge to the samurai way of life from their perspective. The samurai opposed guns for aesthetic and culture reasons. A gun was, for instance, foreign in both conception and form, whereas the sword embodied honor and dignity. In fact, the right to wear a sword was a sign of high social position. Moreover, the use of a sword required a delicate coordination of body, strength, suppleness,

---

16. Shōji, "Myth of Zen," 56.
17. Wu, *Butterfly as Companion*, 38.
18. Kim, *Dōgen Kigen*, 73.

rhythm, and mental faculties, which cannot be claimed for a gun.[19] To enhance these features, warriors stopped using the scabbard to hold their sword by the fifteenth century. They instead thrust their swords through their midriff sashes to save time when they were attacked by an enemy warrior.

Technical control and spiritual awareness are the two main components of the art of swordsmanship. These two components form a unity. Spiritual awareness manifests itself as the natural simplicity of the heart. Undistracted and un-diverted by emotions or intentions, the swordsman must spontaneously conform to each new situation. His reaction must follow, for instance, as immediately as a mirror reflects an image. The sword functions in two ways to help the warrior achieve his ability to react swiftly. In the first instance, it functions to destroy anything that opposes the will of its owner. It also functions symbolically and practically to sacrifice impulses that derived from the instinct for self-preservation.

When practicing the art of swordsmanship, the goal of a student was to become one with his weapon. During training to become a master of the art, the warrior became identified with his weapon to the extent that his sword, arm, body, and mind became unified. Once this goal was achieved, the swordsman could act instinctively and simultaneously without having to logically think about his moves. This is possible because his technical moves had become part of his very being. The genuine master reaches a point in his art of realizing non-self. The selflessness involved possesses important results: there is no thought of killing in the act of killing someone and there is no thought of giving life when bestowing life. The spirit of this unity and selflessness is expressed in the writings of Daitō Kokushi:

> I thought all the time I was learning how to win;
> But I realize now:
> To win is no more,
> No less, than to lose.[20]

This warrior gives expression to the ultimate emptiness of winning and losing with a saying explicitly expressing his thoughts this way. This quotation also suggests that the genuine master is selfless. The lack of a sharp distinction between winning and losing evokes the risky nature of play.

19. Wu, *Butterfly as Companion*, 91–92.
20. Suzuki, *Zen and Japanese Culture*, 216.

The risky feature of play recalls its ability to transform a person despite its autotelic nature, suggesting an action devoid of personal goals or purposes. The archer and swordsman do not adhere to a fixed purpose with respect to their artistic ways. There remains a sense that these figures enter play for the pure sake of playing that can be comprehended as leaping into emptiness from the Zen viewpoint. In both the ways of the sword and archery, the aspirant practiced for many years to become a master that enabled one to act without thinking or the slightest deliberation. The artistic master of the sword or archery achieves a mental harmony and integration that benefits the conscious and unconscious mind.[21] This mental achievement helps one attain the unification of the mind, body, and energy (*qi*) of a practitioner. Although centered in the lower abdomen, the *qi* is an energy that flows throughout one's body. It is the duty of the practitioner to unify this energy with their body and mind.

In the arts of swordsmanship and archery, there are elements of play, such as being unproductive activities because they produce no goods or wealth. These arts are indicative of play as disposition, a pattern of attentiveness, readiness, or psychological commitment that accommodates behavior.[22] Swordsmanship and archery exemplify play as, for example, a satisfactory experience that can be pleasurable. These types of artistic ways are an example of play that is performative.

DEATH AND HUMOR

Because the life of a samurai warrior was often short and violent, we cannot expect to find tales of samurai clown figures, madcap, fun-loving, and humorous guys. But this does not mean that Zen Buddhism did not perceive some humor in death. This does not mean that death itself is funny or humorous. But how people relate to it, anticipate it, and react to death can be humorous. With respect to death, humor is not something insensitive or frivolous. On the contrary, it is a matter of insight and freedom. For instance, when the dying Nanquan was asked by his head monk, "Where are you going after your death?" He replied, "I am going down the hill to be a water buffalo!" "Would it be possible to follow you there?" inquired the devoted monk. Nanquan responded, "If you want

---

21. See Yusa, *Body, Self-Cultivation*.
22. Henricks, *Play and the Human Condition*, 29.

to follow me, please come with straw in your mouth!"[23] As witnessed in chapter 6, humor is a sign of enlightenment and liberation. Zhaozhou, for instance, seeing the somberness of the funeral procession for one of his monks, exclaimed: "What a long train of dead bodies follows in the wake of a single living being."[24]

In terms of spiritual freedom, humor suggests liberation from clinging to life and anxiety over the self. This is illustrated by the story of Dengyanfeng as he was about to die asking his fellow monks, "I have seen monks die in various positions; some lying down, some sitting, some standing. But has anyone ever died standing on his head?" The monks could recall no stories to this effect. Whereupon, Deng stood on his head and died. When it was time to carry him to the funeral pyre he was still upside-down, to the wonder of those who came to view the remains, and to the consternation of those who would properly dispose of the body. Finally, his younger sister, a nun, came to the monastery and chiding him said: "When you were alive you took no notice of laws and customs, and even now that you are dead you are making a nuisance of yourself." And with that she poked him with her finger, felling him with a thud.[25] The freedom suggested by this narrative implies that the degree to which you are free, you are free to laugh. This narrative does not suggest laughter that is cynical or bitter. It is rather laughter of acceptance. This laughter affirms both the transience of life and the naturalness of death. It is laughter that expresses the joy of life.

It is also the laughter of non-ego and non-attachment. This means that a person is free to embrace death as well as life. The spirit of this type of laughter is embodied in the narrative of the Master Taji. As Taji neared death, his senior disciples assembled at his bedside. One of them, remembering that the master was fond of a certain kind of cake, spent half a day searching the pastry shops of Tokyo for this confection, which he now presented to the master. With a wan smile the dying master accepted a piece of the cake and slowly began munching it. As the old master grew weaker, his disciples leaned close and inquired whether he had any final words for them. "Yes," the master replied. The disciples leaned forward eagerly. "Please tell us." The master said, "My, but this cake is delicious!" And with that he died.[26]

23. Dumoulin, *History of Zen Buddhism*, 165.
24. Hamayon, *Why We Play*, 105.
25. Sicart, *Play Matters*, 8.
26. Sicart, *Play Matters*, 16.

As we noted in chapter 6, seriousness is a lucid sign of attachment and thus bondage. The Zen monk knows how to die because he knows how to live, which means being immersed in life without clinging to it. This non-attachment is combined with an iconoclastic spirit by Ikkyū in one of his poems:

> Dimly for thirty years;
> Faintly for thirty years—Dimly and faintly for sixty years;
> At death, I pass my feces and offer them to Brahma.[27]

Based on his entire life, Ikkyū thinks that it is important to celebrate each moment of life as it presents itself. Dōgen expresses this succinctly when he states, "In life identify yourself with life; at death with death."[28] In part, this suggests that there is a beauty of life and a beauty of death. Moreover, there is no separation of life and death, time and eternity. If there is no separation between life and death, there is no reason to lament one's situation and to simply accept what is given. It is this spirit of acceptance and lack of anxiety in the face of death that impressed the samurai.

ZEN AND THE WAY OF WAR

Images of meditating monks and nuns in secluded locations in the countryside meditating and leading an ascetic lifestyle do not evoke thoughts of conflict and war. These types of images are misleading and inaccurate, if one examines the history of the nineteenth and twentieth centuries. But the historical background story of Zen and its relation to modern warfare is rooted in the Tokugawa period (1600–1868). During the Tokugawa era, Buddhism reached the pinnacle of its power by becoming the de facto state religion to the consternation of Shinto and Confucian followers. All Japanese households were required to affiliate with a nearby Buddhist temple, of which there were over 450,000. The evolution of Buddhism into a state religion during this period of history resulted in clergy becoming government functionaries and increased government control over the religion. Moreover, religious membership became a matter of political obligation rather than religious conviction. From this pinnacle of influence and power, Buddhism declined after the Meiji Restoration beginning in 1868.

---

27. Henricks, *Play and the Human Condition*, 184.
28. Wu, *Golden Age of Zen*, 45.

On April 6, 1868, the emperor issued the Charter Oath that consisted of five articles that seemed to be innocuous on the surface of it, even though it promoted anti-feudal aspirations. This was the start of legislation that led to other royal edicts that undermined Buddhism and strengthened Shinto. Examples of subverting Buddhism included removing Buddhist monks from Shinto shrines, only allowing Shinto priests the right to perform duties related to such shrines, prohibiting the use of Buddhist names for Shinto deities (*kami*), and decreeing that Buddhist statues could no longer represent Shinto deities. Thus, a process of separating the two religions was attempted. The national Office of Rites took further aggressive action against Buddhism by closing 40,000 Buddhist temples, destroying religious artifacts, and laicizing thousands of Buddhist priests and nuns. In addition to these actions, the Office of Rites, which was dominated by Shinto leaders, promoted national learning by teaching, for instance, that the Japanese nation and throne were of divine origin. The reason that people did not know this was due to the acceptance by the people of foreign accretions and influences coming from China in the form of Buddhism.

Various Buddhist sects responded to these imperially directed changes. The devotional Shin sect, for example, lent substantial sums of money to the cash-starved Meiji government, an attempt to ameliorate policies by bribing the government. Most Buddhists recognized that their best hope for a positive outcome was to align themselves with the rising nationalistic spirit. Buddhists attempted to ingratiate themselves to the nation by joining, for example, the anti-Christian campaign, during a historical period when anything foreign was treated with suspicion. When peasants began to protest government actions against Buddhism this led to riots. In response to the riots and unrest among the populace, the government decided that its suppression of Buddhism was neither possible nor safe. Thus, the government changed course again and prudently incorporated Buddhism into the new state religion, although it continued to be controlled by the Shinto elite.

After attempting to originally separate Buddhism from Shinto and then trying to synthesize them, the government devised a more subversive plan when it issued Order Number 133 on April 25, 1812. In part, the order stated that Buddhist priests could eat meat, get married, grow their hair long, and wear ordinary clothing. This was obviously an attempt to undermine Buddhism from the inside by promoting a separation of Buddhism from itself.

Although Buddhism did not die out, Shinto did continue to gain power and influence. In 1882, Shinto split into State Shinto and Sect Shinto. The former entity represented a cult of national morality, politics, and patriotism that was centered on the emperor. Sect Shinto represented the religious and less political side of the religion. State Shinto was actively supported by the government with financial assistance, whereas Sect Shinto received no government support.

Having been dethroned by national government forces favorable to Shinto, Buddhist sects responded to the anti-Buddhist critique by showing that Buddhist priests and temples could make a valuable contribution to the nation's social and economic life. Buddhists also insisted that it could promote loyalty to the emperor, patriotism, and national unity. Moreover, the Buddhist leaders claimed that their basic doctrines and practices were compatible with western science and technology, which were considered indispensable for military success and national progress.

During the twentieth century, there was a rapid growth of Japanese militarism that culminated in victory with the Russo-Japanese War, marking the first time that an Asian country had defeated a western power, which set Japan down the road toward building a political empire. Embolden by its military success against Russia, Japan forced the Korean king to sign a Treaty of Annexation in 1910, resulting in Korea's loss of independence. These events transformed Japan into a world power. Support for Japan's militarism was not shared by everyone. Originating with mostly laity, some people, for example, formed the Youth League for Revitalizing Buddhism, an organization that advocated social action, although other Buddhists joined the national bandwagon celebrating the cult of the emperor. The national cult of the divine emperor, who was also the head priest of the nation, turned World War II into a holy crusade. A small suggestion of this crusade could be found on ships with their Shinto shrine room.[29] Even the *banzai* battle charge shout was connected to the imperial cult because the shout was an abbreviated version of statement "May the Emperor live a thousand years" (*Tenno Heika Banzai*). When Japanese troops used the shortened version in a battle charge, they had no planned objective other than to frighten their opponent and they hoped to inflict some damage. What the soldiers really wanted was to die like a warrior and gain honor for themselves, their families, and their nation. The so-called *kamikaze* (divine wind) fighter pilots' ethos was

---

29. Blyth, *Oriental Humor*, 93–94.

even more self-sacrificial because it was basically a suicide strategy not intended to win the war as much as end the war in an honorable way. For both the fighter pilots and foot-soldiers, anyone who surrendered was considered a coward, treated with contempt, and despised, an attitude that helps to partially explain the root cause of the brutally inhuman treatment of Allied prisoners of war.[30]

The 1930s reflected the emergence of an imperial way for Buddhism that was evident in literature published supporting the cult of the emperor. Some Buddhists even published works supporting war, arguing that war was a method for accomplishing Buddhist goals by oddly saving sentient beings. These writers also argued that the emperor, a sacred king of old, was a protector of Buddhism and called the "Golden Wheel-Turning Sacred King." What these Buddhist writers meant was that the emperor represented a fully enlightened being of the secular world who had to use laws, taxes, and weapons because his subjects lack wisdom. Instead of hatred or anger toward other countries, they argued that the emperor stood for the force of compassion. In fact, war was a compassionate act. Finally, these Buddhist writers argued that the true goal of war was to transform the world into a Buddha Land.

Within the context of Japan's war effort, some Zen writers linked the old *Bushidō* code with military success by following the code, which they associated with the essence of being Japanese and adhering to its sacrificial ethos, loyalty to the emperor, and deep filial piety. Masunaga Reiho (1902–1981), a Sōtō priest and scholar, equated the suicidal spirit of *kamikaze* (divine winds) airplane pilots with complete enlightenment.[31] Furukawa Taigo, a popular commentator on Buddhism, published in 1934 a book entitled *Rapidly Advancing Japan and the New Mahayana Buddhism* in which he conceptually linked Zen, the *Bushidō* code, and the imperial military. This author argued that Zen was valuable to the military because it was realistic and this-worldly, it embodied a simple and optimistic spirit, it was atheistic and self-reliant, it resonated with the independent and virile spirit of warriors, it promoted a simple and frugal life that appealed to warrior temperament, and it was a vehicle for warriors to enter the realm of selflessness. These types of ideas led Furukawa to conclude that the Meiji Restoration did not mark the disappearance of the samurai warriors because all Japanese males have become samurai.

30. Hyers, *Laughing Buddha*, 96.
31. Sanford, *Zen-Man Ikkyū*, 191.

To fit Zen Buddhism to his political agenda and promote war, Furukawa redefined the religion and distorted it for his own nefarious purposes.

Some Zen Buddhists joined other Buddhist sects to hold special services designed to ensure victory in battle. A common practice was recitation of the Perfection of Wisdom Sūtras, an action that created merit that was then transferred to the Japanese military. Other activities to benefit the war effort included transforming Avalokiteśvara into a martial figure from his former status as an infinitely compassionate being. And the Rinzai sect even elevated this compassionate *bodhisattva* into a shōgun. Other Zen sects raised money for the war effort. It was not until the 1980s that the Sōtō sect expressed its sorrow for actively supporting their role in the war effort that ended in tragedy for countless people on both sides of the conflict.

In the post–World War II era, Zen forms of discipline were put to new uses by Japanese business corporations. The Zen ethos was used by corporations to instill discipline, obedience, and loyalty to superiors. Other monastic features like conformity and physical and mental endurance were also popular with corporations. Today, Zen meditation techniques are advocated to reduce the stress of contemporary life and pressures associated with work.

In the twentieth century Zen found an interested audience in the West because westerners were eagerly seeking new exotic experiences within the context of a religion that called into question many western cultural assumptions about life and reality. As we have observed in this book, there was also a playful spirit that is integral to Zen that appealed to a western audience. Who among us would not like to play in emptiness?

BIBLIOGRAPHY

Adamek, Wendi L. *The Mystique of Transmission: On the Early Chan History and Its Contexts.* New York: Columbia University Press, 2007.
Allinson, Robert A. *Chuang Tzu for Spiritual Transformation: An Analysis of the Inner Chapters.* Albany: State University of New York Press, 1989.
Ames, Roger T., and David L. Hall, trans. *Dao De Ching: A Philosophical Translation.* New York: Ballantine, 2003.
Arai, Paula K. R. "Women and Dōgen: Rituals Actualizing Empowerment and Healing." In *Zen Ritual: Studies of Zen Buddhist Theory in Practice*, edited by Steven Heine and Dale S. Wright, 196–201. New York: Oxford University Press, 2008.
Arntzen, Sonja. *Ikkyū Sōjun: A Zen Monk and His Poetry.* Bellingham, WA: Western Washington State College, 1973.
Austin, J. L. *How to Do Things with Words.* Cambridge, MA: Harvard University Press, 1967.
Barnhill, David Landis, trans. *Bashō's Haiku: Selected Poems of Matsuo Bashō.* Albany: State University of New York Press, 2004.
———. *Bashō's Journey: The Literary Prose of Matsuo Bashō.* Albany: State University of New York Press, 2005.
Baroni, Helen J. *Iron Eyes: The Life and Teachings of the Obaku Zen Master Tetsugen Dōkō.* Albany: State University of New York Press, 2006.
———. *Obaku Zen: The Emergence of the Third Sect of Zen in Tokugawa Japan.* Honolulu: University of Hawaii Press, 2000.
Berthier, François. *Reading Zen in the Rocks: The Japanese Dry Landscape Garden.* Translated by Graham Parkes. Chicago: University of Chicago Press, 2000.
Blackburn, Simon. *The Oxford Dictionary of Philosophy.* New York: Oxford University Press, 1994.
Blacker, Carmen. *The Catalpa Bow: A Study of Shamanistic Practices in Japan.* London: Routledge Curzon, 1982.
Blyth, R. H. *Haiku.* 4 vols. Tokyo: Hokuseido, 1949–52.
———. "Ikkyū's 'Skeletons.'" *The Eastern Buddhist* 6.1 (May 1973) 111–25.
———. *Oriental Humour.* Tokyo: Hokuseido, 1959.
———. *Zen and Zen Classics.* 3 vols. Tokyo: Hokuseido, 1964.
Bodiford, William M. "Dharma Transmission in Theory and Practice." In *Zen Ritual: Studies of Zen Buddhist Theory in Practice*, edited by Steven Heine and Dale S. Wright, 261–82. New York: Oxford University Press, 2008.
———. *Sōtō Zen in Medieval Japan.* Studies in East Asian Buddhism 8. Honolulu: University of Hawaii Press, 1993.

Bowring, Richard. *The Religious Traditions of Japan 500–1600*. Cambridge, UK: Cambridge University Press, 2005.

Broughton, Jeffery L. *The Bodhidharma Anthology: The Earliest Records of Zen*. Berkeley: University of California Press, 1999.

Broughton, Jeffery L., and Elise Yoko Watanabe, trans. *The Chan Whip Anthology: A Companion to Zen Practice*. New York: Oxford University Press, 2015.

Caillois, Roger. *Man, Play, and Games*. Translated by Meyer Barash. New York: Free Press, 1961.

Carter, Robert T. *The Japanese Arts and Self-Cultivation*. Albany: State University of New York Press, 2008.

Chang, Garma C. C., ed. *A Treasury of Mahāyāna Sūtras: Selections from the Mahāratnakūṭa Sūtra*. Translated by The Buddhist Association of the United States. University Park: Pennsylvania State University, 1983.

Cheng, Chung-ying. "On Zen (Ch'an) Language and Zen Paradoxes." *Journal of Chinese Philosophy* 3.1 (1973) 77–102.

Chen, Kenneth. *The Chinese Transformation of Buddhism*. Princeton: Princeton University Press, 1973.

Chun-fang, Yu. *Chinese Buddhism: A Thematic History*. Honolulu: University of Hawaii Press, 2020.

Chung-yuan, Chang. "Ch'an Teachings of the Yun-men School." *Chinese Culture* 4.4 (1964) 12–15.

———, trans. *Original Teachings of Ch'an Buddhism*. New York: Pantheon, 1969.

Cleary, J. C., trans. *The Recorded Sayings of Linji*. In *Three Chan Classics*. Berkeley, CA: Numata Center for Buddhist Translation and Research, 1999.

———, trans. *Wumen's Gate*. In *Three Chan Classics*. Berkeley, CA: Numata Center for Buddhist Tradition and Research, 1999.

Cleary, Thomas, trans. *The Blue Cliff Records*. Berkeley, CA: Numata Center for Buddhist Translation and Research, 1998.

———, trans. *Code of the Samurai: A Modern Translation of the Bushido Shoshinshu of Taira Shigesuke*. North Clarendon, VT: Tuttle, 1999.

Collins, Randall. *Violence: A Micro-Sociological Theory*. Princeton: Princeton University Press, 2008.

Conze, Edward, trans. *Heart Sutra*. In *Buddhist Wisdom Books*, 25–38. New York: Harper Torchbooks, 1958.

Cook, Francis H., trans. *Sounds of Valley Streams: Enlightenment in Dōgen's Zen Translation of Nine Essays from the Shōbōgenzō*. Albany: State University of New York Press, 1989.

Davids, T. W. Rhys, trans. *Dialogues of the Buddha* (*Digha Nikāya*). 3 vols. London: Luzac, 1966–71.

Davids, Mrs. Rhys, and F. L. Woodward, trans. *The Book of the Kindred Sayings* (*Sanyutta Nikāya*). 5 vols. London: Luzac, 1962–72.

Dōgen. *A Primer of Sōtō Zen: A Translation of Dōgen's Shōbōgenzō Zuimonki*. Translated by Reiho Masunaga. Honolulu: East-West Center Press, 1971.

———. *Shōbōgenzō* (*The Eye and Treasury of the True Law*). 4 vols. Translated by Kōsen Nishiyama. Tokyo: Nakayma Shobo, 1986.

Droogers, André. "The Third Bank of the River: Play, Methodological Ludism, and the Definition of Religion." In *Playful Religion: Challenges for the Study of Religion*, edited by Anton van Harskamp et al., 75–96. Delft, The Netherlands: Eburon Academic, 2008.

Dumoulin, Heinrich. *A History of Zen Buddhism*. Translated by Paul Peachey. New York: Pantheon, 1963.

———. *Zen Buddhism: A History*. Vol. 1, *Indian and China*. Translated by James W. Heisig and Paul Knitter. New York: Macmillan, 1990.

———. *Zen Buddhism: A History*. Vol. 2, *Japan*. Translated by James W. Heisig and Paul Knitter. New York: Macmillan, 1990.

———. *Zen Enlightenment: Origins and Meaning*. Translated by John C. Maraldo. New York: Weatherhill, 1979.

Eisai, Myōan. *A Treatise on Letting Zen Flourish to Protect the State*. In *Zen Texts*, translated by Gishin Tokiwa. Berkeley, CA: Numata Center for Buddhist Translation and Research, 2005.

Eliade, Mircea. *The Sacred and the Profane: The Nature of Religion*. Translated by Willard Trask. New York: Harcourt, Brace, 1959.

Falk, Nancy. "An Image of Woman in Old Buddhist Literature: The Daughters of Māra." In *Women and Religion*, edited by Judith Plaskow and Joan Arnold, 95–115. Missoula, MT: Scholars Press, 1974.

Faure, Bernard. *Chan Insights and Oversights: An Epistemological Critique of the Chan Tradition*. Princeton: Princeton University Press, 1993.

———. *The Power of Denial: Buddhism, Purity, and Gender*. Princeton: Princeton University Press, 2001.

———. *Rhetoric of Immediacy: A Cultural Critique of Chan/Zen Buddhism*. Princeton: Princeton University Press, 1991.

———. *The Will to Orthodoxy: A Critical Genealogy of Northern Chan Buddhism*. Translated by Phyllis Brooks. Stanford, CA: Stanford University Press, 1997.

Fink, Eugen. *Play as Symbol of the World and Other Writings*. Translated by Ian Alexander Moore and Christopher Turner. Bloomington: Indiana University Press, 2016.

Foulk, T. Griffin. "The Form and Function of Kōan Literature: A Historical Overview." In *The Kōan: Texts and Contexts in Zen Buddhism*, edited by Steven Heine and Dale S. Wright, 15–45. Oxford: Oxford University Press, 2000.

———. "Ritual in Japanese Zen Buddhism." In *Zen Ritual: Studies of Zen Buddhist Theory in Practice*, edited by Steven Heine and Dale S. Wright, 21–82. New York: Oxford University Press, 2008.

———. "Sung Controversies Concerning 'Separate Transmission' of Ch'an." In *Buddhism in the Sung*, edited by Peter N. Gregory and Daniel A. Getez, 210–94. Studies in East Asian Buddhism 13. Honolulu: University of Hawaii Press, 1999.

Gimello, Robert M. "Apophatic and Kataphatic Discourse in Mahāyāna: A Chinese View." *Philosophy East and West* 26.2 (1976) 116–36.

Girard, René. *Violence and the Sacred*. Translated by Patrick Gregory. Baltimore: Johns Hopkins University Press, 1989.

Goffman, Erving. *From Analysis: An Essay on the Organization of Experience*. Cambridge, MA: Harvard University Press, 1974.

Gregory, Peter N. *Tsung-mi and the Sinification of Buddhism*. Princeton: Princeton University Press, 1991.

———. "The Vitality of Buddhism in the Sung." In *Buddhism in the Sung*, edited by Peter N. Gregory and Daniel A. Getz, 1–26. Studies in East Asian Buddhism 13. Honolulu: University of Hawaii Press, 1999.

Gregory, Peter N., and Patricia Buckley Ebrey. "The Religious and Historical Landscape." In *Religion and Society in T'ang and Sung China*, edited by Patricia Buckley Ebrey and Peter N. Gregory, 1–49. Honolulu: University of Hawaii Press, 1993.

Hamayon, Roberte. *Why We Play: An Anthropological Study*. Translated by Damien Simon. Chicago: HAV Books, 2016.

Haskel, Peter. *Bankei Zen: Translations from the Record of Bankei*. Edited by Yohito Hakeda. New York: Grove Press, 1984.

———. *Sword of Zen: Master Takuan and His Writings on Immovable Wisdom and the Sword of Taie*. Honolulu: University of Hawaii Press, 2013.

Heine, Steven. *Zen Skin, Zen Marrow: Will the Real Zen Buddhism Stand Up?* New York: Oxford University Press, 2008.

Henderson, Harold G. *An Introduction to Haiku*. Garden City, NY: Doubleday, 1958.

Henricks, Thomas S. *Play and the Human Condition*. Urbana: University of Illinois Press, 2016.

———. *Play Reconsidered: Sociological Perspectives on Human Expression*. Urbana: University of Illinois Press, 2006.

Hershock, Peter D. *Liberating Intimacy: Enlightenment and Social Virtuosity in Ch'an Buddhism*. Albany: State University of New York Press, 1996.

Holmer, Paul. "Something about What Makes It Funny." *Soundings* 57.2 (Summer 1974) 151–74.

Hori, Ichiro. *Folk Religion in Japan: Continuity and Change*. Chicago: University of Chicago Press, 1968.

Horner, I. B., trans. *The Book of Discipline* (*Vinaya-Piṭaka*). 6 vols. London: Luzac, 1966–70.

———, trans. *The Middle Length Sayings* (*Majjhima Nikāya*). 3 vols. London: Luzac, 1969–70.

Huizinga, Johan. *Homo Ludens: A Study of the Play Element in Culture*. Boston: Beacon Press, 1955.

Hyers, Conrad, ed. *Holy Laughter: Essays in Religion in the Comic Perspective*. New York: Seabury, 1996.

———. *The Laughing Buddha*. Eugene, OR: Wipf & Stock, 2004.

———. *Zen and the Comic Spirit*. Philadelphia: Westminster, 1973.

Ichimura, Shohei, trans. *The Baizhang Zen Monastic Regulations*. Berkeley, CA: Numata Center for Buddhist Translation and Research, 2006.

Kasulis, Thomas. *Shinto: The Way Home*. Honolulu: University of Hawaii Press, 2004.

Keene, Donald. *Appreciations of Japanese Culture*. Tokyo: Kodansha International, 1971.

———. "The Portrait of Ikkyū." *Archives of Asian Art* 20 (Mar. 1966–67) 54–65.

Kieschnick, John. *The Impact of Buddhism on Chinese Material Culture*. Princeton: Princeton University Press, 2003.

Kim, Hee-jen. *Dōgen Kigen: Mystical Realist*. Tucson: University of Arizona Press, 1975.

Kitagawa, Joseph M. *Religion in Japanese History*. New York: Columbia University Press, 1966.

Kraft, Kenneth. *Eloquent Zen: Daitō and Early Japanese Zen*. Honolulu: University of Hawaii Press, 1992.

Lakoff, George, and Mark Johnson. *Philosophy in the Flesh: The Embodied Mind and Its Challenge to Western Thought*. New York: Basic Books, 1999.

LeFleur, William R. *The Karma of Words: Buddhism and the Literary Arts of Medieval Japan*. Berkeley: University of California Press, 1986.

Legge, James, trans. *Li Chi: Book of Rites*. Vol. 2. Hong Kong: Hong Kong University Press, 1960.
Leighton, Taigen Daniel, and Shokaku Okumura, trans. *Dōgen's Standards for the Zen Community: A Translation of Eihei Shingi*. Albany: State University of New York Press, 1996.
Ludwig, Theodore M. "Chanoyu and Momoyama: Conflict and Transformation in Rikyū's Art." In *Tea in Japan: Essays in the History of Chanoyu*, edited by Paul Varley and Kumakura Isao, 71–100. Honolulu: University of Hawaii Press, 1989.
Luk, Charles. *Ch'an and Zen Teachings*. 3 vols. London: Rider, 1949–53.
McRae, John R. *Seeing through Zen: Encounter, Transformations, and Genealogy in Chinese Chan Buddhism*. Berkeley: University of California Press, 2003.
Merleau-Ponty, Maurice. *Phenomenology of Perception*. Translated by Colin Smith. London: Routledge and Kegan Paul, 1974.
Miller, Samuel. "The Clown in Contemporary Art." *Theology Today* 24.3 (Oct. 1967) 318–28.
Monge, Rico G. "Saints, Truth, and the 'Use and Abuse' of Hagiography." In *Hagiography and Religious Truth: Case Studies in the Abrahamic and Dharmic Traditions*, edited by Rico G. Monge et al., 7–22. London: Bloomsbury, 2016.
Nagatomo, Shigenori. "An Analysis of Dōgen's 'Casting Off Body and Mind.'" *International Philosophical Quarterly* 27.3 (1987) 227–42.
Nauman, Nelly. "The State Cult of the Nara and Early Heian Periods." In *Shinto in History: Ways of the Kami*, edited by John Breen and Mark Teeuwen, 41–67. Honolulu: University of Hawaii Press, 2000.
Needham, Joseph. *Science and Civilization of China*. Vol. 2, *History of Scientific Thought*. Cambridge, UK: University of Cambridge Press, 1956.
Ohnuki-Tierney, Emiko. *Illness and Healing among the Sakalin-Ainu: A Symbolic Interpretation*. Cambridge, UK: Cambridge University Press, 1981.
Olson, Carl. "The Human Body as a Boundary Symbol: A Comparison of Merleau-Ponty and Dōgen." *Philosophy East and West* 36.2 (Apr. 1986) 102–20.
———. *Indian Asceticism: Power, Violence, and Play*. New York: Oxford University Press, 2015.
———. "The Leap of Thinking: A Comparison of Heidegger and the Zen Master Dōgen." *Philosophy Today* 25 (1981) 55–62.
———. "The Ludic Life: A Comparison of the *Caitanya-caritāmṛta* and the *Zhuangzi*." In *Brahman and Dao: Comparative Studies of Indian and Chinese Philosophy and Religion*, edited by Ithamar Theodor and Zhihua Yao, 247–62. Lanham, MD: Lexington, 2014.
———. *Zen and the Art of Postmodern Philosophy: Two Paths of Liberation from the Representational Mode of Thinking*. Albany: State University of New York Press, 2000.
Ogata, Sohaku. *The Transmission of the Lamp*. Vol. 2, *The Early Masters*. Woliboro, NH: Longwood Academic, 1989.
Parkes, Graham. "The Role of Rock in the Japanese Dry Landscape Garden." In *Reading Zen in the Rocks: The Japanese Dry Landscape Garden*, by François Berthier, 85–145. Chicago: University of Chicago Press, 2000.
Poceski, Mario, trans. *The Record of Mazu and the Making of Classical Chan Literature*. Oxford: Oxford University Press, 2015.

Quinn, Shelly Fenno. *Developing Zeami: The Noh Actor's Attainment in Practice.* Honolulu: University of Hawaii Press, 2005.
Ricoeur, Paul. *Figuring the Sacred: Religion, Narrative, and Imagination.* Translated by David Pellaur. Minneapolis: Fortress, 1995.
———. *The Role of Metaphor.* Translated by Robert Czermy. Toronto: University of Toronto Press, 1977.
Rimer, J. Thomas, and Masakazu Yamazaki, trans. *On the Art of the Nō Drama: The Major Treatises of Zeami.* Princeton: Princeton University Press, 1984.
Sanford, James H. *Zen-Man Ikkyū.* Studies in World Religions 2. Chico, CA: Scholars Press, 1981.
Sasaki, Ruth Fuller, trans. *The Recorded Sayings of Ch'an Master Lin-chi Hui-chao of Chen Prefecture.* Kyoto: Institute for Zen Studies, 1975.
———. *The Record of Linji.* Honolulu: University of Hawaii Press, 2009.
Schlütter, Morten. *How Zen Became Zen: The Dispute over Enlightenment and the Formation of Chan Buddhism in the Song Dynasty China.* Kuroda Institute Studies in East Asian Buddhism. Honolulu: University of Hawaii Press, 2008.
Shih, Hu. "Ch'an (Zen) Buddhism in China: Its History and Method." *Philosophy East and West* 3.1 (1953) 3–24.
Shirane, Harubo. *Traces of Dreams: Landscape, Cultural Memory and Poetry of Bashō.* Stanford, CA: Stanford University Press, 1998.
Shōji, Yamada. "The Myth of Zen in the Art of Archery." *Japanese Journal of Religious Studies* 29.1–2 (2004) 1–30.
Sicart, Miguel. *Play Matters.* Cambridge: MIT Press, 2014.
Smith, Rachel J. "Devotion, Critique and the Reading of Saint's Lives." In *Hagiography and Religious Truth: Case Studies in the Abrahamic and Dharma Traditions,* edited by Rico G. Monge et al., 30–34. London: Bloomsbury, 2016.
Sōshitsu XV, Sen. *Japanese Way of Tea: From Its Origins in China to Sen Rikyū.* Translated by V. Dixon Morris. Honolulu: University of Hawaii Press, 1998.
Stone, Jacqueline I. *Original Enlightenment and the Transformation of Medieval Japanese Buddhism.* Studies in East Asian Buddhism 12. Honolulu: University of Hawaii Press, 1999.
Strickmann, Michel. "Saintly Fools and Chinese Masters (Holy Fools)." *Asia Major* 7.1 (1994) 35–57.
Stryk, Lucien, and Takashi Ikemoto. *Zen Poems, Prayers, Sermons, Anecdotes and Interviews.* Garden City, NY: Doubleday, 1963.
Suzuki, D. T. *Essays in Zen Buddhism First Series.* Reprint, New York: Grove Press, 1961.
———. *Essays in Zen Buddhism Second Series.* Edited by Christmas Humphreys. New York: Samuel Weiser, 1971.
———. *Essays in Zen Buddhism Third Series.* Edited by Christmas Humphreys. New York: Samuel Weiser, 1971.
———. *Sengai: The Zen Master.* Greenwich, CT: New York Graphic Society, 1971.
———. *Zen Buddhism: Selected Writings of D. T. Suzuki.* Edited by William Barrett. New York: Doubleday, 1956.
———. *Zen and Japanese Culture.* Bollingen Series 69. New York: Pantheon, 1965.
Teeuwen, Mark. "From Jindō to Shinto." *Japanese Journal of Religious Studies* 29 (2002) 233–63.
Turner, Victor. *The Anthropology of Performance.* New York: PAJ, 1987.
———. *The Ritual Process: Structure and Anti-Structure.* Chicago: Aldine, 1969.

Tyler, Royell. "'The Path of My Mountain': Buddhism in Nō." In *Flowing Traces: Buddhism in the Literary and Visual Arts of Japan*. Edited by James H. Sanford et al., 149–79. Princeton: Princeton University Press, 1993.
Varley, H. Paul. "Chanoyu: From the Genroku Epoch to Modern Times." In *Tea in Japan: Essays on the History of Chanoyu*, edited by Paul Varley and Kumakura Isao, 161–94. Honolulu: University of Hawaii Press, 1998.
———. *Japanese Culture*. 3rd ed. Honolulu: University of Hawaii Press, 1973.
Victoria, Brian Daizen. *Zen at War*. 2nd ed. Lanham, MD: Rowman and Littlefield, 2006.
Vos, Nelvin. *The Drama of Comedy: Victim and Victor*. Richmond, VA: John Knox, 1966.
Warren, Henry Clarke, ed. *Visuddhimagga of Buddhaghosacariya*. Harvard Oriental Series 41. Cambridge, MA: Harvard University Press, 1950.
Watson, Burton, trans. *The Complete Chuang Tzu*. New York: Columbia University Press, 1968.
———, trans. *The Lotus Sutra*. New York: Columbia University Press, 1993.
———, trans. *Ryōkan: Zen Monk-Poet of Japan*. New York: Columbia University Press, 1977.
Welter, Albert. "Buddhist Rituals for Protecting the Country in Medieval Japan: Myōan Eisai's Regulations of the Zen School." In *Zen Ritual: Studies of Zen Buddhist Theory in Practice*, edited by Steven Heine and Dale S. Wright, 113–38. New York: Oxford University Press, 2008.
———. *Monks, Rulers, and Literati: The Political Ascendancy of Chan Buddhism*. New York: Oxford University Press, 2006.
Whitfield, Randolph S., trans. *Record of the Transmission of the Lamp*. 2 vols. Germany: Books on Demand, 2015.
Williams, Duncan Ryūken. *The Other Side of Zen: A Social History of Sōtō Zen Buddhism in Tokugawa Japan*. Princeton: Princeton University Press, 2005.
Woodward, F. L., trans. *The Book of the Gradual Sayings* (*Anguttara-Nikāya*). 5 vols. London: Luzac, 1962–72.
Wright, Dale S. "Introduction: Rethinking Ritual Practice in Zen Buddhism." In *Zen Ritual: Studies in Zen Buddhist Theory in Practice*, edited by Steven Heine and Dale S. Wright, 3–20. New York: Oxford University Press, 2008.
———. "Kōan History: Transformative Language in Chinese Buddhist Thought." In *The Kōan: Texts and Contexts in Zen Buddhism*, edited by Steven Heine and Dale S. Wright, 200–212. Oxford: Oxford University Press, 2000.
———. *Philosophical Meditations on Zen Buddhism*. Cambridge, UK: Cambridge University Press, 1998.
———. "Rethinking Transcendence: The Role of Language in Zen Experience." *Philosophy East and West* 42.1 (1993) 113–38.
Wu, John C. H. *The Golden Age of Zen*. Taipei: United Publishing Center, 1975.
Wu, Kuang-ming. *The Butterfly as Companion: Meditation on the First Three Chapters of the Chuang Tzu*. Albany: State University of New York Press, 1990.
———. *Chuang Tzu: World Philosopher at Play*. New York: Crossroad, 1982.
Yampolsky, Philip B., trans. *The Platform Sutra of the Sixth Patriarch*. New York: Columbia University Press, 1967.
———, trans. *The Zen Master Hakuin: Selected Writings*. New York: Columbia University Press, 1971.

Yasuda, Kenneth. *Japanese Haiku: Its Essential Nature and History*. Boston: Tuttle, 2001.

Yasuhiko, Murai. "The Development of Chanoyu: Before Rikyū." In *Tea in Japan: Essays on the History of Chanoyu*, translated by Paul Varley, edited by Paul Varley and Kumakura Isao, 3–32. Honolulu: University of Hawaii Press, 1989.

Yokoi, Yuho, and Daizen Victoria. *Zen Master Dogen: An Introduction with Selected Writings*. New York: Weatherhill, 1976.

Yusa, Vatsuo. *The Body, Self-Cultivation and Ki-Energy*. Translated by S. Nagatomo and M. S. Hull. Albany: State University of New York Press, 1993.

Zürcher, Erik. *The Buddhist Conquest of China: The Spread and Adaptation of Buddhism in Early Medieval China*. 2 vols. Sinica Leidensia 11. Leiden: Brill, 1959.

Index

aesthictic categories, 179–182
ahimsā, 113
alaya-vijana, 13
anatta, 6
Aśoka, Kimd, 36
Austin, J. L., 110, 123
Avaghosa, 34
Avalokitesvara, 225
avidya, 11–12
aware, 179

Baoche, 168
Baizhong, 50–52, 89, 112–113, 119–120, 123
Banko, 70
Bashō, 22, 200–206
Bodhidharma, 13, 42–43m, 45, 58–59, 80, 126, 156
bodhisattva, 13–17., 21, 25, 98, 114, 117–118, 125–126, 148, 158–170m, 174, 184, 213m, 225
brahmavirhas, 15
Buddha, 7–8, 12, 103–104
Buddhsm, 2-1-73, 102, 116–118, 123, 138, 221–224
Buddha-nature, 41, 104, 136–141, 145–146, 148, 150
Buddhaghosa, 99, 113
Bushdo Code, 211–212., 224

Caodog House, 56
Chan, 37–60
   major families, 52–57
chanōyu, 195
Charter Oath, 222

*ch*i, 41
chinso, 100, 154
comic, 168–171
Confucianism, 4, 13, 36, 38–39, 58, 69, 101, 184, 195, 217
consciousness, 12–13

Daoan, 22
Daoism, 4, 34, 37, 39, 42, 55, 185, 193, 200, 217
Daoxin, 42, 44, 62
Dayu, 109
dhyna, 410, 15, 23, 47, 91, 102, 149, 198
dharmas, 8–9, 88
Dharmaraksa, 34
Dōgen Kigen, 20–21m, 27, 64., 85–88, 104, 130, 132134–135, 137–139, 142–143, 149–150, 221
on death, 209–225
time, 210–224
Dōsōsōn, 62
Dummeon, H., 21

Eisai, 63, 88
Ej, Emperor, 85
emptiness, 9–10, 35, 146, 185
enlightenment, 131–132, 134, 136, 133, 147, 198
   and madness, 153–55
Enni Beben, 13
erotic, 160–165
evil, 149
existence, 140–141

Fadong, 44

236 INDEX

Fau, 45
Fayuan House, 56
Fazang, 40
fial piey, 36, 48
fine arts, 276–208
Four noble truths, 7
frumai, 295
fushiryō, 144

gadō, 179
Genpei War, 62
Girard, Rene, 114–115
gozan, 86
Guuan, 1
Guzonzong, 53
Gyōhyō, 62

haiku, 22., 200–207
Hakuin, 22, 30, 72, 83, 85–86, 89, 99, 117, 128, 211
Hanazonreō. Emperor, 87
harmomy, 208
Herriigel, Eugene, 216
Hongren, 23, 43–44, 62
Hongzhou, 44
hua hu, 36
Huangbo, 32, 52, 54, 99, 108–110
Huayen, 40
Huineng, 23, 26, 44–49
Huizinga Johan, 28–29, 172
humot, 167–176, 219–221
Hu Shih, 21
Hyers, Conrad, 164

Ikkyū, 25, 33, 87–88, 152–172m, 221
impermanence, 39–40, 139

jiso, 86
jingren, 37
Jizo, 158

Kamakura Period, 62, 195
kadō, 179
kamikaze, 223
Kanonon, 213
kānseki, 197
kami, 59, 182
kamyō, 105, 194

karma, 4–5, 117
Kasō Sōdon, 87, 163
Keirn okin, 75
kika, 95
Kimnrieou, Emperor, 61
kōan, 33, 51., 73, 78–82, 139, 142., 172, 186, 213
  meditating on, 86
konioha, 196
Korea, 61
kśani, 15
kuan, 41–42
kung-an, 79
Kuārajiva, 34–80
kōnyejuku, 140

language, 74–78
Lankavatara School, 44
Li, 38., 101
Lin-ji, 2, 32, 49, 54–55., 76., 108–110, 112, 126

ma, 181, 191
Madhyamika School, 8–14
madness, 165–169
Mahayana Buddhism, 41,
Mahakasya, 132
Mazu, 32., 49–51, 74–76, 111, 123, 126, 166, 170
meditation, 82–10
McRae, John, 126
madness, 151–169
martial arts, 208–225
māyā, 11
medō, 163
micho, 179
miko, 184
mikyp, 191
mio, 61
Minoato Yoritomo no, 64
Mori, 161–162
Mu, 84
Museō Ssoseki, 86
mushi, 192
myō, 191ō

Nāgārjuna, 11
Nanqun, 51, 149, 219

INDEX 237

Naoxin, 23
Neo-Confucianism, 58, 193, 200
Nietzsche, F., 151
nikon, 140–141
Nirvana, 7, 42
Nō theatre, 189–193
nuns, 103–105

obnich, 194
Oda Nobunaga, 68, 195, 200
Onin War, 86, 151, 212
Ox Head School, 57

painting, 187–189
Pang, 1
performative utterance, 122
play, 2–3, 20–32, 151–171, 207, 219
    and comic, 175–176
    and humor, 172–174
    and laugher, 166–167
    and madness, 165–166
    and violence, 125–127
    cpmuc and humor, 167–171
politics, 100–103
prajba, 8
prajnaparamita, 11, 15
prajnā, 87, 148
pratyekthanabuddha, 14
Puke, 155
Puhu, 75–76
Pure Land, 310

qi, 184

radhis, 99
raku, 196
rinka, 86
Rinzai, 26, 33., 63
ritual, 100–103
Rock Gardens, 182–186
ryaken, 86
Ryōken, 25, 167, 183

sabi, 180, 198–199
Saichō, 62
Śakya, 23
sanmon, 93
samurai, 212–215

sangea, 189
Sans, 124h
samadhi, 90, 100, 148., 150
satori, 22, 74, 8181, 94
sangha, 91
sanmon, 93
self, 1460148
Sengoho, 99
Sengai, 171–172
Sen no Rikyyuū, 1950196, 198–199
seppuku, 196, 211–212
Sengpan, 34
Sesshi, 182
sesshin, 91
shaman, 61
Shandhu, 45
*shansrti*184
Shenxiu, 45, 47
Shenhin, 44, 48
shinyō, 144
shite, 191, 184
Shinto, 181–182, 193, 222-
*shiniyō*135, 142
shih, 40., 192
shite, 191, 186
Shingon, 63–64., 95
shentomf, 98
shentomg, 98
Shinto, 61, 200, 217
shodō, 179
Shōtoku,Taishi, 61
Shūdō Mypchō, 87
Shūdō Mypchō, 87
Siddharta, 3
sidhas, 88
śila, 16
skandhas, 146
sokukuto, 97
Sogaku, 169
Song Dynasty, 23, 48, 58—59., 195
Sōtō, 33, 69
sufferings, 5–7
śunyatā, 11–12, 94
Susano, 217
sutra, 8., 11
Suzuki, D. T., 21–22., 25, 117, 165, 192, 200
Suzuki Shosan, 70

svaha, 9, 11

Taina Shigesuke, 213
Takane Sōhō, 69
Taken Sohō, 212
tan, 93
Tang Dynasty, 35, 48–52, 79, 110, 155
tatha, 6, 12, 15
Te, 38
tea ceremony, 193–200
Tendai, 63
Tetsugen Dōkō, 70
Tettsū Grlain, 86
textuality, 24–28
time, 140–141
Tokugawa, 68–69, 200, 221
Tokugawa Leyasy, 68
Toyomi Hideyoshi, 68, 195
Tungshan, 55
Turner, Victor, 29–30

upekka, 16
uji, 140
upaya, 27., 116–117, 158
Upanisad, 102

violence, 109–123
    and play, 125–127

wabi, 180, 198–199
Wangxya, 170
Wu, John C., 21
Wuia, 1
Wuxzhu, 23
Wusomg, Emperor, 38

Wuven, 22

Xuefeng, 112
Xiangy, 121, 130

yamabushi, 193
yang, 40, 185., 199–200
Yang-shan, 169
Yaoshan, 2, 127
yin, 4, 185, 199
Yogacāra School, 8, 10–14
Yōsseŏ Sōe, 160
Yoshida Kamenoe, 60
yūgen, 181, 192., 217
Yunen, 53–54, 76, 109, 112, 119, 167, 170

zazen, 133–137, 147
Zeami, 189–190-192
Zen, 14, 96, 151, 183, 186
    and archery, 2133–217
    and death, 209–225
    and ply, 20–32
    and swordsmanship, 217–219
    and war, 221–223
    History in China, 34–59
    History in Japan, 60–72
    major characteristics, 17–20
    metaphors, 20–25
zendo, 92, 186
Zhaozho, 116, 118, 120, 171, 220
Zhaozhou Conghen, 51, 168
Zhimen, 127
Zhuahzi, 3
Zongmi, 47–48, 56

www.ingramcontent.com/pod-product-compliance
Lightning Source LLC
Chambersburg PA
CBHW051635230426
43669CB00013B/2314